Learn React with TypeScript 3

Beginner's guide to modern React web development with TypeScript 3

Carl Rippon

BIRMINGHAM - MUMBAI

Learn React with TypeScript 3

Copyright © 2018 Packt Publishing

Commissioning Editor: Amarabha Banerjee
Acquisition Editor: Devanshi Doshi
Content Development Editor: Francis Carneiro
Technical Editor: Surabhi Kulkarni
Copy Editor: Safis Editing
Project Coordinator: Kinjal Bari
Proofreader: Safis Editing
Indexer: Rekha Nair
Graphics: Alishon Mendonsa
Production Coordinator: Aparna Bhagat

First published: November 2018

Production reference: 1281118

Published by Packt Publishing Ltd.
Livery Place
35 Livery Street
Birmingham
B3 2PB, UK.

ISBN 978-1-78961-025-3

www.packtpub.com

mapt.io

Mapt is an online digital library that gives you full access to over 5,000 books and videos, as well as industry leading tools to help you plan your personal development and advance your career. For more information, please visit our website.

Why subscribe?

- Spend less time learning and more time coding with practical eBooks and Videos from over 4,000 industry professionals

- Improve your learning with Skill Plans built especially for you

- Get a free eBook or video every month

- Mapt is fully searchable

- Copy and paste, print, and bookmark content

Packt.com

Did you know that Packt offers eBook versions of every book published, with PDF and ePub files available? You can upgrade to the eBook version at www.packt.com and as a print book customer, you are entitled to a discount on the eBook copy. Get in touch with us at customercare@packtpub.com for more details.

At www.packt.com, you can also read a collection of free technical articles, sign up for a range of free newsletters, and receive exclusive discounts and offers on Packt books and eBooks.

Contributors

About the author

Carl Rippon has been involved in the software industry for over 20 years, developing a complex line of business applications in various sectors. He has spent the last eight years building single page applications using a wide range of JavaScript technologies, including Angular, ReactJS, and TypeScript. Carl has written over 100 blog posts on various technologies.

I'd like to thank Sarah, Ellie-Jayne, and Lily-Rose for all the support they've given me while writing this book. Thanks to everyone in the Packt editorial team for their hard work and great feedback, especially Francis Carneiro and Surabhi Kulkarni. Special thanks also to Devanshi Doshi for reaching out to me with this opportunity.

About the reviewers

Ashok Kumar S has been working in the mobile development domain for about six years. In his early days, he was a JavaScript and Node developer. Thanks to his strong web development skills, he has mastered web and mobile development. He is a Google-certified engineer, a speaker at global level conferences (including DroidCon Berlin and MODS), and he also runs a YouTube channel called AndroidABCD for Android developers. He is a computer science and engineering graduate who is passionate about innovation in technology. He contributes to open source heavily with a view to improving his e-karma.

He has also written books on Wear OS programming and mastering the Firebase toolchain. In his spare time, he writes articles and makes videos on programming. Ashok Kumar has also reviewed books on mobile and web development, namely *Mastering JUnit 5*, *Android Programming for Beginners*, and developing Enterprise applications using JavaScript.

> *I would especially like to thank my mother for her boundless support in every possible way, not to mention family members Shylaja, Sumitra, Krishna, Vinisha, and my fiancé, Geetha Shree.*

Dave has had over 16 years' experience as a software engineer. After working for a number of creative agencies in London and then as a contract tech lead for a global e-commerce company, he is now tech lead at Seccl Technology, a start-up based in Bath, UK, that is building pioneering digital services for the financial industry, working with a serverless infrastructure in the cloud, and providing wonderful experiences through their web applications. He has worked with TypeScript for about five years and has seen it mature a lot over the years. Dave has worked specifically on React applications for over two years, as well on serverless code for the Seccl platform.

Pogo Kid is Dave's consultancy where he provides support for companies wanting to improve their serverless, React, and TypeScript applications. He has also reviewed a couple of book proposals for Manning on TypeScript.

He has had the privilege of bringing leadership to development teams across the world, including many household names. He is a firm believer that when systems have the correct architecture and the team has a good mix of passion and skill, users will have a wonderful experience.

Daniel Deutsch is working as a web developer in various companies. Although most of his work is structured around client-side development, he is also able to contribute to different problem areas in software development, like the backend, devops, or project management. Coming from legal fields and also studying law he aims for bringing the 2 areas together and create additional value for both industries. As his personal interest focuses on machine learning, he likes to incorporate more of those disciplines in his day to day work.

Daniel's ultimate goal is to structure a business around motivated people to create something that brings value to humanity and lasts for a long time period.

Packt is searching for authors like you

If you're interested in becoming an author for Packt, please visit `authors.packtpub.com` and apply today. We have worked with thousands of developers and tech professionals, just like you, to help them share their insight with the global tech community. You can make a general application, apply for a specific hot topic that we are recruiting an author for, or submit your own idea.

Table of Contents

Preface

React was built by Facebook in order to provide more structure to their code base and allow it to scale much better. React worked so well for Facebook that they eventually open sourced it. Today, React is one of the most popular JavaScript libraries for building frontends. It allows us to build small, isolated, and highly reusable components that can be composed together in order to create complex frontends.

TypeScript was built by Microsoft to help developers more easily build large frontend applications. It is a superset of JavaScript, bringing a rich type system to it. This type system helps developers to catch bugs early and allows tools to be created to robustly navigate and refactor code.

This book will teach you how you can use both of these technologies to create large sophisticated frontends efficiently that are easy to maintain.

Who this book is for

This book is primarily aimed at web developers who want to create large web applications with React and TypeScript. A basic understanding of JavaScript and HTML is assumed.

What this book covers

Chapter 1, *TypeScript Basics*, introduces the TypeScript type system, covering the basic types. It moves on to cover how we can configure the incredibly flexible TypeScript compiler. Linting and code formatting are also introduced, along with their configuration.

Chapter 2, *What is New in TypeScript 3*, steps through the significant new features that were introduced in version 3 of TypeScript. Tuples feature heavily in this chapter, along with the closely related rest and spread syntax and how we can use these constructs with strong types. Setting up multiple related TypeScript projects efficiently is also covered, before moving on to improvements that have been made when setting default prop values in a React component.

Chapter 3, *Getting Started with React and TypeScript*, begins with how projects that use both these technologies can be created. The chapter then introduces how strongly-typed React components can be built in both a class-based and functional manner. Managing state and hooking into life cycle events are also key topics in this chapter.

Chapter 4, *Routing with React Router*, introduces a library that can help us efficiently create an app with multiple pages. It covers how to create page links, and declare the components that should be rendered. Step by step, the chapter covers how to implement route parameters, query parameters, and nested routes. The chapter also covers how to load components from a route on demand in order to optimize performance in apps entailing lots of large pages.

Chapter 5, *Advanced Types*, focuses solely on TypeScript types. On this occasion, more advanced, but still very useful, types are covered, such as generic types, union types, overload signatures, and keyof and lookup types.

Chapter 6, *Component Patterns*, covers a number of common patterns for building React components while still maintaining strong types. Container components are stepped through first, followed by composite components. The popular render props pattern and higher-order components are also covered in this chapter.

Chapter 7, *Working with Forms*, covers how forms can be implemented efficiently with React and TypeScript. A generic form component is built step by step, including validation and submission.

Chapter 8, *React Redux*, covers how this popular library can help manage state across an app. A strongly typed Redux store is built with actions and reducers. The chapter finishes by looking at how a new React function can allow a Redux style structure within components without Redux.

Chapter 9, *Interacting with RESTful APIs*, begins with detailed coverage of asynchronous code. The chapter then moves on to cover how we can interact with RESTful APIs using a native JavaScript function, as well as a popular open source library.

Chapter 10, *Interacting with GraphQL APIs*, begins by introducing the syntax for reading and writing data. The chapter covers how to interact with a GraphQL server with an HTTP library before moving on to using a popular purpose-built library.

Chapter 11, *Unit Testing with Jest*, covers how to test both pure functions and React components. A popular open source library is looked at to make tests less brittle when the internals of components are refactored. Some of the great features of Jest are stepped through, such as snapshot testing, mocking, and code coverage.

`Answers`, Contains the answers to all the exercises present in the chapters of this book.

To get the most out of this book

You need to know the basics of JavaScript, including the following:

- An understanding of some of the primitive JavaScript types, such as string, number, Boolean, null, and undefined
- An understanding of how to create variables and reference them, including arrays and objects
- An understanding of how to create functions and call them
- An understanding of how to create conditional statements with the if and else keywords

You need to know the basics of HTML, including the following:

- An understanding of basic HTML tags, such as div, ul, p, a, h1, and h2, and how to compose them together to create a web page
- An understanding of how to reference a CSS class to style an HTML element

An understanding of basic CSS is also helpful, but not essential:

- How to size elements and include margins and padding
- How to position elements
- How to color elements

You will need the following technologies installed on your computer:

- **Google Chrome**: This can be installed at `https://www.google.com/chrome/`.
- **Node.js and npm**: These are used throughout this book. You can install them at `https://nodejs.org/en/download/`. If you already have these installed, make sure that Node.js is at least version 8.2 and that npm is at least version 5.2.
- **TypeScript**: This can be installed via npm by entering the following command in a terminal:

  ```
  npm install -g typescript
  ```

- **Visual Studio Code**: You'll need this to write React and TypeScript code. This can be installed from `https://code.visualstudio.com/`.

Download the example code files

You can download the example code files for this book from your account at `www.packt.com`. If you purchased this book elsewhere, you can visit `www.packt.com/support` and register to have the files emailed directly to you.

You can download the code files by following these steps:

1. Log in or register at `www.packt.com`.
2. Select the **SUPPORT** tab.
3. Click on **Code Downloads & Errata**.
4. Enter the name of the book in the **Search** box and follow the onscreen instructions.

Once the file is downloaded, please make sure that you unzip or extract the folder using the latest version of:

- WinRAR/7-Zip for Windows
- Zipeg/iZip/UnRarX for Mac
- 7-Zip/PeaZip for Linux

The code bundle for the book is also hosted on GitHub at `https://github.com/PacktPublishing/Learn-React-with-TypeScript-3`. In case there's an update to the code, it will be updated on the existing GitHub repository.

We also have other code bundles from our rich catalog of books and videos available at `https://github.com/PacktPublishing/`. Check them out!

Download the color images

We also provide a PDF file that has color images of the screenshots/diagrams used in this book. You can download it here: `https://www.packtpub.com/sites/default/files/downloads/9781789610253_ColorImages.pdf`.

Conventions used

There are a number of text conventions used throughout this book.

`CodeInText`: Indicates code words in text, database table names, folder names, filenames, file extensions, pathnames, dummy URLs, user input, and Twitter handles. Here is an example: "Let's create a new file called `tsconfig.json` in the root of our project."

A block of code is set as follows:

```
import * as React from "react";

const App: React.SFC = () => {
  return <h1>My React App!</h1>;
};
```

When we wish to draw your attention to a particular part of a code block, the relevant lines or items are set in bold:

```
interface IProps {
  title: string;
  content: string;
  cancelCaption?: string;
  okCaption?: string;
}
```

Any command-line input or output is written as follows:

```
cd my-components
npm install tslint tslint-react tslint-config-prettier --save-dev
```

Bold: Indicates a new term, an important word, or words that you see on screen. For example, words in menus or dialog boxes appear in the text like this. Here is an example: "We need to click the **Install** option to install the extension."

Warnings or important notes appear like this.

Tips and tricks appear like this.

Get in touch

Feedback from our readers is always welcome.

General feedback: If you have questions about any aspect of this book, mention the book title in the subject of your message and email us at customercare@packtpub.com.

Errata: Although we have taken every care to ensure the accuracy of our content, mistakes do happen. If you have found a mistake in this book, we would be grateful if you would report this to us. Please visit www.packt.com/submit-errata, selecting your book, clicking on the Errata Submission Form link, and entering the details.

Piracy: If you come across any illegal copies of our works in any form on the internet, we would be grateful if you would provide us with the location address or website name. Please contact us at copyright@packt.com with a link to the material.

If you are interested in becoming an author: If there is a topic that you have expertise in, and you are interested in either writing or contributing to a book, please visit authors.packtpub.com.

Reviews

Please leave a review. Once you have read and used this book, why not leave a review on the site that you purchased it from? Potential readers can then see and use your unbiased opinion to make purchase decisions, we at Packt can understand what you think about our products, and our authors can see your feedback on their book. Thank you!

For more information about Packt, please visit packt.com.

TypeScript Basics 1

Facebook has become an incredibly popular app. As its popularity grew, so did the demand for new features. React was Facebook's answer to help more people work on the codebase and deliver features quicker. React worked so well for Facebook that they eventually open sourced it. Today, React is a mature library for building component-based frontends that is extremely popular and has a massive community and ecosystem.

TypeScript is also a popular, mature library maintained by a big company – namely, Microsoft. It allows users to add strong types to their JavaScript code, helping them to be more productive, particularly in large code bases.

This book will teach you how you can use both of these awesome libraries to build robust frontends that are easy to maintain. The first couple of chapters in the book focus solely on TypeScript. You'll then start to learn about React and how you can compose robust frontends using Typescript components with strong typing.

In this chapter, we'll cover TypeScript's relationship to JavaScript and the benefits it brings. A basic understanding of JavaScript is therefore required. We'll also cover the basics of TypeScript that you'll commonly use when writing code for the browser.

You'll come to understand the need to use TypeScript for building a frontend and the sort of projects for which TypeScript really shines. You will also see how to transpile your TypeScript code into JavaScript so that it can run in a browser. Last but not least, you'll learn how you can perform additional checks on your TypeScript code to make it readable and maintainable.

By the end of the chapter, you'll be ready to start learning how you can use TypeScript for building frontends with React.

In this chapter, we'll cover the following topics:

- Understanding the benefits of TypeScript
- Understanding basic types
- Creating interfaces, types aliases, and classes
- Structuring code into modules
- Configuring compilation
- TypeScript linting
- Code formatting

Technical requirements

We will use the following technologies in this chapter:

- **TypeScript playground**: This is a website at `https://www.typescriptlang.org/play/` that allows you to play around with and understand the features in TypeScript without installing it.
- **Node.js and** `npm`: TypeScript and React are dependent on these. You can install them at: `https://nodejs.org/en/download/`. If you already have these installed, make sure Node.js is at least Version 8.2 and `npm` is at least Version 5.2.
- **TypeScript**: This can be installed via `npm`, entering the following command in a terminal:

  ```
  npm install -g typescript
  ```

- **Visual Studio Code**: We'll need an editor to write our TypeScript code. This one can be installed from `https://code.visualstudio.com/`. Other editors that could be used can be found at `https://github.com/Microsoft/TypeScript/wiki/TypeScript-Editor-Support`.

 All the code snippets in this chapter can be found online at: `https://github.com/carlrip/LearnReact17WithTypeScript/tree/master/01-TypeScriptBasics`

Understanding the benefits of TypeScript

When a JavaScript codebase grows, it can become hard to read and maintain. TypeScript is an extension of JavaScript, adding static types. The TypeScript compiler reads in TypeScript code that includes type information and produces clean, readable JavaScript with the type information transformed and removed. The compiled code can then run in our favorite browsers and Node.js.

TypeScript offers several benefits over JavaScript:

- Coding errors can be caught in the development process earlier
- Static types allow tools to be built that improve the developer experience and productivity
- JavaScript features that aren't implemented in all the browsers yet can actually be used in an app that targets those browsers

We'll go through these points in detail in the following sections.

Catching coding errors early

The type information helps the TypeScript compiler catch bugs and typos before our users run into them. In code editors such as Visual Studio Code, a mistake is underlined in red immediately after the user has gone wrong. As an example, create a file called utils.js and paste in the following code, which calculates the total price on an order line:

```
function calculateTotalPrice(product, quantity, discount) {
  var priceWithoutDiscount = product.price * quantity;
  var discountAmount = priceWithoutDiscount * discount;
  return priceWithoutDiscount - discountAmount;
}
```

There is a bug in the code that might be difficult for us to spot. If we open the file in Visual Studio Code, no errors are highlighted. If we change the extension of the file to `.ts`, Visual Studio Code immediately underlines bits of the code that need our attention in red:

```
1   function calculateTotalPrice(product, quantity, discount) {
2     var priceWithoutDiscount = product.price * quantity;
3     var discountAmount = priceWithoutDiscount * discount;
4     return priceWithoutDiscount - discountAmount;
5   }
6
```

Most of the errors are TypeScript asking for some type information. So, let's add some types to our code:

```
interface IProduct {
  name: string;
  unitPrice: number;
}

function calculateTotalPrice(product: IProduct, quantity: number, discount:
number): number {
  var priceWithoutDiscount: number = product.price * quantity;
  var discountAmount: number = priceWithoutDiscount * discount;
  return priceWithoutDiscount - discountAmount;
}
```

Don't worry if you don't understand what we just added; we'll go through types in the next section. The key point is that we now have a single error highlighted to us, which is, in fact, the bug:

```
1   interface IProduct {
2     name: string;
3     unitPrice: number;
4   }
5
6   function calculateTotalPrice(product: IProduct, quantity: number, discount: number): number {
7     var priceWithoutDiscount: number = product.price * quantity;
8     var discountAmount: number = priceWithoutDiscount * discount;
9     return priceWithoutDiscount - discountAmount;
10  }
```

The bug is that our function references a `price` property in the product object that doesn't exist. The property that we should reference is `unitPrice`.

Better developer experience and productivity

Let's fix the bug in the previous section by renaming `price` to `unitPrice`. Notice how Visual Studio Code gives us IntelliSense lists `unitPrice` as an option because it looking at our type definition:

```
function calculateTotalPrice(product: IProduct, quantity: number, discount: number): number {
    var priceWithoutDiscount: number = product. * quantity;
    var discountAmount: number = priceWithoutDi ⬢ name
    return priceWithoutDiscount - discountAmoun ⬢ unitPrice    (property) IProduct.unitPrice: number ⊕
}
```

Here, TypeScript and Visual Studio Code are using the types to provide a better authoring experience for us. As well as IntelliSense, we are provided with code navigation features, and the safe renaming of functions and variables across multiple files. These features increase our productivity, particularly when the code base is large and there is a team of people working on it.

Using future JavaScript features

There is another benefit of TypeScript that is important to understand. TypeScript allows us to use some features in JavaScript that haven't yet been adopted by all browsers but still target those browsers. TypeScript achieves this by transpiling the use of these features down to JavaScript code that the targeted browser does support.

As an example, let's look at the exponentiation operator ($**$) in ES7, which isn't supported in IE. Let's create a file called `future.ts` and enter the following code:

```
var threeSquared: number = 3 ** 2;
console.log(threeSquared);
```

When we run the program in a browser, it should put 9 into the console. Before we do that, let's run the code against the TypeScript compiler to get the transpiled JavaScript. Run the following command in a terminal in the same directory as `future.ts`:

```
tsc future
```

This should generate a file called `future.js` with the following content:

```
var threeSquared = Math.pow(3, 2);
console.log(threeSquared);
```

So, TypeScript converted the exponentiation operator to a call to the `Math.pow` function, which is supported in IE. To confirm that this works, paste the generated JavaScript code into the console in IE and the output should be 9.

This example is purposely simple but probably not that useful. `Async/await`, **spread** operators, **rest** parameters, and **arrow functions** are far more useful features that IE doesn't support but TypeScript allows the use of. Don't worry if you don't know what the features in the last sentence are, as we'll cover them when we need them in the book.

Understanding basic types

We touched on types in the last section. In this section, we'll go through the basic types that are commonly used in TypeScript so that we start to understand what cases we should use in each type. We'll make heavy use of the online TypeScript playground, so be sure to have that ready.

Primitive types

Before understanding how we declare variables and functions with types in TypeScript, let's briefly look at primitive types, which are the most basic types. Primitive types are simple values that have no properties. TypeScript shares the following primitive types with JavaScript:

- `string`: Represents a sequence of Unicode characters
- `number`: Represents both integers and floating-point numbers
- `boolean`: Represents a logical true or false
- `undefined`: Represents a value that hasn't been initialized yet
- `null`: Represents no value

Type annotations

Types for JavaScript variables are determined at runtime. Types for JavaScript variables can also change at runtime. For example, a variable that holds a number can later be replaced by a string. Usually, this is unwanted behavior and can result in a bug in our app.

TypeScript annotations let us declare variables with specific types when we are writing our code. This allows the TypeScript compiler to check that the code adheres to these types before the code executes at runtime. In short, type annotations allow TypeScript to catch bugs where our code is using the wrong type much earlier than we would if we were writing our code in JavaScript.

TypeScript annotations let us declare variables with types using the `:Type` syntax.

1. Let's browse to the TypeScript playground and enter the following variable declaration into the left-hand pane:

```
let unitPrice: number;
```

2. The transpiled JavaScript will appear on the right-hand side as follows:

```
var unitPrice;
```

 That `let` has been converted to `var`. This is because the compiler that the playground uses is set to target a wide range of browsers, some of which don't support `let`. Also, notice that the type annotation has disappeared. This is because type annotations don't exist in JavaScript.

3. Let's add a second line to our program:

```
unitPrice = "Table";
```

Notice that a red line appears under `unitPrice`, and if you hover over it, you are correctly informed that there is a type error:

4. You can also add type annotations to function parameters for the return value using the same `:Type` syntax. Let's enter the following function into the playground:

```
function getTotal(unitPrice: number, quantity: number,
discount: number): number {
  const priceWithoutDiscount = unitPrice * quantity;
  const discountAmount = priceWithoutDiscount * discount;
  return priceWithoutDiscount - discountAmount;
}
```

We've declared `unitPrice`, `quantity`, and `discount` parameters, all as numbers. The `return` type annotation comes after the function's parentheses, which is also a number in the preceding example.

 We have used both `const` and `let` to declare variables in different examples. `let` will allow the variable to change the value after the declaration, whereas `const` variables can't change. In the preceding function, `priceWithoutDiscount` and `discountAmount` never change the value after the initial assignment, so we have used `const`.

5. Let's call our function with an incorrect type for `quantity` and assign the result to a variable with an incorrect type:

```
let total: string = getTotal(500, "one", 0.1);
```

We find that `one` is underlined in red, highlighting that there is a type error:

```
1 function getTotal(unitPrice: number, quantity: number, discount: number): number {
2   const priceWithoutDiscount = unitPrice * quantity;
3   const discountAmount = priceWithoutDiscount * discount;
4   return priceWithoutDiscount - di
5 }                                   Argument of type '"one"' is not assignable to par
6                                     ameter of type 'number'.
7 let total: string = getTotal(500, "one", 0.1);
```

6. If we then correct `one` to `1`, `total` should be underlined in red, highlighting that there is a type problem with that:

```
1  function getTotal(unitPrice: number, quantity: number, discount: number): number {
2     const priceWithoutDiscount = unitPrice * quantity;
3     const discountAmount = priceWithoutDiscount * discount;
4     re┌─────────────────────────────────────────────┐
5  }   │ Type 'number' is not assignable to type 'string'. │
6     │ let total: string                              │
       └─────────────────────────────────────────────┘
7  let total: string = getTotal(500, 1, 0.1);
```

The TypeScript compiler uses type annotations to check whether values assigned to variables and function parameters are valid for their type.

This strong type checking is something that we don't get in JavaScript, and it is very useful in large code bases because it helps us immediately detect type errors.

Type inference

We have seen how type annotations are really valuable, but they involve a lot of extra typing. Luckily, TypeScript's powerful type inference system means we don't have to provide annotations all the time. We can use type inference when we immediately set a variable value.

Let's look at an example:

1. Let's add the following variable assignment in the TypeScript playground:

   ```
   let flag = false;
   ```

2. If we hover our mouse over the `flag` variable, we can see that TypeScript has inferred the type as `boolean`:

3. If we add another line beneath this, to incorrectly set `flag` to `Table`, we get a type error:

```
Sel  Type '"Table"' is not assignable to type 'boolean'.
1    let flag: boolean
2    flag = "Table";
```

So, when we declare a variable and immediately set its type, we can use type inference to save a few keystrokes.

Any

What if we declare a variable with no type annotation and no value? What does TypeScript infer as the type? Let's enter the following code in the TypeScript playground and find out:

```
let flag;
```

If we hover our mouse over `flag`, we see it has been given the `any` type:

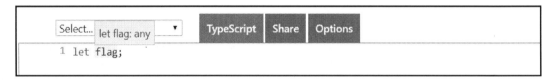

So, the TypeScript compiler gives a variable with no type annotation and no immediately assigned value, the `any` type. The `any` type is specific to TypeScript; it doesn't exist in JavaScript. It is a way of opting out of type checking on a particular variable. It is commonly used for dynamic content or values from third-party libraries. However, TypeScript's increasingly powerful type system means that we need to use `any` less often these days.

Void

void is another type that doesn't exist in JavaScript. It is generally used to represent a non-returning function.

Let's look at an example:

1. Let's enter the following function into the TypeScript playground:

```
function logText(text: string): void {
    console.log(text);
}
```

The function simply logs some text into the console and doesn't return anything. So, we've marked the return type as void.

2. If we remove the return type annotation and hover over the function name, logText, we'll see that TypeScript has inferred the type to be void:

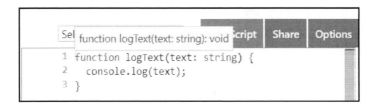

This saves us a few keystrokes while writing functions that don't return anything.

Never

The never type represents something that would never occur and is typically used to specify unreachable areas of code. Again, this doesn't exist in JavaScript.

Time for an example:

1. Type the following code into the TypeScript playground:

```
function foreverTask(taskName: string): never {
    while (true) {
        console.log(`Doing ${taskName} over and over again ...`);
    }
}
```

The function invokes an infinite loop and never returns, and so we have given it a type annotation of `never`. This is different to `void` because void means it will return, but with no value.

 In the preceding example, we used a JavaScript template literal to construct the string to log to the console. Template literals are enclosed by back-ticks (` `` `) and can include a JavaScript expression in curly braces prefixed with a dollar sign (`${expression}`). Template literals are great when we need to merge static text with variables.

2. Let's change the `foreverTask` function to break out of the loop:

```
function foreverTask(taskName: string): never {
  while (true) {
    console.log(`Doing ${taskName} over and over again ...`);
    break;
  }
}
```

The TypeScript compiler quite rightly complains:

```
                                    A function returning 'never' cannot have a
  Select...                ▼  TypeScript  Share  reachable end point.
1 function foreverTask(taskName: string): never {
2   while (true) {
3     console.log(`Doing ${taskName} over and over again ...`);
4     break;
5   }
6 }
```

3. Let's now remove the `break` statement and the `never` type annotation. If we hover over the `foreverTask` function name with our mouse, we see that TypeScript has inferred the type to be `void`, which is not what we want in this example:

```
  Select...    function foreverTask(taskName: string): void  tions
1 function foreverTask(taskName: string) {
2   while (true) {
3     console.log(`Doing ${taskName} over and over again ...`);
4   }
5 }
```

The `never` type is useful in places where the code never returns. However, we will probably need to explicitly define the `never` type annotation because the TypeScript compiler isn't smart enough yet to infer that.

Enumerations

Enumerations allow us to declare a meaningful set of friendly names that a variable can be set to. We use the `enum` keyword, followed by the name we want to give to it, followed by the possible values in curly braces.

Here's an example:

1. Let's declare an `enum` for order statuses in the TypeScript playground:

```
enum OrderStatus {
    Paid,
    Shipped,
    Completed,
    Cancelled
}
```

2. If we look at the transpiled JavaScript, we see that it looks very different:

```
var OrderStatus;
(function (OrderStatus) {
    OrderStatus[OrderStatus["Paid"] = 1] = "Paid";
    OrderStatus[OrderStatus["Shipped"] = 2] = "Shipped";
    OrderStatus[OrderStatus["Completed"] = 3] = "Completed";
    OrderStatus[OrderStatus["Cancelled"] = 4] = "Cancelled";
})(OrderStatus || (OrderStatus = {}));
```

This is because enumerations don't exist in JavaScript, so the TypeScript compiler is transpiling the code into something that does exist.

3. Let's declare a `status` variable, setting the value to the `shipped` status:

```
let status = OrderStatus.Shipped;
```

Notice how we get nice IntelliSense when typing the value:

```
1  enum OrderStatus {
2    Paid,
3    Shipped,
4    Completed,
5    Cancelled
6  }
7  let status = OrderStatus.
```
```
         🔧 Cancelled
         🔧 Completed
         🔧 Paid
         🔧 Shipped          (enum member) OrderStatus.Shipped = 1
```

4. By default, the numerical values start from 0 and increment. However, the starting value can be explicitly declared in the enum, as in the following example, where we set Paid to 1:

```
enum OrderStatus {
   Paid = 1,
   Shipped,
   Completed,
   Cancelled
}
```

5. Let's set our status variable to the shipped status and log this to the console:

```
let status = OrderStatus.Shipped;
console.log(status);
```

If we run the program, we should see **2** output in the console:

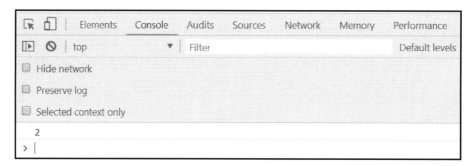

6. In addition, all the values can be explicitly declared, as in the following example:

```
enum OrderStatus {
    Paid = 1,
    Shipped = 2,
    Completed = 3,
    Cancelled = 0
}
```

Enumerations are great for data such as a status that is stored as a specific set of integers but actually has some business meaning. They make our code more readable and less prone to error.

Objects

The object type is shared with JavaScript and represents a non-primitive type. Objects can contain typed properties to hold bits of information.

Let's work through an example:

1. Let's enter the following code into the TypeScript playground, which creates an object with several properties of information:

```
const customer = {
    name: "Lamps Ltd",
    turnover: 2000134,
    active: true
};
```

If we hover over `name`, `turnover`, and `active`, we'll see that TypeScript has smartly inferred the types to be `string`, `number`, and `boolean` respectively.

2. If we hover over the `customer` variable name, we see something interesting:

```
Select...
    const customer: { name: string; turnover: number; active: boolean; }
1  const customer = {
2      name: "Lamps Ltd",
3      turnover: 2000134,
4      active: true
5  };
```

3. Rather than the type being `object`, it is a specific type with `name`, `turnover`, and `active` properties. On the next line, let's set the `turnover` property to some other value:

```
customer.turnover = 500000;
```

As we type the turnover property, IntelliSense provides the properties that are available on the object:

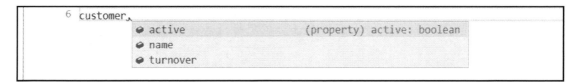

 We used `const` to declare the `customer` variable and then was able to change one of its property values later in the program. Shouldn't this have thrown an error? Well, the customer variable reference hasn't changed — just some properties within it. So, this is fine with the TypeScript compiler.

4. This line of code is perfectly fine, so we don't get any complaints from the compiler. If we set the `turnover` to a value that has an incorrect type, we'll be warned as we would expect:

```
1  const customer = {
2    name: "Lamns Ltd"
3
     Type '"500,000"' is not assignable to type 'number'.
4
5    (property) turnover: number
6  customer.turnover = "500,000";
```

5. Now let's set a property on `customer` that doesn't exist yet:

```
customer.profit = 10000;
```

We'll see that TypeScript complains:

```
Select...                    ▼    TypeScript   Share   Options

1  const cus+omon  - f
2    name: " Property 'profit' does not exist on type '{ name: string; turno
3    turnove ver: number; active: boolean; }'.
4    active:
5  };         any
6  customer.profit = 10000;
```

This makes sense if we think about it. We've declared `customer` with `name`, `turnover`, and `active` properties, so setting a `profit` property should cause an error. If we wanted a `profit` property, we should have declared it in the original declaration.

In summary, the `object` type is flexible because we get to define any properties we require, but TypeScript will narrow down the type to prevent us incorrectly typing a property name.

Arrays

Arrays are structures that TypeScript inherits from JavaScript. We add type annotations to arrays as usual, but with square brackets at the end to denote that this is an array type.

Let's take a look at an example:

1. Let's declare the following array of numbers in the TypeScript playground:

```
const numbers: number[] = [];
```

Here, we have initialized the array as empty.

2. We can add an item to the array by using the array's `push` function. Let's add the number 1 to our array:

```
numbers.push(1);
```

We used `const` to declare the `numbers` variable and was able to change its array elements later in the program. The array reference hasn't changed – just the elements within it. So, this is fine with the TypeScript compiler.

3. If we add an element with an incorrect type, the TypeScript compiler will complain, as we would expect:

```
Select...                    TypeScript   Share   Options
                   Argument of type '"two"' is not assignable to parameter of type
1  const numbers    'number'.
2  numbers.push(
3  numbers.push("two");
```

4. We can use type inference to save a few keystrokes if we declare an array with some initial values. As an example, if we type in the following declaration and hover over the `numbers` variable, we'll see the type has been inferred as `number[]`.

```
const numbers = [1, 3, 5];
```

5. We can access an element in an array by using the element number in square brackets. Element numbers start at `0`.

Let's take an example:

1. Let's log out the number of elements under the numbers variable declaration, as follows:

```
console.log(numbers[0]);
console.log(numbers[1]);
console.log(numbers[2]);
```

2. Let's now click the **Run** option on the right-hand side of the TypeScript playground to run our program. A new browser tab should open with a blank page. If we press *F12* to open the **Developer tools** and go to the console section, we'll see **1**, **3**, and **5** output to the console.

3. There are several ways to iterate through elements in an array. One option is to use a `for` loop, as follows:

```
for (let i in numbers) {
  console.log(numbers[i]);
}
```

If we run the program, we'll see **1**, **3**, and **5** output to the console again.

4. Arrays also have a useful function for iterating through their elements, called `forEach`. We can use this function as follows:

```
numbers.forEach(function (num) {
  console.log(num);
});
```

5. `forEach` calls a nested function for each array element, passing in the array element. If we hover over the `num` variable, we'll see it has been correctly inferred as a `number`. We could have put a type annotation here, but we have saved ourselves a few keystrokes:

```
1 const numbers = [1, 3, 5];
2                              (parameter) num: number
3 numbers.forEach(function (num) {
4   console.log(num);
5 });
```

Arrays are one of the most common types we'll use to structure our data. In the preceding examples, we've only used an array with elements having a number type, but any type can be used for elements, including objects, which in turn have their own properties.

Creating interfaces, types aliases, and classes

In the *Understanding basic types* section, we introduced ourselves to objects, which are types that can have their own properties. Interfaces, type aliases, and classes are ways that we can define an object structure before we start using it.

Following here is the `customer` object we worked with, where we declared the `customer` variable with an initial object value:

```
const customer = {
  name: "Lamps Ltd",
  turnover: 2000134,
  active: true
};
```

1. Let's try to declare the customer variable and set its value on a subsequent line:

```
let customer: object;
customer = {
  name: "Lamps Ltd",
  turnover: 2000134,
  active: true
};
```

2. So far, so good. However, let's see what happens when we try to change the customers `turnover` value:

```
customer.turnover = 2000200;
```

3. The lack of IntelliSense when we type `turnover` isn't what we are used to. When we've finished typing the line, we get a compiler error:

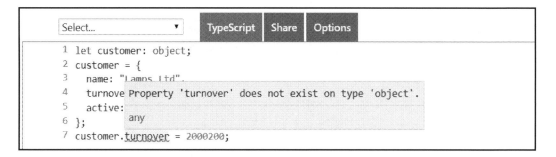

The TypeScript compiler doesn't know about the properties in the `customer` object and so thinks there's a problem.

So, we need another way of defining an object structure with the ability to set property values later in the program. That's where interfaces, type aliases, and classes come in; they let us define the structure of an object by letting us define our own types.

Interfaces

An interface is a contract that defines a type with a collection of property and method definitions without any implementation. Interfaces don't exist in JavaScript, so they are purely used by the TypeScript compiler to enforce the contract by type checking.

We create an interface with the `interface` keyword, followed by its name, followed by the bits that make up the `interface` in curly braces:

```
interface Product {
   ...
}
```

Properties

Properties are one of the elements that can be part of an interface. Properties can hold values associated with an object. So, when we define a property in an interface, we are saying that objects that implement the interface must have the property we have defined.

Let's start to play with an interface in the TypeScript playground:

1. Enter the following interface:

```
interface Product {
   name: string;
   unitPrice: number;
}
```

2. The preceding example creates a `Product` interface with `name` and `unitPrice` properties. Let's go on to use this interface by using it as the type for a `table` variable:

```
const table: Product = {
   name: "Table",
   unitPrice: 500
}
```

3. Let's try to set a property that doesn't exist in the interface:

```
const chair: Product = {
   productName: "Table",
   price: 70
}
```

As expected, we get a type error:

```
Select...                ▼    TypeScript   Share   Options
 1  interface Product {
 2    name: string;
 3    unitPrice: number;
 4  }
 5
 6  const table: Product = {
 7       Type '{ productName: string; price: number; }' is not assignabl
 8       e to type 'Product'.
 9  }       Object literal may only specify known properties, and 'produc
10          tName' does not exist in type 'Product'.
11  co
12       productName: "Table",
13     price: 70
14  }
```

4. Properties on an interface can reference another interface because an interface is just a type. The following example shows an `OrderDetail` interface making use of a `Product` interface:

```
interface Product {
  name: string;
  unitPrice: number;
}

interface OrderDetail {
  product: Product;
  quantity: number;
}

const table: Product = {
  name: "Table",
  unitPrice: 500
}

const tableOrder: OrderDetail = {
  product: table,
  quantity: 1
};
```

This gives us the flexibility to create complex object structures, which is critical when writing large, complex apps.

Method signatures

Interfaces can contain method signatures as well. These won't contain the implementation of the method; they define the contracts for when interfaces are used in an implementation.

Let's look at an example:

1. Let's add a method to the `OrderDetail` interface we just created. Our method is called `getTotal` and it has a `discount` parameter of type `number` and returns a `number`:

```
interface OrderDetail {
  product: Product;
  quantity: number;
  getTotal(discount: number): number;
}
```

Notice that the `getTotal` method on the interface doesn't specify anything about how the total is calculated – it just specifies the method signature that should be used.

2. Having adjusted our `OrderDetail` interface, our `tableOrder` object, which implemented this interface, will now be giving a compilation error. So, let's resolve the error by implementing `getTotal`:

```
const tableOrder: OrderDetail = {
  product: table,
  quantity: 1,
  getTotal(discount: number): number {
    const priceWithoutDiscount = this.product.unitPrice *
    this.quantity;
    const discountAmount = priceWithoutDiscount * discount;
    return priceWithoutDiscount - discountAmount;
    }
};
```

Notice that the implemented method has the same signature as in the `OrderDetail` interface.

The method implementation uses the `this` keyword to get access to properties on the object. If we simply referenced `product.unitPrice` and `quantity` without `this`, we would get a compilation error, because TypeScript would assume these variables are local within the method.

3. Let's tweak the method signature to discover what we can and can't do. We'll start by changing the parameter name:

```
getTotal(discountPercentage: number): number {
  const priceWithoutDiscount = this.product.unitPrice *
   this.quantity;
  const discountAmount = priceWithoutDiscount *
  discountPercentage;
  return priceWithoutDiscount - discountAmount;
}
```

4. We'll see that we don't get a compilation error. Let's change the method name now:

```
total(discountPercentage: number): number {
  const priceWithoutDiscount = this.product.unitPrice *
this.quantity;
  const discountAmount = priceWithoutDiscount *
discountPercentage;
  return priceWithoutDiscount - discountAmount;
}
```

5. This does cause an error because a `total` method doesn't exist on the `OrderDetail` interface:

```
12  co  Type '{ product: Product; quantity: number; total(discountPerce
13      ntage: number): number; }' is not assignable to type 'OrderDeta
14      il'.
15  }     Object literal may only specify known properties, and 'total'
16      does not exist in type 'OrderDetail'.
17  co
18
19      (method) total(discountPercentage: number): number
20    total(discountPercentage: number): number {
21      const priceWithoutDiscount = this.product.unitPrice * this.quantity;
22      const discountAmount = priceWithoutDiscount * discountPercentage;
23      return priceWithoutDiscount - discountAmount;
24    }
```

6. We could try changing the return type:

```
const tableOrder: OrderDetail = {
  product: table,
  quantity: 1,
  getTotal(discountPercentage: number): string {
    const priceWithoutDiscount = this.product.unitPrice *
this.quantity;
```

```
      const discountAmount = priceWithoutDiscount *
discountPercentage;
         return (priceWithoutDiscount - discountAmount).toString();
      }
   };
```

This actually doesn't produce a compilation error in the TypeScript playground, but it should do!

7. So, let's use Visual Studio Code for this example. After we've opened Visual Studio Code in a folder of our choice, let's create a file called `interfaces.ts` and paste in the interface definitions for the `Product` and `OrderDetail` interfaces, along with the `table` variable declaration.

8. We can then enter the preceding implementation of the `OrderDetail` interface. As expected, we get a compilation error:

```
1    interface Product {
2      name: string;
3      unitPrice: number;
4    }
5
6    interface OrderDetail {
7      product: Product;
8      quantity: number;
9      getTotal(discount: number): number;
10   }
11
12   co [ts]
13     Type '(discountPercentage: number) => string' is not assignable
14     to type '(discount: number) => number'.
15   };   Type 'string' is not assignable to type 'number'.
16
17   co  • interfaces.ts(9, 3): The expected type comes from property 'getTotal' which
18        is declared here on type 'OrderDetail'
19
     (method) getTotal(discountPercentage: number): string
20   getTotal(discountPercentage: number): string {
21     const priceWithoutDiscount = this.product.unitPrice * this.quantity;
22     const discountAmount = priceWithoutDiscount * discountPercentage;
23     return (priceWithoutDiscount - discountAmount).toString();
24   }
25   };
```

9. Changing the parameter type also results in a compilation error:

```
[ts]
Type '(discountPercentage: string) => number' is not assignable
to type '(discount: number) => number'.
  Types of parameters 'discountPercentage' and 'discount' are i
ncompatible.
    Type 'number' is not assignable to type 'string'.

• interfaces.ts(9, 3): The expected type comes from property 'getTotal' which
  is declared here on type 'OrderDetail'

(method) getTotal(discountPercentage: string): number
getTotal(discountPercentage: string): number {
    const priceWithoutDiscount = this.product.unitPrice * this.quantity;
    const discountAmount = priceWithoutDiscount * parseInt(discountPercentage);
    return priceWithoutDiscount - discountAmount;
}
};
```

The errors provided by TypeScript are fantastic—they are very specific about where the problem is, allowing us to quickly correct our mistakes.

10. So, when implementing a method from an interface, the parameter names aren't important, but the other parts of the signature are. In fact, we don't even need to declare the parameter names in the interface:

```
interface OrderDetail {
    ...
    getTotal(number): number;
}
```

However, omitting the parameter names arguably makes the interface harder to understand—how do we know exactly what the parameter is for?

Optional properties and parameters

We might want to make a property optional because not every situation where the interface is implemented requires it. Let's take the following steps in our `OrderDetail` interface:

1. Let's create an optional property for the date it was added. We specify an optional value by putting a ? at the end of the property name but before the type annotation:

```
interface OrderDetail {
    product: Product;
    quantity: number;
    dateAdded?: Date,
```

```
    getTotal(discount: number): number;
}
```

We'll see that our implementation of this interface, `tableOrder`, isn't broken. We can choose to add `dateAdded` to `tableOrder` but it isn't required.

2. We might also want to make a method parameter optional. We do this in a similar way by putting a `?` after the parameter name. In our example, let's make `discount` optional in the `OrderDetail` interface:

```
interface OrderDetail {
    product: Product;
    quantity: number;
    dateAdded?: Date,
    getTotal(discount?: number): number;
}
```

3. We can change the method implementation signature as well:

```
getTotal(discount?: number): number {
    const priceWithoutDiscount = this.product.unitPrice *
this.quantity;
    const discountAmount = priceWithoutDiscount * (discount ||
0);
    return priceWithoutDiscount - discountAmount;
}
```

We've also dealt with the case when a discount isn't passed into the method by using `(discount || 0)` in the `discountAmount` variable assignment.

 `x || y` is shorthand for *if x is* truthy *then use x, otherwise, use y*. The following values are falsy values: `false`, `0`, `""`, `null`, `undefined`, and `NaN`. All other values are truthy.

4. With our optional parameter in place, we can call `getTotal` without passing a value for the discount parameter:

```
tableOrder.getTotal()
```

The preceding line doesn't upset the TypeScript compiler.

Readonly properties

We can stop a property from being changed after it has initially been set by using the readonly keyword before the property name.

1. Let's give this a try on our Product interface by making the name property readonly:

```
interface Product {
  readonly name: string;
  unitPrice: number;
}
```

2. Let's also make sure we have an instance of the Product interface in place:

```
const table: Product = {
  name: "Table",
  unitPrice: 500
};
```

3. Let's change the name property table now on the next line:

```
table.name = "Better Table";
```

As expected, we get a compilation error:

```
1  interface Product {
2    readonly name: string;
3    unitPrice: number;
4  }
5
6  const table: Product = {
7    name  Cannot assign to 'name' because it is a constant or a read-only
8    unit  property.
9  };
10         (property) Product.name: string
11  table.name = "Better Table";
```

readonly properties are a simple way of freezing their values after being initially set. A common use case is when you want to code in a functional way and prevent unexpected mutations to a property.

Extending interfaces

Interfaces can *extend* other interfaces so that they inherit all the properties and methods from its parent. We do this using the `extends` keyword after the new interface name and before the interface name that is being extended.

Let's look at the following example:

1. We create a new interface, taking `Product` as a base, and add information about discount codes:

```
interface Product {
  name: string;
  unitPrice: number;
}

interface DiscountCode {
  code: string;
  percentage: number;
}

interface ProductWithDiscountCodes extends Product {
  discountCodes: DiscountCode[];
}
```

2. We can create an instance of the interface in the usual way, filling in properties from the base interface as well as the child interface:

```
const table: ProductWithDiscountCodes = {
  name: "Table",
  unitPrice: 500,
  discountCodes: [
    { code: "SUMMER10", percentage: 0.1 },
    { code: "BFRI", percentage: 0.2 }
  ]
};
```

Interfaces allow us to create complex but flexible structured types for our TypeScript program to use. They are a really important feature that we can use to create a robust, strongly-typed TypeScript program.

Type aliases

In simple terms, a type alias creates a new name for a type. To define a type alias, we use the `type` keyword, followed by the alias name, followed by the type that we want to alias.

We'll explore this with the following example:

1. Let's create a type alias for the `getTotal` method in the `OrderDetail` interface we have been working with. Let's try this in the TypeScript playground:

```typescript
type GetTotal = (discount: number) => number;

interface OrderDetail {
  product: Product;
  quantity: number;
  getTotal: GetTotal;
}
```

   Nothing changes with objects that implement this interface – it is purely a way we can structure our code. It arguably makes the code a little more readable.

2. Type aliases can also define the shape of an object. We could use a type alias for our `Product` and `OrderDetail` types that we previously defined with an interface:

```typescript
type Product = {
  name: string;
  unitPrice: number;
};

type OrderDetail = {
  product: Product;
  quantity: number;
  getTotal: (discount: number) => number;
};
```

3. We use these types in exactly the same way as we used our interface-based types:

```typescript
const table: Product = {
  name: "Table",
  unitPrice: 500
};

const orderDetail: OrderDetail = {
  product: table,
  quantity: 1,
  getTotal(discount: number): number {
```

```
    const priceWithoutDiscount = this.product.unitPrice *
this.quantity;
    const discountAmount = priceWithoutDiscount * discount;
    return priceWithoutDiscount - discountAmount;
  }
};
```

So, type aliases seem very similar to interfaces. What is the difference between a type alias and an interface? The main difference is that type aliases can't be extended or implemented from like you can with interfaces. So, for a simple structure that doesn't require inheritance, should we use an interface or should we use a type alias? There isn't strong reasoning to prefer either approach. However, we should be consistent with whichever approach we choose to improve the readability of our code.

Classes

Classes feature in many programming languages, including JavaScript. They let us shape objects with type annotations in a similar way to interfaces and type aliases. However, classes have many more features than interfaces and type aliases, which we'll explore in the following sections.

Basic classes

Classes have lots of features. So, in this section we'll look at the basic features of a class. We use the `class` keyword followed by the class name, followed by the definition of the class.

Let's look at this in more depth with the following example:

1. We could use a class to define the `Product` type we previously defined as an interface and as a type alias:

```
class Product {
  name: string;
  unitPrice: number;
}
```

2. We create an instance of our `Product` class by using the `new` keyword followed by the class name and parentheses. We then go on to interact with the class, setting property values or calling methods:

```
const table = new Product();
table.name = "Table";
table.unitPrice = 500;
```

Notice that when we use this approach we don't need a type annotation for the table variable because the type can be inferred.

Classes have many more features than type aliases and interfaces though. One of these features is the ability to define the implementation of methods in a class.

Let's explore this with an example:

1. Let's change the `OrderDetail` type we have been working within previous sections to a class. We can define the implementation of the `getTotal` method in this class:

```
class OrderDetail {
  product: Product;
  quantity: number;

  getTotal(discount: number): number {
    const priceWithoutDiscount = this.product.unitPrice *
this.quantity;
    const discountAmount = priceWithoutDiscount * discount;
    return priceWithoutDiscount - discountAmount;
  }
}
```

2. We can create an instance of `OrderDetail`, specifying a `product` and `quantity`, and then calling the `getTotal` method with a `discount` to get the total price:

```
const table = new Product();
table.name = "Table";
table.unitPrice = 500;

const orderDetail = new OrderDetail();
orderDetail.product = table;
orderDetail.quantity = 2;

const total = orderDetail.getTotal(0.1);

console.log(total);
```

If we run this and look at the console, we should see an output of 900.

Implementing interfaces

We can use classes and interfaces together by defining the contract in an interface and then implementing the class as per the interface. We specify that a class is implementing a particular interface using the `implements` keyword.

As an example, we can define an interface for the order detail and then a class that implements this interface:

```
interface IOrderDetail {
  product: Product;
  quantity: number;
  getTotal(discount: number): number;
}

class OrderDetail implements IOrderDetail {
  product: Product;
  quantity: number;

  getTotal(discount: number): number {
    const priceWithoutDiscount = this.product.unitPrice *
      this.quantity;
    const discountAmount = priceWithoutDiscount * discount;
    return priceWithoutDiscount - discountAmount;
  }
}
```

In the preceding example, we've prefixed the interface with `I` so that readers of the code can quickly see when we are referencing interfaces.

Why would we use this approach? It seems like more code than we need to write. So, what's the benefit? This approach allows us to have multiple implementations of an interface, which can be useful in certain situations.

Constructors

Constructors are functions that perform the initialization of new instances of a class. In order to implement a constructor, we implement a function called `constructor`. It's common to set property values in the constructor to simplify consumption of the class.

Let's look at the following example:

1. Let's create a constructor in the `OrderDetail` class that allows us to set the product and quantity:

    ```
    class OrderDetail implements IOrderDetail {
      product: Product;
      quantity: number;

      constructor(product: Product, quantity: number) {
        this.product = product;
        this.quantity = quantity;
      }

      getTotal(discount: number): number {
        ...
      }
    }
    ```

2. If we create an instance of the class, we are forced to pass in the product and quantity:

    ```
    const orderDetail = new OrderDetail(table, 2);
    ```

3. This is nice because we've reduced three lines of code to one line. However, we can make our class even nicer to work with by making the default quantity parameter 1 if nothing is passed in:

    ```
    constructor(product: Product, quantity: number = 1) {
      this.product = product;
      this.quantity = quantity;
    }
    ```

4. We now don't have to pass in a quantity if it is 1:

    ```
    const orderDetail = new OrderDetail(table);
    ```

5. We can save ourselves a few keystrokes and let the TypeScript compiler implement the product and quantity properties by using the public keyword before the parameters in the constructor:

    ```
    class OrderDetail implements IOrderDetail {
      constructor(public product: Product, public quantity: number
      = 1) {
        this.product = product;
        this.quantity = quantity;
      }
    ```

```
getTotal(discount: number): number {
  ...
}
}
```

Extending classes

Classes can extend other classes. This is the same concept as interfaces extending other interfaces, which we covered in the *Extending interfaces* section. This is a way for class properties and methods to be shared with child classes.

As with interfaces, we use the extends keyword followed by the class we are extending. Let's look at an example:

1. Let's create a ProductWithDiscountCodes from our Product class:

```
class Product {
  name: string;
  unitPrice: number;
}

interface DiscountCode {
  code: string;
  percentage: number;
}

class ProductWithDiscountCodes extends Product {
  discountCodes: DiscountCode[];
}
```

2. We can then consume the ProductWithDiscountCodes class as follows, leveraging properties from the base class as well as the child class:

```
const table = new ProductWithDiscountCodes();
table.name = "Table";
table.unitPrice = 500;
table.discountCodes = [
  { code: "SUMMER10", percentage: 0.1 },
  { code: "BFRI", percentage: 0.2 }
];
```

3. If the parent class has a constructor, then the child class will need to pass the constructor parameters using a function called `super`:

```
class Product {
  constructor(public name: string, public unitPrice: number) {
  }
}

interface DiscountCode {
  code: string;
  percentage: number;
}

class ProductWithDiscountCodes extends Product {
  constructor(public name: string, public unitPrice: number) {
    super(name, unitPrice);
  }
  discountCodes: DiscountCode[];
}
```

Abstract classes

Abstract classes are a special type of class that can only be inherited from and not instantiated. They are declared with the `abstract` keyword, as in the following example:

1. We can define a base `Product` class as follows:

```
abstract class Product {
  name: string;
  unitPrice: number;
}
```

2. If we try to create an instance of this, the compiler will complain, as we would expect:

```
1 abstract class Product {
2   name: string;
3   unitPrice: number;
4 }
5
6 const bread = new Product();
```
Cannot create an instance of an abstract class.

3. We can create a more specific usable class for food products by extending `Product`:

```
class Food extends Product {
    constructor(public bestBefore: Date) {
        super();
    }
}
```

4. Here, we are adding a `bestBefore` date in our `Food` class. We can then create an instance of `Food`, passing in the `bestBefore` date:

```
const bread = new Food(new Date(2019, 6, 1));
```

Abstract classes can have `abstract` methods that child classes must implement. Abstract methods are declared with the `abstract` keyword in front of them, as in the following example:

1. Let's add an `abstract` method to our base `Product` class:

```
abstract class Product {
    name: string;
    unitPrice: number;
    abstract delete(): void;
}
```

2. After we add the `abstract` method, the compiler immediately complains about our `Food` class because it doesn't implement the `delete` method:

```
1  abstract class Product {
2      name: string;
3      unit  Non-abstract class 'Food' does not implement inherited abstract
4      abst  member 'delete' from class 'Product'.
5  }
6            class Food
7  class Food extends Product {
8      constructor(public bestBefore: Date) {
9          super();
10     }
11 }
```

3. So, let's fix this and implement the `delete` method:

```
class Food extends Product {
  deleted: boolean;
  constructor(public bestBefore: Date) {
    super();
  }
  delete() {
    this.deleted = false;
  }
}
```

Access modifiers

So far, all our class properties and methods have automatically had the `public` access modifier. This means they are available to interact with class instances and child classes. We can explicitly set the `public` keyword on our class properties and methods immediately before the property or method name:

```
class OrderDetail {
  public product: Product;
  public quantity: number;

  public getTotal(discount: number): number {
    const priceWithoutDiscount = this.product.unitPrice * this.quantity;
    const discountAmount = priceWithoutDiscount * discount;
    return priceWithoutDiscount - discountAmount;
  }
}
```

As you might have guessed, there is another access modifier, called `private`, which allows the member to only be available to interact with inside the class and not on class instances or child classes.

Let's look at an example:

1. Let's add a `delete` method in our `OrderDetail` class, which sets a private `deleted` property:

```
class OrderDetail {
  public product: Product;
  public quantity: number;
  private deleted: boolean;

  public delete(): void {
    this.deleted = true;
```

```
    }
    ...
  }
```

2. Let's create an instance of `OrderDetail` and try to access the `deleted` property:

```
const orderDetail = new OrderDetail();
orderDetail.deleted = true;
```

As expected, the compiler complains:

```
        Property 'deleted' is private and only accessible within class
        'OrderDetail'.

const orderD (property) OrderDetail.deleted: boolean
orderDetail.deleted = true;
```

There is a third access modifier, `protected`, which allows the member to be available to interact with inside the class and on child classes, but not on class instances.

Property setters and getters

Our classes so far have had simple property declarations. However, for more complex scenarios, we can implement a property with a `getter` and a `setter`. When implementing `getters` and `setters`, generally, you'll need a private property to hold the property value:

- `getter` is a function with the property name and the `get` keyword at the beginning and no parameters. Generally, this will return the value of the associated private property.
- `setter` is a function with the same name with the `set` keyword at the beginning and a single parameter for the value. This will set the value of the associated private property.
- The `private` property is commonly named the same as the `getter` and `setter` with an underscore in front.

Let's take a look at an example:

1. Let's create `getters` and `setters` for the `unitPrice` property in our `Product` class. The `setter` ensures the value is not less than 0. The `getter` ensures `null` or `undefined` is never returned:

```
class Product {
  name: string;

  private _unitPrice: number;
  get unitPrice(): number {
    return this._unitPrice || 0;
  }
  set unitPrice(value: number) {
    if (value < 0) {
      value = 0;
    }
    this._unitPrice = value;
  }
}
```

2. Let's consume the `Product` class and try this out:

```
const table = new Product();
table.name = "Table";
console.log(table.unitPrice);
table.unitPrice = -10;
console.log(table.unitPrice);
```

If we run this, we should see two **0**'s in the console.

Static

Static properties and methods are held in the class itself and not in class instances. They can be declared using the `static` keyword before the property or method name.

Let's look at the following example:

1. Let's make the `getTotal` method static on the `OrderDetail` class we have been using:

```
class OrderDetail {
  product: Product;
  quantity: number;

  static getTotal(discount: number): number {
```

```
        const priceWithoutDiscount = this.product.unitPrice *
this.quantity;
        const discountAmount = priceWithoutDiscount * discount;
        return priceWithoutDiscount - discountAmount;
    }
}
```

2. We get compilation errors where we try to reference the properties on the class. This is because the `static` method isn't in the class instance and therefore can't access these properties:

```
class OrderDetail {
  product: Product;              Property 'product' does not exist on type 'ty
  quantity: number;              peof OrderDetail'.

  static getTotal(discount: number): n any
    const priceWithoutDiscount = this.product.unitPrice * this.quantity;
    const discountAmount = priceWithoutDiscount * discount;
    return priceWithoutDiscount - discountAmount;
  }
}
```

3. To make the `static` method work, we can move its dependencies on the class instance to parameters in the function:

```
static getTotal(unitPrice: number, quantity: number, discount:
number): number {
  const priceWithoutDiscount = unitPrice * quantity;
  const discountAmount = priceWithoutDiscount * discount;
  return priceWithoutDiscount - discountAmount;
}
```

4. We can now call the static method on the class type itself, passing in all the parameter values:

```
const total = OrderDetail.getTotal(500, 2, 0.1);
console.log(total);
```

If we run the preceding program, we should get an output of 900 in the console.

Structuring code into modules

By default, TypeScript generated JavaScript code that executes in what is called the global scope. This means code from one file is automatically available in another file. This in turn means that the functions we implement can overwrite functions in other files if the names are the same, which can cause our applications to break.

Let's look at an example in Visual Studio Code:

1. Let's create a file called `product.ts` and enter the following interface for a product:

```
interface Product {
  name: string;
  unitPrice: number;
}
```

2. Let's create another file, called `orderDetail.ts`, with the following content:

```
class OrderDetail {
  product: Product;
  quantity: number;
  getTotal(discount: number): number {
    const priceWithoutDiscount = this.product.unitPrice *
this.quantity;
    const discountAmount = priceWithoutDiscount * discount;
    return priceWithoutDiscount - discountAmount;
  }
}
```

The compiler doesn't give us any complaints. In particular, the reference to the `Product` interface in the `OrderDetail` class is able to be resolved, even though it's in a different file. This is because both `Product` and `OrderDetail` are in the global scope.

Operating in the global scope is problematic because item names can conflict across different files, and as our code base grows, this is harder to avoid. Modules resolve this issue and help us write well organized and reusable code.

Module formats

Modules feature in JavaScript as part of ES6, which is great. However, lots of code exists in other popular module formats that came before this standardization. TypeScript allows us to write our code using ES6 modules, which can then transpile into another module format if specified.

Here is a brief description of the different module formats that TypeScript can transpile to:

- **Asynchronous Module Definition (AMD)**: This is commonly used in code targeted for the browser and uses a `define` function to define modules.
- **CommonJS**: This format is used in Node.js programs. It uses `module.exports` to define modules and `require` to define dependencies.
- **Universal Module Definition (UMD)**: This can be used in both browser apps and Node.js programs.
- **ES6**: This is the native JavaScript module format and uses the `export` keyword to define modules and `import` to define dependencies.

In the following sections (and, in fact, this whole book), we'll write our code using ES6 modules.

Exporting

Exporting code from a module allows it to be used by other modules. In order to export from a module, we use the `export` keyword. We can specify that an item is exported using `export` directly before its definition. Exports can be applied to interfaces, type aliases, classes, functions, constants, and so on.

Let's start to adjust our example code from the previous section to operate in modules rather than the global scope:

1. Firstly, let's export the `Product` interface:

```
export interface Product {
  name: string;
  unitPrice: number;
}
```

2. After we make this change, the compiler will complain about the reference to the `Product` interface in the `OrderDetail` class:

```
product.ts          orderDetail.ts  ✖
1    class Order [ts] Cannot find name 'Product'.
2    ··product: Product;
3    ··quantity: number;
4    ··getTotal(discount: number): number {
5    ····const priceWithoutDiscount = this.product.unitPrice * this.quantity;
6    ····const discountAmount = priceWithoutDiscount * discount;
7    ····return priceWithoutDiscount - discountAmount;
8    ··}
9    }
```

This is because `Product` is no longer in the global scope but `OrderDetail` still is. We'll resolve this in the next section, but let's look at alternative ways we can export the `Product` interface first.

3. We can use an `export` statement beneath the item declarations. We use the `export` keyword followed by a comma-delimited list of item names to export in curly braces:

```
interface Product {
  name: string;
  unitPrice: number;
}

export { Product }
```

4. With this approach, we can also rename exported items using the `as` keyword:

```
interface Product {
  name: string;
  unitPrice: number;
}

export { Product as Stock }
```

Importing

Importing allows us to import items from an exported module. We do this using an `import` statement that includes the item names to import in curly braces and the file path to get the items from (excluding the `ts` extension). We can only import items that are exported in the other module file.

1. Let's resolve the issue with our `OrderDetail` class by importing the `Product` interface:

```typescript
import { Product } from "./product";

class OrderDetail {
  product: Product;
  quantity: number;
  getTotal(discount: number): number {
    const priceWithoutDiscount = this.product.unitPrice *
this.quantity;
    const discountAmount = priceWithoutDiscount * discount;
    return priceWithoutDiscount - discountAmount;
  }
}
```

2. We can rename imported items using the `as` keyword in an `import` statement. We then reference the item in our code using the new name:

```typescript
import { Product as Stock } from "./product";

class OrderDetail {
  product: Stock;
  quantity: number;
  getTotal(discount: number): number {
    const priceWithoutDiscount = this.product.unitPrice *
this.quantity;
    const discountAmount = priceWithoutDiscount * discount;
    return priceWithoutDiscount - discountAmount;
  }
}
```

Default exports

We can specify a single item that can be exported by default using the `default` keyword:

```
export default interface {
  name: string;
  unitPrice: number;
}
```

Notice that we don't need to name the interface. We can then import a default exported item using an `import` statement without the curly braces with a name of our choice:

```
import Product from "./product";
```

Configuring compilation

We need to compile our TypeScript code before it can be executed in a browser. We do this by running the TypeScript compiler, `tsc`, on the files we want to compile. TypeScript is very popular and is used in many different situations:

- It is often introduced into large existing JavaScript code bases
- It comes by default in an Angular project
- It is often used to add strong types to a React project
- It can even be used in Node.js projects

All these situations involve slightly different requirements for the TypeScript compiler. So, the compiler gives us lots of different options to hopefully meet the requirements of our particular situation.

1. Let's give this a try by opening Visual Studio Code in a new folder and creating a new file, called `orderDetail.ts`, with the following content:

```
export interface Product {
  name: string;
  unitPrice: number;
}

export class OrderDetail {
  product: Product;
  quantity: number;
  getTotal(discount: number): number {
    const priceWithoutDiscount = this.product.unitPrice *
this.quantity;
```

```
        const discountAmount = priceWithoutDiscount * discount;
        return priceWithoutDiscount - discountAmount;
    }
}
```

2. We can open a **Terminal** in Visual Studio Code by going to the **View** menu and choosing **Terminal**. Let's enter the following command in the **Terminal**:

    tsc orderDetail

3. Hopefully, no errors should be output from the compiler and it should generate a file called `orderDetail.js`, containing the following transpiled JavaScript:

```
"use strict";
exports.__esModule = true;
var OrderDetail = (function () {
    function OrderDetail() {
    }
    OrderDetail.prototype.getTotal = function (discount) {
        var priceWithoutDiscount = this.product.unitPrice *
this.quantity;
        var discountAmount = priceWithoutDiscount * discount;
        return priceWithoutDiscount - discountAmount;
    };
    return OrderDetail;
}());
exports.OrderDetail = OrderDetail;
```

We'll continue to use `orderDetail.ts` in the following sections as we explore how the compiler can be configured.

Common options

As mentioned earlier, there are lots of configuration options for the TypeScript compiler. All the configuration options can be found at `https://www.typescriptlang.org/docs/handbook/compiler-options.html`. The following sections detail some of the more common options that are used.

--target

This determines the ECMAScript version the transpiled code will be generated in.

The default is ES3, which will ensure the code works in a wide range of browsers and their different versions. However, this compilation target will generate the most amount of code because the compiler will generate polyfill code for features that aren't supported in ES3.

The ESNext option is the other extreme, which compiles to the latest supported proposed ES features. This will generate the least amount of code, but will only work on browsers that have implemented the features we have used.

As an example, let's compile orderDetail.ts targeting ES6 browsers. Enter the following in the terminal:

```
tsc orderDetail --target es6
```

Our transpiled JavaScript will be very different from the last compilation and much closer to our source TypeScript because classes are supported in es6:

```
export class OrderDetail {
    getTotal(discount) {
        const priceWithoutDiscount = this.product.unitPrice *
this.quantity;
        const discountAmount = priceWithoutDiscount * discount;
        return priceWithoutDiscount - discountAmount;
    }
}
```

--outDir

By default, the transpiled JavaScript files are created in the same directory as the TypeScript files. --outDir can be used to place these files in a different directory.

Let's give this a try and output the transpiled orderDetail.js to a folder called dist. Let's enter the following in the terminal:

```
tsc orderDetail --outDir dist
```

A dist folder will be created containing the generated orderDetail.js file.

--module

This specifies the module format that the generated JavaScript should use. The default is the **CommonJS** module format if ES3 or ES5 are targeted. ES6 and ESNext are common options today when creating a new project.

--allowJS

This option tells the TypeScript compiler to process JavaScript files as well as TypeScript files. This is useful if we've written some of our code in JavaScript and used features that haven't been implemented yet in all browsers. In this situation, we can use the TypeScript compiler to transpile our JavaScript into something that will work with a wider range of browsers.

--watch

This option makes the TypeScript compiler run indefinitely. Whenever a source file is changed, the compiling process is triggered automatically to generate the new version. This is a useful option to switch on during our developments:

1. Let's give this a try by entering the following in a terminal:

    ```
    tsc orderDetail --watch
    ```

2. The compiler should run and, when completed, give the message Watching for file changes. Let's change the getTotal method in the OrderDetail class to handle situations when discount is undefined:

    ```
    getTotal(discount: number): number {
      const priceWithoutDiscount = this.product.unitPrice *
    this.quantity;
      const discountAmount = priceWithoutDiscount * (discount ||
    0);
      return priceWithoutDiscount - discountAmount;
    }
    ```

3. When we save orderDetail.ts, the compiler will say File change detected. Starting incremental compilation... and carry out the compilation.

To exit the watch mode, we can kill the terminal by clicking the bin icon in the **Terminal**.

--noImplicitAny

This forces us to explicitly specify the any type where we want to use it. This forces us to think about our use of any and whether we really need it.

Let's explore this with an example:

1. Let's add a doSomething method to our OrderDetail class that has a parameter called input with no type annotation:

   ```
   export class OrderDetail {
     . . .
     doSomething(input) {
       input.something();
       return input.result;
     }
   }
   ```

2. Let's do a compilation with the --noImplicitAny flag in the Terminal:

   tsc orderDetail --noImplicitAny

   The compiler outputs the following error message because we haven't explicitly said what type the input parameter is:

   ```
   orderDetail.ts(14,15): error TS7006: Parameter 'input'
   implicitly has an 'any' type.
   ```

3. We can fix this by adding a type annotation with any or, better still, something more specific:

   ```
   doSomething(input: {something: () => void, result: string}) {
     input.something();
     return input.result;
   }
   ```

If we do a compilation with --noImplicitAny again, the compiler is happy.

--noImplicitReturns

This ensures we return a value in all branches of a function if the return type isn't `void`.

Let's see this in action with an example:

1. In our `OrderDetail` class, let's say we have the following implementation for our `getTotal` method:

```
getTotal(discount: number): number {
  if (discount) {
    const priceWithoutDiscount = this.product.unitPrice *
this.quantity;
    const discountAmount = priceWithoutDiscount * discount;
    return priceWithoutDiscount - discountAmount;
  } else {
    // We forgot about this branch!
  }
}
```

2. We've forgotten to implement the branch of code that deals with the case where there is no discount. If we compile the code without the `--noImplicitReturns` flag, it compiles fine:

```
tsc orderDetail
```

3. However, let's see what happens if we compile the code with the `--noImplicitReturns` flag:

```
tsc orderDetail --noImplicitReturns
```

We get the following error, as expected:

```
orderDetail.ts(9,31): error TS7030: Not all code paths return a
value.
```

--sourceMap

When this is set, `*.map` files are generated during the transpilation process. This will allow us to debug the TypeScript version of the program (rather than the transpiled JavaScript). So, this is generally switched on during development.

--moduleResolution

This tells the TypeScript compiler how to resolve modules. This can be set to `classic` or `node`. If we are using ES6 modules, this defaults to `classic`, which means the TypeScript compiler struggles to find third-party packages such as Axios. So, we can explicitly set this to `node` to tell the compiler to look for modules in `"node_modules"`.

tsconfig.json

As we have seen, there are lots of different switches that we can apply to the compilation process, and repeatedly specifying these on the command line is a little clunky. Luckily, we can specify these options in a file called `tsconfig.json`. The compiler options we have looked at in previous sections are defined in a `compilerOptions` field without the `"--"` prefix.

Let's take a look at an example:

1. Let's create a `tsconfig.json` file with the following content:

```
{
  "compilerOptions": {
    "target": "esnext",
    "outDir": "dist",
    "module": "es6",
    "moduleResolution": "node",
    "sourceMap": true,
    "noImplicitReturns": true,
    "noImplicitAny": true
  }
}
```

2. Let's run a compile without specifying the source file and any flags:

```
tsc
```

The compilation will run fine, with the transpiled JavaScript being output to the `dist` folder along with a source map file.

Specifying files for compilation

There are several ways to tell the TypeScript compiler which files to process. The simplest method is to explicitly list the files in the `files` field:

```
{
  "compilerOptions": {
    ...
  },
  "files": ["product.ts", "orderDetail.ts"]
}
```

However, that approach is difficult to maintain as our code base grows. A more maintainable approach is to define file patterns for what to include and exclude with the `include` and `exclude` fields.

The following example looks at the use of these fields:

1. Let's add the following `include` fields, which tell the compiler to compile TypeScript files found in the `src` folder and its subfolders:

   ```
   {
     "compilerOptions": {
       ...
     },
     "include": ["src/**/*"]
   }
   ```

2. At the moment, our source files aren't in a folder called `src`, but let's run a compile anyway:

   ```
   tsc
   ```

3. As expected, we get `No inputs were found in the config file...` from the compiler.

Let's create an `src` folder and move `orderDetail.ts` into this folder. If we do a compile again, it will successfully find the files and do a compilation.

So, we have lots of options for adapting the TypeScript compiler to our particular situation. Some options, such as `--noImplicitAny`, force us to write good TypeScript code. We can take the checks on our code to the next level by introducing linting into our project, which we'll look at in the next section.

TypeScript linting

As we have seen, the compiler does lots of useful checks against our TypeScript code to help us write error-free code. We can take this a step further and lint the code to help us make our code even more readable and maintainable. TSLint is a linter that is very popular in TypeScript projects, and we will explore it in this section.

The home page for TSLint is at `https://palantir.github.io/tslint/`.

We'll install TSLint in the next section.

Installing TSLint

We'll install TSLint in this section, along with a Visual Studio Code extension that will highlight linting problems right in the code:

1. Let's install TSLint globally via `npm`, as follows:

   ```
   npm install -g tslint
   ```

2. Now, we can open Visual Studio Code and go to the extensions area (*Ctrl + Shift + X*) and type `tslint` in the search box at the top-left. The extension is called TSLint and was published by egamma:

3. We need to click the **Install** option to install the extension.

4. After it has been installed, we'll need to reload Visual Studio Code for the extension to become enabled.

Now that this extension is installed, along with TSLint globally, linting errors will be highlighted right in our code, as we'll see in the following sections.

Configuring rules

The rules that `tslint` uses when checking our code are configurable in a file called `tslint.json`. In order to explore some of the rules, we first need a TypeScript file:

1. So, let's create a file called `orderDetail.ts` with the following content in Visual Studio Code:

```
export interface Product {
  name: string;
  unitPrice: number;
}

export class OrderDetail {
  product: Product;
  quantity: number;
  getTotal(discount: number): number {
    const priceWithoutDiscount = this.product.unitPrice *
this.quantity;
    const discountAmount = priceWithoutDiscount * discount;
    return priceWithoutDiscount - discountAmount;
  }
}
```

2. Let's now create a `tslint.json` file. We define the rules we want to implement in a `rules` field. Let's add the following rule:

```
{
  "rules": {
    "member-access": true
  }
}
```

3. A full list of the rules can be found at: `https://palantir.github.io/tslint/rules/`. The `member-access` rule forces us to explicitly declare the access modifier for classes. We haven't explicitly defined the property and method access modifiers in the `OrderDetail` class because they are `public` by default. So, with our linting rule in place, Visual Studio Code will highlight the lack of access modifiers to us:

```
 6   export class OrderDetail {
 7     product: Product;
 8     quantity: number;
 9     getTotal(discount: number): number {
10       const priceWithoutDiscount = this.product.unitPrice * this.quantity;
11       const discountAmount = priceWithoutDiscount * discount;
12       return priceWithoutDiscount - discountAmount;
13     }
14   }
```

PROBLEMS (3)   OUTPUT   DEBUG CONSOLE   TERMINAL

orderDetail.ts (3)

❌ [tslint] The class property 'product' must be marked either 'private', 'public', or 'protected' (member-access) (7, 3)

❌ [tslint] The class property 'quantity' must be marked either 'private', 'public', or 'protected' (member-access) (8, 3)

❌ [tslint] The class method 'getTotal' must be marked either 'private', 'public', or 'protected' (member-access) (9, 3)

4. As we put a `public` access modifier in front of the properties and method, the warnings go away:

```
export class OrderDetail {
  public product: Product;
  public quantity: number;
  public getTotal(discount: number): number {
    const priceWithoutDiscount = this.product.unitPrice *
this.quantity;
    const discountAmount = priceWithoutDiscount * discount;
    return priceWithoutDiscount - discountAmount;
  }
}
```

The `member-access` rule forces us to write more code – how can this be a good thing? The rule is useful if you're reading the code and don't know TypeScript well enough to understand that class members without access modifiers are public. So, it's great if our team consists of developers who don't know TypeScript that well yet, but not necessarily for an experienced team of TypeScript developers.

Lots of the `tslint` rules are like `member-access` – in some teams, they will work well and in others, they don't really add value. This is why rules are configurable!

Built-in rules

`tslint` has a handy collection of built-in rulesets that can be used. We can use these by specifying the ruleset name in the `extends` field. We can use multiple rulesets by putting all their names in the array:

1. Let's adopt the opinionated set of rules that `tslint` ships with, called `"tslint:recommended"`. So, in our `tslint.json` file, let's remove the `rules` field and add an `extends` field, as follows:

   ```
   {
       "extends": ["tslint:recommended"]
   }
   ```

   We immediately get lint errors when `tslint.json` is saved. The error is complaining about the lack of an `I` prefix on our `Product` interface. The logic behind the rule is that, while reading code, if a type starts with an `I`, we immediately know that it is an interface.

2. Let's pretend that this rule isn't valuable to us. We can override this rule from `"tslint:recommended"` in the `"rules"` field. The rule is called `"interface-name"`. So, let's override this to `false`:

   ```
   {
       "extends": ["tslint:recommended"],
       "rules": {
         "interface-name": false
       }
   }
   ```

When `tslint.json` is saved, the linting errors immediately go away.

Excluding files

We can exclude files from the linting process. This is useful for excluding third-party code. We do this by specifying an array of files in an `exclude` field in the `linterOptions` field:

```
{
  "extends": ["tslint:recommended"],
  "linterOptions": {
  "exclude": ["node_modules/**/*.ts"]
  }
}
```

The preceding configuration excludes third-party `node` packages from the linting process.

Now that we've added TSLint to our tool belt, we are going to add another tool that will automatically format our code for us. This will help our code adhere to some of the code formattings TSLint rules.

Code formatting

In this section, we are going to install another extension in Visual Studio Code, called Prettier, which will automatically format our code. As well as putting a stop to all the ongoing debates over styles, it will help us adhere to some of the TSLint rules:

1. Let's open Visual Studio Code, go to the **Extensions** area, and type **prettier** in the search box. The extension is called **Prettier - Code formatter** and was published by Esben Petersen:

2. We need to click the **Install** option to install the extension.

3. After it has been installed, we'll need to reload Visual Studio Code for the extension to become enabled.

4. The last step is to make sure the **Format on Save** option is ticked in **User Settings**. Press *Ctrl +,* (comma) to open the settings screen and type **Format On Save** in the search box to find the setting. If the setting isn't ticked, then tick it:

Now that this extension is installed, when we save our TypeScript code, it will automatically be formatted nicely for us.

Summary

At the start of this chapter, there was a section on why we would use TypeScript to build a frontend. We now have first-hand experience of TypeScript catching errors early and giving us productivity features such as IntelliSense. We learned that TypeScript is just an extension of JavaScript. So, we get to use all of the features in JavaScript plus additional stuff from TypeScript. One of these additional things is type annotations, which help the compiler spot errors and light up features such as code navigation in our code editor.

We haven't covered everything about types yet, but we have enough knowledge to build fairly complex TypeScript programs now. Classes, in particular, allow us to model complex real-world objects nicely. We learned about modules and how they keep us out of that dangerous global scope. Modules allow us to structure code nicely and make it reusable. We can even use these if we need to support IE, because of that magical TypeScript compiler.

We learned a fair bit about the TypeScript compiler and how it can work well in different use cases because it is very configurable. This is going to be important for when we start to use TypeScript with React later in the book.

`TSLint` and `Prettier` were the icings on the cake. It's down to us and our team to debate and decide the TSLint rules we should go with. The benefit of both these tools is that they force consistency across our code base, which makes it more readable.

Now that we understand the basics of TypeScript, we'll dive into the new features that have been added in TypeScript 3.

Questions

Here are some questions to test what you have learned in this first chapter. The answers can be found in the appendix.

Good luck!

1. What are the 5 primitive types?
2. What would the inferred type be for the `flag` variable be in the following code?

```
const flag = false;
```

3. What's the difference between an interface and a type alias?
4. What is wrong with the following code? How could this be resolved?

```
class Product {
  constructor(public name: string, public unitPrice: number) {}
}

let table = new Product();
table.name = "Table";
table.unitPrice = 700;
```

5. If we want our TypeScript program to support IE11, what should the compiler-- `target` option be?
6. Is it possible to get the TypeScript compiler to transpile ES6 `.js` files? If so, how?
7. How can we prevent `console.log()` statements from getting into our code?

Further reading

http://www.typescriptlang.org has great documentation on TypeScript. It is worth looking at the following pages of this site to cement your knowledge, or using them as a quick reference guide:

- **Basic types**: https://www.typescriptlang.org/docs/handbook/basic-types.html
- **Interfaces**: https://www.typescriptlang.org/docs/handbook/interfaces.html
- **Classes**: https://www.typescriptlang.org/docs/handbook/classes.html
- **Modules**: https://www.typescriptlang.org/docs/handbook/modules.html
- **Compiler Options**: https://www.typescriptlang.org/docs/handbook/compiler-options.html

The full list of tslint rules can be found at https://palantir.github.io/tslint/rules/.

What is New in TypeScript 3

In its six years of existence, TypeScript has continued to move forward and mature nicely. Is TypeScript 3 a significant release for React developers? What exactly are the new features that we have to add to our toolkit in TypeScript 3? These questions will be answered in this chapter, starting with the `tuple` type and how it can now be successfully used with the **rest** and **spread** JavaScript syntax, which is very popular in the React community. We'll then move on to the new `unknown` type and how it can be used as an alternative to the `any` type. Further more, we'll break TypeScript projects up into smaller projects with the new project references in TypeScript. Finally, we'll go about defining default properties in a strongly-typed React component that has improved in TypeScript 3.

By the end of the chapter, we'll be ready to start learning how you can use TypeScript 3 to build frontends with React. In this chapter, we'll cover the following topics:

- Tuples
- The unknown type
- Project references
- Default JSX properties

Technical requirements

In this chapter, we will use the same technologies as in Chapter 1, *TypeScript Basics*:

- **TypeScript playground**: This is a website at `https://www.typescriptlang.org/play/`, which allows us to play around with and understand the features in TypeScript without installing it.
- **Node.js and** `npm`: TypeScript and React are dependent on these. You can install them from `https://nodejs.org/en/download/`. If you already have these installed, make sure `npm` is at least version 5.2.

- **TypeScript**: This can be installed via `npm`, entering the following command in a terminal:

  ```
  npm install -g typescript
  ```

- It is important that we are using TypeScript 3 in this chapter. You can check your TypeScript version by using the following command in a terminal:

  ```
  tsc -v
  ```

  If you need to upgrade to the latest version, you can run the following command:

  ```
  npm install -g typescript@latest
  ```

- **Visual Studio Code**: We'll need an editor to write our React and TypeScript code. This one can be installed from `https://code.visualstudio.com/`. We will also need the TSLint (by egamma) and Prettier (by Estben Petersen) extensions installed in Visual Studio Code.

 All the code snippets in this chapter can be found at `https://github.com/carlrip/LearnReact17WithTypeScript/tree/master/02-WhatsNewInTS3`.

Tuples

Tuples have had a few enhancements in TypeScript 3, so that they can be used with the popular `rest` and `spread` JavaScript syntax. Before we get into the specific enhancements, we'll go through what tuples are, along with what the `rest` and `spread` syntax is. A tuple is like an array but the number of elements are fixed. It's a simple way to structure data and use some type safety.

Let's have a play with tuples:

1. In the TypeScript playground, let's enter the following example of a tuple variable:

   ```
   let product: [string, number];
   ```

   We've initialized a `product` variable to a tuple type with two elements. The first element is a string and the second a number.

2. We can store a product name and its unit price in the `product` variable on the next line, as follows:

```
product = ["Table", 500];
```

3. Let's try to store the product name and unit price the other way around:

```
product = [500, "Table"];
```

Not surprisingly, we get a compilation error. If we hover over `500`, the compiler quite rightly complains that it was expecting a string. If we hover over `"Table"`, the compiler complains that it expects a number:

```
Select...                    ▼    TypeScript   Share   Options

1 let product: [string, number];
2
3 product = ["Tabl" ─────┐
4                   Type 'string' is not assignable to type 'number'.
5 product = [500, "Table"];
```

So, we do get type safety, but tuples tell us nothing about what should be in the elements. So, they are nice for small structures or structures where the elements are obvious.

4. The following examples are arguably fairly readable:

```
let flag: [string, boolean];
flag = ["Active", false]

let last3Scores: [string, number, number, number]
last3Scores = ["Billy", 60, 70, 75];

let point: [number, number, number];
point = [100, 200, 100];
```

5. However, the following example is not so readable:

```
let customer: [string, number, number];
customer = ["Tables Ltd", 500100, 10500];
```

What exactly do those last two numbers represent?

6. We can access items in a tuple in the same way as an array, by using the element's index. So, let's access the product name and unit price in our `product` variable in the TypeScript playground:

```
let product: [string, number];
product = ["Table", 500];
console.log(product[0]);
console.log(product[1]);
```

If we run the program, we'll get **"Table"** and **500** output to the console.

7. We can iterate through elements in a tuple like we can an array, using a `for` loop or the array `forEach` function:

```
let product: [string, number];
product = ["Table", 500];

for (let element in product) {
  console.log(product[element]);
}

product.forEach(function(element) {
  console.log(element);
});
```

Running the program, will output `Table` and `500` to the console twice. Notice that we don't need to add a type annotation to the `element` variable because the TypeScript compiler cleverly infers this.

So, that's the tuple type, but's what's new in TypeScript 3? The enhancements have been largely driven by the popularity of JavaScript's `rest` and `spread` syntax, so let's briefly cover this in the next section.

JavaScript rest and spread syntax

In JavaScript, a `rest` parameter collects multiple arguments and condenses them into a single argument. It is called `rest` because it collects the `rest` of the arguments into a single argument.

 A `rest` parameter has nothing to do with **Representational state transfer protocol (REST)**.

This syntax was introduced in ES6 and allows us to nicely implement functions that have an indefinite number of parameters.

We define a `rest` parameter with three dots preceding the parameter name.

Let's go through a quick example:

1. Let's create a `logScores` function that takes in a `scores` rest parameter that just outputs the parameter to the console:

```
function logScores(...scores) {
  console.log(scores);
}
```

 This is pure JavaScript - we'll introduce types to `rest` parameters when we look at the new features in TypeScript 3.

2. We can call `logScores` as follows:

```
logScores(50, 85, 75);
```

If we run this, we'll get an array of the three elements we passed in as parameters output to the console. So, our `scores` parameter has collected all the arguments into an array.

The `spread` syntax is the opposite of `rest` parameters. It allows an iterable, such as `array`, to be expanded into function arguments.

Let's look at an example:

1. Let's redefine our `logScore` function with specific parameters:

```
function logScore(score1, score2, score3) {
  console.log(score1, score2, score3);
}
```

Note that this is still pure JavaScript – no types just yet!

2. Let's define a `scores` array:

```
const scores = [75, 65, 80];
```

3. Finally, let's use the `spread` syntax to pass our `scores` variable into our `logScore` function:

```
logScore(...scores);
```

If you are using the TypeScript playground, you'll get the compilation error, `expected 3 arguments, but got 0 or more`. The program still runs though, because this is perfectly valid JavaScript. `75, 65, 80` will be output to the console if we do run it.

In the following sections, we'll see how the new features in TypeScript 3 help us help the compiler to better understand what we are trying to do when using `rest` and `spread`. This will allow us to resolve the compilation errors seen in the preceding example.

Open-ended tuples

Before TypeScript 3, tuples had to have a fixed amount of elements. TypeScript 3 gives us a little more flexibility with `rest` elements. `rest` elements are similar to `rest` parameters, described in the last section, but they work with tuple element types. A `rest` element allows us to define an open-ended tuple.

Time to go through an example:

1. In the TypeScript playground, let's create a tuple with the first element being a string and subsequent elements being numbers:

```
type Scores = [string, ...number[]];
```

2. We should be able to use this structure to store someone's name with an infinite amount of scores. Let's give this a go for `Billy` and three scores:

```
const billyScores: Scores = ["Billy", 60, 70, 75];
```

3. Let's move on to try `Sally` and four scores:

```
const sallyScores: Scores = ["Sally", 60, 70, 75, 70];
```

Both these variables compile fine, as we would expect, because we have defined the numbers as open-ended.

Tuple function parameters

Tuple `function` parameters in TypeScript 3 allow us to create strongly-typed `rest` parameters.

Time for an example:

1. When we first looked at `rest` parameters, we created a pure JavaScript version of `logScores` that collected an unlimited amount of arguments in a `scores` variable:

   ```
   function logScores(...scores) {
     console.log(scores);
   }
   ```

2. In TypeScript 3, we can now make this example strongly-typed with a tuple `rest` parameter. Let's give this a try in the TypeScript playground:

   ```
   function logScores(...scores: [...number[]]) {
     console.log(scores);
   }
   ```

3. Let's call our function with some scores:

   ```
   logScores(50, 85, 75);
   ```

   We don't get a compiler error, and if we run the program, we get an array containing 50, 85, 75 output in the console.

We can create an enhanced version of our function that uses the `Scores` type from the *Open-ended tuples* section.

1. The `function` will take in the name, as well as an unlimited set of scores:

   ```
   type Scores = [string, ...number[]];

   function logNameAndScores(...scores: Scores) {
     console.log(scores);
   }
   ```

2. Let's try to call our function with some scores from `Sally`:

   ```
   logNameAndScores("Sally", 60, 70, 75, 70);
   ```

If we run the program, `Sally` and her array of scores will be output to the console.

Spread expressions

TypeScript 3 allows us to use tuples with spread expressions.

Let's look at an example:

1. Let's go back to the problematic pure JavaScript example we looked at for using the spread syntax:

```
function logScore(score1, score2, score3) {
  console.log(score1 + ", " + score2 + ", " + score3);
}

const scores = [75, 65, 80];

logScore(...scores);
```

The TypeScript compiler raised the error Expected 3 arguments, but got 0 or more.

2. Let's resolve this now with enhanced tuples in TypeScript 3. We'll start by adding types to the function parameters:

```
function logScore(score1: number, score2: number, score3:
number) {
  console.log(score1, score2, score3);
}
```

There's nothing new yet, and we're still getting the compilation error.

3. Let's change the scores variable into a fixed tuple:

```
const scores: [number, number, number] = [75, 65, 80];
```

That's it – the compilation error has gone! All we needed to do was tell the compiler how many items were in scores for it to successfully spread into the logScore function.

So, in TypeScript 3, we can spread into fixed tuples. What about open-ended tuples? Let's give that a try:

```
const scoresUnlimited: [...number[]] = [75, 65, 80];

logScore(...scoresUnlimited);
```

Unfortunately, the compiler is not yet quite clever enough to let us do this. We get the compilation error Expected 3 arguments, but got 0 or more.:

```
1  function logScore(score1: number, score2: number, score3: number) {
2    console.log(score1, score2, score3);
3  }
4
5                                    , 65, 80];
6    Expected 3 arguments, but got 0 or more.
7  logScore(...scoresUnlimited);
8
```

Empty tuples

In TypeScript 3, we can now define an empty tuple type. Let's have a little play with this in the TypeScript playground:

1. Let's create the following type alias for an empty tuple:

   ```
   type Empty = [];
   ```

2. Let's declare a variable of this type and assign it to an empty array:

   ```
   const empty: Empty = [];
   ```

3. Now, let's try to declare a variable of this type and assign it to a non-empty array:

   ```
   const notEmpty: Empty = ["Billy"];
   ```

As expected, we get a compilation error:

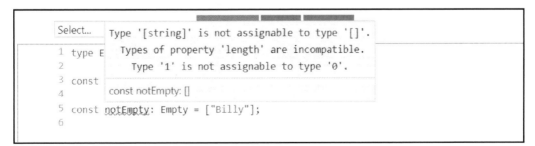

Why is an empty tuple type useful, though? On its own, it perhaps is not that useful, but it can be used as part of a union type, which we'll cover in detail later in the book. As a quick example for now, we can create a type for no more than three scores, where no scores is also acceptable:

```
type Scores = [] | [number] | [number, number] | [number, number, number]

const benScores: Scores = [];
const samScores: Scores = [55];
const bobScores: Scores = [95, 75];
const jayneScores: Scores = [65, 50, 70];
const sarahScores: Scores = [95, 50, 75, 75];
```

All the scores are valid except Sarah's, because four scores aren't allowed in the Scores type.

Optional tuple elements

The final tuple enhancement in TypeScript 3 is the ability to have optional elements. Optional elements are specified using a ? at the end of the element type.

Let's look at another example using our scores theme:

1. Let's create a type for between one and three scores:

    ```
    type Scores = [number, number?, number?];
    ```

2. So, we should be able to create variables to hold between one and three scores:

    ```
    const samScores: Scores = [55];
    const bobScores: Scores = [95, 75];
    const jayneScores: Scores = [65, 50, 70];
    ```

    As expected, this compiles just fine.

3. What about four elements? Let's give this a go:

    ```
    const sarahScores: Scores = [95, 50, 75, 75];
    ```

We get a compilation error, as we would expect:

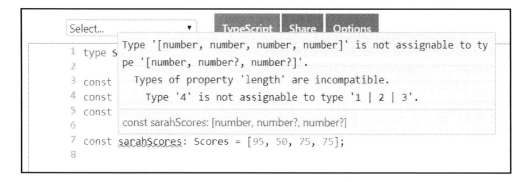

4. If we try no elements, we again get a compilation error:

```
const benScores: Scores = [];
```

When defining optional elements in a tuple, they are restricted to the end of the tuple. Let's try to define a required element after an optional element:

```
type ProblematicScores = [number?, number?, number];
```

We get a compilation error, as expected:

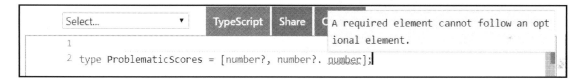

Optional elements also work in a function `rest` parameter. Let's try this:

1. Let's use our `scores` type in our `logScores` function we worked with in earlier sections:

```
type Scores = [number, number?, number?];

function logScores(...scores: Scores) {
  console.log(scores);
}
```

2. If we try to pass in two scores, the code will compile just fine, because the last parameter is optional:

```
logScores(45, 80);
```

3. As expected, if we pass in four scores, we receive `Expected 1-3 arguments, but got 4`:

```
logScores(45, 70, 80, 65);
```

When we have optional parameters, it is likely our function's implementation will need to know which arguments have been passed. We can use the tuple's `length` property to do this:

1. Let's create an enhanced version of our scores logger, called `logScoresEnhanced`, which thanks us if we log all 3 scores:

```
type Scores = [number, number?, number?];

function logScoresEnhanced(...scores: Scores) {
  if (scores.length === 3) {
    console.log(scores, "Thank you for logging all 3 scores");
  } else {
    console.log(scores);
  }
}
```

2. Now, let's call this function with various parameters:

```
logScoresEnhanced(60, 70, 75);
logScoresEnhanced(45, 80);
logScoresEnhanced(95);
```

If we run the program, we only get thanked after the first call when we pass all three scores.

All the enhancements to tuples in TypeScript 3 allow us to use the `rest` and `spread` syntax in a strongly-typed fashion. We'll make use of this feature later in the book, when we work with React components.

The unknown type

unknown is a new type that has been added in TypeScript 3. Before TypeScript 3, we may have used the any type when we weren't sure of all the properties and methods in an object from a third-party library. However, when we declare a variable with the any type, the TypeScript compiler won't do any type checking on it. The unknown type can be used in these situations to make our code more type-safe. This is because unknown types are type-checked. So, unknown can often be used as an alternative to any.

In the TypeScript playground, let's go through an example of a function using any and an improved version using unknown:

1. First, let's create a logScores function that takes in a parameter of type any. It logs out the name and scores properties from the argument to the console:

```
function logScores(scores: any) {
  console.log(scores.firstName);
  console.log(scores.scores);
}
```

2. Let's call this function with the following:

```
logScores({
  name: "Billy",
  scores: [60, 70, 75]
});
```

If we run the program, we get undefined followed by [60, 70, 75] in the console. We passed in a correct object parameter, but our function logs firstName instead of name to the console. The program compiled just fine and didn't produce an error at runtime, but didn't give the result we wanted. This is all because we told the compiler not to check any types with the any type.

3. Let's start to create a better version of this function with the unknown type:

```
function logScoresBetter(scores: unknown) {
  console.log(scores.firstName);
  console.log(scores.scores);
}
```

We immediately get compiler warnings where we reference the properties in `scores`:

```
Select...                                                    Options
  1  function logSc
  2     console.log(      Object is of type 'unknown'.
  3     console.log(scores.scores);   (parameter) scores: unknown
  4  }
  5
```

So, the compiler is checking our `scores` variable now, which is great, and is even warning us about the `firstName` property. However, the `scores` property is also giving a complication error but is valid. So, how do we tell the compiler this? We need to explicitly do some type checking ourselves in our code. We'll cover a couple of ways of doing this in the following sections.

Type checking with a type predicate

One way we can perform type checking in a function is with another function that has a return type as a type predicate. Let's explore this and eventually create a new version of our `logScores` function:

1. First, we'll define a new function called `scoresCheck` to do the necessary type checking:

```
const scoresCheck = (
  scores: any
): scores is { name: string; scores: number[] } => {
  return "name" in scores && "scores" in scores;
};
```

This takes in a `scores` parameter that has a type predicate, `scores is { name: string; scores: number[] }`, ensuring it contains the correctly typed `name` and `scores` properties. The function simply returns whether the `scores` parameter contains the `name` and `scores` properties.

2. Let's use this function in our `logScores` function:

```
function logScores(scores: unknown) {
  if (scoresCheck(scores)) {
    console.log(scores.firstName);
    console.log(scores.scores);
  }
}
```

We immediately get the compilation error we want:

```
1  const scoresCheck = (
2    scores: any
3  ): scores is { name: string; scores: number[] } => {
4    return "name" in scores && "scores" in scores;
5  };
6
7  function logScores(scor
8    if (scoresCheck(score any
9      console.log(scores.firstName);
10     console.log(scores.scores);
11   }
12 }
```

> Property 'firstName' does not exist on type '{ name: string; scores: number[]; }'.

The type predicate, `scores is { name: string, scores: number[] }`, allows the TypeScript compiler to narrow down the type in the `if` block that logs the properties to the console. This results in `scores.scores` compiling fine, but `scores.firstName` is giving an error, which is just what we want.

The type predicate is the key bit. Without it, the TypeScript compiler will still throw errors on the valid `scores.scores` reference. Try removing the type predicate and see for yourself.

Note that we can make the predicate a little more readable with a type alias:

```
type Scores = { name: string; scores: number[] }

const scoresCheck = (
  scores: any
): scores is Scores => {
  return "name" in scores && "scores" in scores;
};
```

Using a type predicate in this way is called a type guard. There are other ways of implementing type guards, which we'll cover later in the book.

Type narrowing with a type assertion

The other way of performing type checking we are going to look at when using `unknown` is to use type assertion. Type assertion lets us tell the compiler what the type is with the `as` keyword.

Let's create yet another version of our `logScores` function as an example:

1. First, let's create a type alias for the structure we want the function parameter to be:

```
type Scores = {
  name: string;
  scores: number[]
};
```

2. In our `logScores` function, we can now use the `as` keyword to tell the compiler what type to expect:

```
function logScores(scores: unknown) {
  console.log((scores as Scores).firstName);
  console.log((scores as Scores).scores);
}
```

That's enough information for the compiler to pinpoint the problem:

```
Select...                    ▾    TypeScript | Share | Options

1  type Scores = { name: string; scores: number[] };
2
3  function logScores(scores: unknown) {
4    console.log((scores as Scores).firstName);
5    console.log((scores as Scores).scores);
6  }
7
```

The `unknown` type allows us to reduce our use of the `any` type and create more strongly-typed and robust TypeScript programs. We do have to write more code, though, when referencing `unknown` types. The additional code we need to write needs to check the type of the `unknown` variable so that the TypeScript compiler can be sure we are accessing valid members within it.

Project references

TypeScript 3 allows TypeScript projects to depend on other TypeScript projects by allowing `tsconfig.json` to reference other `tsconfig.json` files.

This makes it easier to split our code up into smaller projects. Our frontend code might be in TypeScript, in addition to having our backend in TypeScript. With TypeScript 3, we can have a frontend TypeScript project, a backend TypeScript project, and a shared TypeScript project that contains code that is used in both the frontend and backend. Splitting our code up into smaller projects can also can give us faster builds, because they can work incrementally.

Setting up an example

In order to explore this, we are going to work through an example of a TypeScript project referencing another project in Visual Studio Code:

1. Firstly, let's create a new folder called `Shared`. This is going to be the project for shared code that could potentially be used in many other projects.
2. In our `Shared` folder, let's create the following `tsconfig.json` as a starting point:

```
{
  "compilerOptions": {
    "target": "es5",
    "outDir": "dist",
    "module": "es6",
    "sourceMap": true,
    "noImplicitReturns": true,
    "noImplicitAny": true,
    "rootDir": "src"
  },
  "include": ["src/**/*"]
}
```

3. Let's create an `src` folder containing a TypeScript file called `utils.ts` with the following function, `randomString`:

```
export function randomString() {
  return Math.floor((1 + Math.random()) *
0x10000).toString(16);
}
```

This is a function that creates a random string of characters, as the name suggests. We are going to use this function in another project.

4. Let's start to create our second project now, so go back up to the root of our solution, and create a folder called `ProjectA`.

5. Inside `ProjectA`, let's create the following `tsconfig.json` as a starting point:

```
{
  "compilerOptions": {
    "target": "es5",
    "outDir": "dist",
    "module": "es6",
    "sourceMap": true,
    "noImplicitReturns": true,
    "noImplicitAny": true
  },
  "include": ["src/**/*"]
}
```

6. Let's also create a folder called `src` in `ProjectA`, containing a TypeScript file called `person.ts`, with the following code:

```
import { randomString } from "../../Shared/dist/utils";

class Person {
  id: string;
  name: string;
  constructor() {
    this.id = randomString();
  }
}
```

The code defines a simple class of information about a person. The unique identifier of the person is set to a random string in the constructor using the `randomString` function from our `Shared` project.

7. Let's open up the terminal, go to our `Shared` folder, and compile our `Shared` project:

```
cd Shared
tsc
```

The `Shared` project compiles just fine.

8. Let's try to compile `ProjectA` now:

```
cd ..
cd ProjectA
tsc
```

We get a compilation error:

```
error TS7016: Could not find a declaration file for module
'../../Shared/dist/utils'. '.../Shared/dist/utils.js'
implicitly has an 'any' type.
```

So, we created two dependent projects, but they don't properly understand each other yet, which is why we are getting the error. We'll resolve this in the following sections, using TypeScript 3's new features for multiple projects.

Referencing projects

The first step in setting up TypeScript 3's multiple projects feature is to reference projects using a new field called `references` in `tsconfig.json`. This field is an array of objects that specify projects to reference.

In our working example, let's make `ProjectA` start to understand the `Shared` project:

1. Let's change the `tsconfig.json` in `ProjectA` to reference the `Shared` project:

```
{
  "compilerOptions": {
    ...
  },
  "references": [
    { "path": "../shared" }
  ]
}
```

If we want the dependent project's generated JavaScript code to be included in the same file as the current project, we can set `prepend` to `true` on the dependency.

```
"references": [
  { "path": "../shared", "prepend": true }
]
```

We're not going to use `prepend` in our example though.

2. If we compile `ProjectA` again, a different error is raised:

```
error TS6306: Referenced project '.../shared' must have setting
"composite": true
```

The error gives a great clue as to what is wrong. We'll resolve this problem with the missing `composite` setting in the next section.

Additions to compiler options

Just referencing another project isn't enough for the TypeScript compiler to properly handle multiple projects. We need to add some additional compiler options in the dependent project.

The `compilerOptions` field has a new field called `composite`, which must be set to `true` if we are using multiple projects. This ensures certain options are enabled so that this project can be referenced and built incrementally for any project that depends on it.

When `composite` is `true`, `declaration` must also be set to `true`, forcing the corresponding `.d.ts` file to be generated, containing the project's types. This allows TypeScript to only build dependent projects when types are changed and not rebuild all the dependent projects all the time.

Let's make the following changes to our working example:

1. Let's open up `tsconfig.json` in the `Shared` project and make the following changes:

   ```
   {
     "compilerOptions": {
       "composite": true,
       "declaration": true,
       ...
     },
   }
   ```

2. In the terminal, let's go to the `Shared` project directory and compile our `Shared` project:

   ```
   cd ..
   cd Shared
   tsc
   ```

   The project compiles okay. Let's now try to compile `ProjectA` again in the terminal:

   ```
   cd ..
   cd ProjectA
   tsc
   ```

   This time, `ProjectA` compiles just fine.

So, we have successfully tied together two projects using TypeScript 3's multiple projects feature. In the next section, we'll improve the setup of our projects even more.

Cross-project Go to Definition

In order for the **Go to Definition** feature in Visual Studio Code to work across projects, we need to set the `declarationMap` setting in `tsconfig.json`.

Let's continue with our multiple project example:

1. Let's open person.ts in ProjectA, right-click on the randomString reference, and select **Go to Definition**:

```
person.ts            ✖
    1│  import { randomString } from "../../Shared/dist/utils";
    2
    3   class Person {
    4     id: string;
    5     name: string;
    6     constructor() {
    7│      this.id = randomString();
    8     }                          Navigate to test/snapshot   Alt+Ctrl+F12
    9   }
   10                               Go to Definition                  F12

                                    Peek Definition               Alt+F12

                                    Go to Type Definition

                                    Find All References          Shift+F12
```

We are taken to the declaration file rather than the source file:

```
utils.d.ts        ✖
    1  export declare function randomString(): string;
    2
```

2. We can resolve that by setting declarationMap in tsconfig.json in the Shared project:

```
{
  "compilerOptions": {
    "composite": true,
    "declaration": true,
    "declarationMap": true,
    ...
  },
}
```

If we compile the Shared project and try the **Go to Definition** feature again, we are taken to the source file, as we would want.

So, by setting `declarationMap` to `true` in the dependent project, along with `composite` and `declaration`, we get great support for multiple TypeScript projects.

Build mode

The TypeScript 3 compiler includes the ability to perform smart incremental builds using the `--build` flag. Let's give this a try in our example multiple project solution:

1. First, let's go to the root of the solution, open the terminal, and enter the following:

   ```
   tsc --build ProjectA --verbose
   ```

   The `--verbose` flag tells the compiler to tell us the details of what it's doing. The messages confirm to us that it has picked up the `Shared` project as well as `ProjectA`:

   ```
   Projects in this build:
       * Shared/tsconfig.json
       * ProjectA/tsconfig.json
   ```

   The compiler then checks each project to see if it's up to date. If the project is up to date, we get something like the following:

   ```
   Project 'Shared/tsconfig.json' is up to date because newest
   input 'Shared/src/utils.ts' is older than oldest output
   'Shared/dist/utils.js'
   ```

2. Let's make a change in the `utils.ts` file in the `Shared` project by adding a space somewhere, removing it, and then saving the file.
3. Let's build `ProjectA` again:

   ```
   tsc --build ProjectA --verbose
   ```

   As expected, we get a message to indicate that the `Shared` project is out of date and will be rebuilt:

   ```
   Project 'Shared/tsconfig.json' is out of date because oldest
   output 'Shared/dist/utils.js' is older than newest input
   'Shared/src/utils.ts

   Building project '.../Shared/tsconfig.json'
   ```

4. If we want to force a rebuild, even if projects are up to date, we can use the `--force` flag. Let's give this a try:

```
tsc --build ProjectA --force --verbose
```

When we do this, the compiler will still check whether projects are up to date (and tell us), but then it goes on to build each project.

So, in addition to great multiple-project support, we can speed up solution builds using the `--build` flag. As the solution grows over time, this becomes increasingly valuable. If ever we want to force a rebuild of a project, we can use the `--force` flag along with `--build`.

Default JSX properties

TypeScript 3 has also improved how we can set default properties on React components with `--strictNullChecks`. Before TypeScript 3, we had to set properties that had default values as optional and perform `null` checks when referencing them. We haven't introduced React yet in this book, so we'll only touch on this briefly at this point.

Let's look through an example to get a feel for the improvement:

1. The following is a React component with some default properties in TypeScript 2.9. The component is called `SplitText` and it takes in some text, splits it, and renders the bits that have been split in a list:

```
interface IProps {
  text: string;
  delimiter?: string;
}

class SplitText extends Component<IProps> {
  static defaultProps = {
    delimiter: ","
  };
  render() {
    const bits = this.props.text.split(this.props.delimiter!);
    return (
      <ul>
        {bits.map((bit: string) => (
          <li key={bit}>{bit}</li>
        ))}
      </ul>
    );
  }
```

```
    }

const App = () => (
  <div>
    <SplitText text="Fred,Jane,Bob" />
  </div>
);

export default App;
```

The component has a `delimiter` property that defaults to `","`. In TypeScript 2.9, we need to make `delimiter` an optional property, otherwise we get a compiler error if we don't specify it in the calling component (even though there is a `default`).

Also notice that we need to put a `!` after we reference `delimiter` in the `bits` variable declaration. This is to tell the compiler that this will never be undefined.

2. Here's the component that calls `SplitText`:

```
const App = () => (
  <div>
    <SplitText text="Fred,Jane,Bob" />
  </div>
);
```

Here's what it looks like when rendered:

3. Now, let's look at the component in TypeScript 3:

```
interface IProps {
  text: string;
  delimiter: string;
}

class SplitText extends React.Component<IProps> {
  static defaultProps = {
    delimiter: ","
  };
```

```
render() {
  const bits = this.props.text.split(this.props.delimiter);
  return (
    <ul>
      {bits.map((bit: string) => (
        <li key={bit}>{bit}</li>
      ))}
    </ul>
  );
}
}
```

Notice that we didn't need to make the `delimiter` property optional. Also notice that we didn't need to tell the compiler that `this.props.delimiter` can't be undefined.

So, in summary, we don't have to fiddle around to make default properties work nicely in TypeScript 3!

This is our first taste of React. Don't worry if the code examples don't make much sense at this point. We'll start to learn about React components in Chapter 3, *Getting Started with React and TypeScript*.

Summary

Using the `rest` and `spread` syntax is very common nowadays, particularly when building React apps. We've seen how TypeScript 3, with the enhancement of tuples, allows us to use `rest` and `spread` in a strongly-typed fashion.

We've also seen how we can use the `unknown` type to reduce our use of the `any` type. The `unknown` type does require us to write more code, but it also allows us to create a more strongly-typed, more maintainable code base.

TypeScript has always made working with large code bases easier. With the introduction of project references, we can now split our solution into smaller projects more easily. This approach makes large solutions even more maintainable and flexible, and also yields faster build times with the new `--build` flag.

We briefly went through how using `defaultprops` in a React component has improved. We'll be using this frequently as we start to learn how to build strongly-typed React components in subsequent chapters.

So, now that we are starting to get comfortable with TypeScript, in the next chapter, we'll get started with React. We'll start by learning how to create a React and TypeScript project, and then move on to how to create React and TypeScript components.

Questions

In order to cement what we have learned about TypeScript 3, have a go at the following questions:

1. We have the following function, which draws a point:

```
function drawPoint(x: number, y: number, z: number) {
    ...
}
```

We also have the following `point` variable:

```
const point: [number, number, number] = [100, 200, 300];
```

How can we call the `drawPoint` function in a terse manner?

2. We need to create another version of the `drawPoint` function, where we can call it by passing the *x*, *y*, and *z* point values as parameters:

```
drawPoint(1, 2, 3);
```

Internally, in the implementation of `drawPoint`, we draw the point from a tuple type [number, number, number]. How can we define the method parameter(s) with the required tuple?

3. In your implementation of `drawPoint`, how can you make z in the point optional?

4. We have a function called `getData`, which calls a web API to get some data. The number of different API resources is still growing, so we've chosen to use `any` as the return type:

```
function getData(resource: string): any {
  const data = ... // call the web API
  if (resource === "person") {
    data.fullName = `${data.firstName} ${data.surname}`;
  }
  return data;
}
```

How can we make `getData` more type-safe by leveraging the `unknown` type?

5. What `build` flag can we use to determine which projects are out of date and need to be rebuilt without doing a rebuild?

Further reading

The following links are good resources for further information on TypeScript 3.0:

- The Microsoft blog post that announced the TypeScript 3.0 release is worth a read: `https://blogs.msdn.microsoft.com/typescript/2018/07/30/announcing-typescript-3-0/`

- The TypeScript documentation has got good information on project references, which is worth looking at: `https://www.typescriptlang.org/docs/handbook/project-references.html`

3
Getting Started with React and TypeScript

React is a JavaScript library that helps us build the frontend of an app. It allows us to structure our apps using powerful and reusable components. It helps us manage the data that the components use, and their state, in a structured fashion. It uses something called a virtual DOM to efficiently render our frontend.

TypeScript can work beautifully with React, giving us the ability to add static types to our React components. The types help our code editor to surface problems while we write our React components, and give us tools to safely refactor them.

In this chapter, we'll look at two different ways to create a React and TypeScript project. We'll create our first React component, which will be a confirmation dialog. Early topics we'll cover are JSX and strongly typed props. We'll look at handling the dialog's button click events.

We'll then look at declaring and interacting with strongly typed states, which will be used to hide and show the dialog. We'll discuss component life cycle methods, and touch on the ones that have been removed in React 17.

Finally, we'll look at function components, and when these are used.

In this chapter, we'll cover the following topics:

- Creating a React and TypeScript project
- Creating a class component
- Handling class component events
- Class component states
- Class component life cycle methods
- Creating a function component

Technical requirements

We use the following technologies in this chapter:

- **Node.js and** `npm`: TypeScript and React are dependent on these. Install them from the following link: `https://nodejs.org/en/download/`. If you already have these installed, make sure `npm` is at least version 5.2.

- **Visual Studio Code**: We'll need an editor to write our React and TypeScript code, which can be installed from `https://code.visualstudio.com/`. We'll also need the TSLint extension (by egamma) and the Prettier extension (by Estben Petersen).

- **Babel Repl**: We'll use this online tool briefly to explore JSX. This can be found at `https://babeljs.io/repl`.

All the code snippets in this chapter can be found online at `https://github.com/carlrip/LearnReact17WithTypeScript/tree/master/03-GettingStartedWithReactAndTypeScript`.

Creating a React and TypeScript project

There are several ways to create a React and TypeScript project. We'll start by quickly creating a project using a popular tool called `create-react-app`.

We'll then create a project in a more manual way, helping us to understand all the different pieces in play.

Using create-react-app

`create-react-app` is a command-line tool that we can use to quickly create a React and TypeScript app with lots of useful pieces.

Open Visual Studio Code in an empty folder of your choice. Let's create an app using this tool:

1. We use the `create-react-app` npm package to create a React and TypeScript project by entering the following:

```
npx create-react-app my-react-ts-app --typescript
```

The `npx` tool temporarily installs the `create-react-app` npm package and uses it to create our project.

We chose to call our project `my-react-ts-app`. We also specified `--typescript`, which is the bit that tells the tool to set the project up with TypeScript.

The tool will take a minute or so to create your project.

Note that the version of React we use needs to be at least version `16.7.0-alpha.0`. We can check this in the `package.json` file. If the version of React in `package.json` is less that `16.7.0-alpha.0` then we can install this version using the following command:

```
npm install react@16.7.0-alpha.0
npm install react-dom@16.7.0-alpha.0
```

2. When the project is created, add TSLint as a development dependency, along with some rules that work well with React and Prettier:

```
cd my-react-ts-app
npm install tslint tslint-react tslint-config-prettier --save-dev
```

3. Now add a `tslint.json` file, containing some rules:

```
{
  "extends": ["tslint:recommended", "tslint-react", "tslint-config-prettier"],
  "rules": {
    "ordered-imports": false,
    "object-literal-sort-keys": false,
    "no-debugger": false,
    "no-console": false,
  },
  "linterOptions": {
    "exclude": [
      "config/**/*.js",
```

```
      "node_modules/**/*.ts",
      "coverage/lcov-report/*.js"
    ]
  }
}
```

Here we are merging the generally recommended rules with specific ones for React and Prettier. We've enabled the use of `debugger` and `console` statements, which will come in handy from time to time as we develop our app.

We've also suppressed the rule about the ordering of `import` statements and object literal keys, to make life easier as we copy bits of code from this book.

4. We can now start the app running in a development server, by entering the following command:

   npm start

   After a few seconds, a browser window opens, with our app running:

Our React code is in the `src` folder.

5. With our app still running, open the `App.tsx` file. You'll immediately see a linting error on the `render` method, because we haven't specified the modifier:

```
App.tsx    ✕
1    import React, { Component } from 'react';
2    im  [tslint] The class method 'render' must be marked either 'priva
3    im  te', 'public', or 'protected'
4
5    cl (method) App.render(): JSX.Element
6       render() {
```

So, let's fix that by adding `public` as the modifier:

```
class App extends Component {
  public render() {
    return ( ... );
  }
}
```

6. While we are still in `App.tsx`, let's change the anchor tag to the following:

```
<a className="App-link" href="https://reactjs.org"
target="_blank" rel="noopener noreferrer">
 Learn React and TypeScript
</a>
```

7. Save the file, and go back to the app in the browser. The app has automatically changed, showing the new content. Nice!

`create-react-app` has configured a lot of great stuff for us in our project. This is great if we just want to quickly start learning React, and skip over how the React and TypeScript code is packaged up to be served from a web server.

In the next section, we'll do manually do some of what `create-react-app` did for us automatically. This will start to give us an understanding of what needs to happen when React and TypeScript apps are packaged up.

Creating a project manually

In this section, we'll create a React and TypeScript project manually, step by step. We'll start by creating our folder structure.

Creating our folder structure

We need a folder structure that gives us decent separation between the project's configuration files, source code, and files to distribute to our web server.

All our configuration files will go in our project route:

1. Open Visual Studio Code in an empty folder of your choice, and create a folder called `src`. This will hold our source code.

2. Let's also create a folder called `dist`. This will hold the files to distribute to our web server.

Creating package.json

The `package.json` file defines our project name, description, build commands, dependent `npm` modules, and much more.

Open a terminal window, and run the following command:

```
npm init
```

This will prompt you for various bits of information about the project, and then create a `package.json` file containing that information.

Adding TypeScript

We installed TypeScript globally in Chapter 1, *TypeScript Basics*. In this section, we are going to install it locally within our project. Having TypeScript locally simplifies the build process a little bit.

We can install TypeScript just within our project by running the following command in the terminal:

```
npm install typescript --save-dev
```

> The --save-dev command marks the TypeScript dependency as being only for development purposes.

Creating tsconfig.json

As outlined in Chapter 1, *TypeScript Basics*, tsconfig.json specifies how our TypeScript code is compiled and transpiled.

Let's create a new file called tsconfig.json in the root of our project, and enter the following:

```
{
  "compilerOptions": {
    "target": "es5",
    "module": "es6",
    "moduleResolution": "node",
    "lib": ["es6", "dom"],
    "sourceMap": true,
    "jsx": "react",
    "strict": true,
    "noImplicitReturns": true,
    "rootDir": "src",
    "outDir": "dist",
  },
  "include": ["**/*.ts", "**/*.tsx"],
  "exclude": ["node_modules"]
}
```

Adding TSLint

in Chapter 1, *TypeScript Linting*, introduced us to TSLint. Add it to your project as follows:

1. Install TSLint by entering the following command in the terminal:

```
npm install tslint --save-dev
```

2. Add a basic tslint.json file at the root of our project, and enter the following:

```
{
  "extends": ["tslint:recommended", "tslint-react", "tslint-
config-prettier"],
  "linterOptions": {
    "exclude": ["node_modules/**/*.ts"]
  }
}
```

Adding React with types

Let's add the React library to our project, by running the following command in the terminal:

```
npm install react react-dom
```

We also want the TypeScript types for React. So, add these to our project as a development dependency, as follows:

```
npm install @types/react @types/react-dom --save-dev
```

Creating a root web page

We need an HTML page that is going to host our React app. Create a file called index.html in our dist folder, and enter the following:

```
<!DOCTYPE html>
<html>
<head>
  <meta charset="utf-8"/>
</head>
<body>
  <div id="root"></div>
  <script src="bundle.js"></script>
</body>
</html>
```

The HTML from our React app will be injected into the `div` with `id ="root"`. All the app's JavaScript code will eventually be bundled together into a file called `bundle.js` in the `dist` folder.

Of course, neither of these exist at the moment—we'll do this in a later section.

Creating a simple React component

Let's create a very simple React component. Create a file called `index.tsx` in your `src` folder, and enter the following:

```
import * as React from "react";

const App: React.SFC = () => {
  return <h1>My React App!</h1>;
};
```

Our component simply returns `My React App!` in an h1 tag.

 The `tsx` extension distinguishes TypeScript React components from vanilla JavaScript React components, which have a `jsx` extension. `React.SFC` is a TypeScript type we can use for React components that don't have any internal state. We'll learn more about these components later in this book, and we'll look at state later in this chapter.

The next step is to inject our React component into `index.html`. We can do that by using the `ReactDOM.render` function. `ReactDOM.render` takes in our component as the first parameter, and the HTML element to inject it into as the next element.

Let's add the highlighted lines into `index.tsx`:

```
import * as React from "react";
import * as ReactDOM from "react-dom";

const App: React.SFC = () => {
  return <h1>My React App!</h1>;
};

ReactDOM.render(<App />, document.getElementById("root") as HTMLElement);
```

Now that we have a small app in place, we need to package it up. We'll cover that in the next section.

Adding webpack

Webpack is a popular tool that we can use to bundle all our JavaScript code into the `bundle.js` file that our `index.html` is expecting.

1. Install webpack and its command-line interface into our project as development dependencies, by entering the following command in the terminal:

   ```
   npm install webpack webpack-cli --save-dev
   ```

2. Webpack also has a handy web server that we can use during development. So, let's install that as well via the terminal:

   ```
   npm install webpack webpack-dev-server --save-dev
   ```

3. There's one final task to complete before we can start configuring webpack. This is to install a webpack plugin called `ts-loader`, which will help it load our TypeScript code. Install this as follows:

   ```
   npm install ts-loader --save-dev
   ```

4. Now that we have all this webpack stuff in our project, it's time to configure it. Create a file called `webpack.config.js` in the project root, and enter the following into it:

   ```js
   const path = require("path");

   module.exports = {
     entry: "./src/index.tsx",
     module: {
       rules: [
         {
           test: /\.tsx?$/,
           use: "ts-loader",
           exclude: /node_modules/
         }
       ]
     },
     resolve: {
       extensions: [".tsx", ".ts", ".js"]
     },
     output: {
       path: path.resolve(__dirname, "dist"),
       filename: "bundle.js"
     },
     devServer: {
       contentBase: path.join(__dirname, "dist"),
   ```

```
        compress: true,
        port: 9000
    }
};
```

There's a fair bit going on here, so let's break it down:

- The `module.exports` is our webpack configuration object.
- The `entry` field tells webpack where to start looking for modules to bundle. In our project, this is `index.tsx`.
- The `module` field tells webpack how different modules will be treated. Our project is telling webpack to use `ts-loader` to handle files with `ts` and `tsx` extensions.
- The `resolve` field tells webpack how to resolve modules. In our project, we need to process `tsx` and `.ts` files, as well as the standard `.js` files.
- The `output` field tells webpack where to bundle our code. In our project, this is the file called `bundle.js` in the `dist` folder.
- The `devServer` field configures the webpack development server. We are telling it that the root of the web server is the `dist` folder, and to serve files on `port 9000`.

Project folders and files

We should now have the following folders, with the following files within them:

```
├── dist/
│   ├── bundle.js
│   ├── index.html
├── node_modules/
├── src/
│   ├── index.tsx
├── package.json
├── tsconfig.json
├── tslint.json
├── webpack.config.js
```

We are nearly ready to run our app now—there's just one more thing to do, as we'll discuss in the next section.

Creating start and build scripts

We are going to leverage npm scripts to start our app in development mode, and also to build a production version of our app:

1. Let's open up package.json—there should be quite a bit of content in there now. We need to find the scripts section, which will probably have a single script called test in place. Add the highlighted scripts for start and build:

```
{
  ...
  "scripts": {
    "test": "echo \"Error: no test specified\" && exit 1"
    "start": "webpack-dev-server --env development",
    "build": "webpack --env production"
  },
  ..
}
```

2. Run the following command, which produces a production version of our app:

```
npm run build
```

Now, webpack will kick in and do its stuff. If we look in the dist folder, eventually a file called bundle.js will appear. This file contains all the JavaScript minified code, including code from the React library and our simple React component.

3. Now, enter the following command:

```
npm start
```

The webpack development server will start.

4. If we browse to http://localhost:9000/ we'll see our web app:

5. With our app still running, in `index.tsx`, let's change our `App` component to the following:

```
const App: React.SFC = () => {
  return <h1>My React and TypeScript App!</h1>;
};
```

6. If we save `index.tsx` and go to the browser, we'll see that our app automatically updates with the new content:

We'll leave our manually-configured project there. It doesn't do as much as the `create-react-app` project, but we have started to gain an understanding of how React and TypeScript projects are packaged up.

Creating a class component

So far we have created some very simple components. In this section, we are going to build a component that is a little more complex, and start to get more familiar with some of the different parts of a component.

Together, we'll start to build a component called `Confirm` that will allow a user to either continue with an operation or stop.

Our component will look like the following screenshot when we've finished:

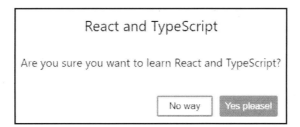

We're going to use `create-react-app` to spin up a project quickly, as follows:

1. Open up Visual Studio Code in a folder of your choice and enter the following in the terminal:

```
npx create-react-app my-components --typescript
```

This time we chose to call our project `my-components`.

2. Let's add TSLint with some rules as a development dependency to our project:

```
cd my-components
npm install tslint tslint-react tslint-config-prettier --save-
dev
```

3. Now add a `tslint.json` file, containing the following rules:

```
{
  "extends": ["tslint:recommended", "tslint-react", "tslint-
config-prettier"],
  "rules": {
    "ordered-imports": false,
    "object-literal-sort-keys": false,
    "no-debugger": false,
    "no-console": false,
  },
  "linterOptions": {
    "exclude": [
      "config/**/*.js",
      "node_modules/**/*.ts",
      "coverage/lcov-report/*.js"
    ]
  }
}
```

4. Fix the linting error in `App.tsx` by adding the missing access modifier on the `render` method:

```
class App extends Component {
  public render() {
    return ( ... );
  }
}
```

5. We can now start a development server and start our app:

```
npm start
```

6. Next we'll shrink and fix the app header, so that there is enough space for our confirmation component. Change the highlighted lines in app.css:

```css
.App-logo {
  animation: App-logo-spin infinite 20s linear;
  height: 80px;
}

.App-header {
  background-color: #282c34;
  height: 200px;
  display: flex;
  flex-direction: column;
  align-items: center;
  justify-content: center;
  font-size: 16px;
  color: white;
}
```

The app header should now be a little shorter.

We'll keep our app running while we develop our component in the following sections.

Creating a basic class component

Let's look at App.tsx, which has been created for us. This is an example of a class component. We're going to create our own class component now. Follow these steps:

1. Create a file called Confirm.tsx in the src folder, and enter the following into it:

```tsx
import * as React from "react";

class Confirm extends React.Component {
}

export default Confirm;
```

We learned all about classes in Chapter 1, *TypeScript Basics.* Here we are creating a class that extends the standard Component class from React. Note that we've imported React at the top of our file, and also that we are exporting our class component using a default export at the bottom of our file.

2. Let's start to implement our Confirm class component now, by creating a render method:

```
class Confirm extends React.Component {
  public render() {
    return (
    );
  }
}
```

The render method determines what the component needs to display. We define what needs to be displayed using JSX. In simple terms, JSX is a mix of HTML and JavaScript. We'll explore it in more detail in the next section.

3. For the time being, let's enter the following in our render method:

```
public render() {
  return (
    <div className="confirm-wrapper confirm-visible">
      <div className="confirm-container">
        <div className="confirm-title-container">
          <span>This is where our title should go</span>
        </div>
        <div className="confirm-content-container">
          <p>This is where our content should go</p>
        </div>
        <div className="confirm-buttons-container">
          <button className="confirm-cancel">Cancel</button>
          <button className="confirm-ok">Okay</button>
        </div>
      </div>
    </div>
  );
}
```

At the moment, our render method looks a lot more like HTML than JavaScript, apart from that funny className attribute—shouldn't that be class?

We'll cover this and JSX in a little more detail in the next section, but before that, let's consume our Confirm component in the App component.

4. In `App.tsx`, we need to import our `Confirm` component class, as follows:

```
import Confirm from "./Confirm";
```

5. Our `Confirm` component can be referenced as `<Confirm />` in JSX. So, let's add this to the JSX in `App.tsx`:

```
<div className="App">
  <header className="App-header">
    . . .
  </header>
  <Confirm />
</div>
```

If we look at the browser page where our app is running, it should now look like the following:

6. We are going to make our component look more like a dialog using CSS. Let's create a file called `Confirm.css`, and enter the following into it:

```
.confirm-wrapper {
  position: fixed;
  left: 0;
  top: 0;
  width: 100%;
  height: 100%;
  background-color: gray;
  opacity: 0;
```

```
    visibility: hidden;
    transform: scale(1.1);
    transition: visibility 0s linear 0.25s, opacity 0.25s 0s,
transform 0.25s;
    z-index: 1;
}
.confirm-visible {
  opacity: 1;
  visibility: visible;
  transform: scale(1);
  transition: visibility 0s linear 0s, opacity 0.25s 0s,
transform 0.25s;
}
.confirm-container {
  background-color: #fff;
  position: absolute;
  top: 50%;
  left: 50%;
  transform: translate(-50%, -50%);
  border-radius: 0.2em;
  min-width: 300px;
}
.confirm-title-container {
  font-size: 1.3em;
  padding: 10px;
  border-top-left-radius: 0.2em;
  border-top-right-radius: 0.2em;
}
.confirm-content-container {
  padding: 0px 10px 15px 10px;
}
.confirm-buttons-container {
  padding: 5px 15px 10px 15px;
  text-align: right;
}
.confirm-buttons-container button {
  margin-left: 10px;
  min-width: 80px;
  line-height: 20px;
  border-style: solid;
  border-radius: 0.2em;
  padding: 3px 6px;
  cursor: pointer;
}
.confirm-cancel {
  background-color: #fff;
  border-color: #848e97;
}
```

```
.confirm-cancel:hover {
  border-color: #6c757d;
}
.confirm-ok {
  background-color: #848e97;
  border-color: #848e97;
  color: #fff;
}
.confirm-ok:hover {
  background-color: #6c757d;
  border-color: #6c757d;
}
```

7. Now let's import our CSS in our `Confirm.tsx`:

```
import "./Confirm.css";
```

Our component in the browser page should now look like the following:

So, a React class component has a special method called `render`, where we define what our component displays in JSX.

In the next section, we'll take a little break from our confirmation component while we learn a little more about JSX.

JSX

As mentioned in the previous section, JSX looks a bit like HTML. We can have JSX in our JavaScript (or TypeScript) code, as we did in the last section in our `render` function. JSX isn't valid JavaScript though—we need a preprocessor step to convert it into JavaScript.

We're going to use an online Babel REPL to play with JSX:

1. Open a browser, go to `https://babeljs.io/repl`, and enter the following JSX in the left-hand pane:

   ```
   <span>This is where our title should go</span>
   ```

   The following appears in the right-hand pane, which is what our JSX has compiled down to:

   ```
   React.createElement(
     "span",
     null,
     "This is where our title should go"
   );
   ```

   We can see that it compiles down to a call to `React.createElement`, which has three parameters:

   - The element type, which can be an HTML tag name string (such as `"span"`), a React component type, or a React fragment type
   - An object containing the props to be applied to the element
   - The children for the element

2. Let's expand our example by putting `div` tags around our `span`:

   ```
   <div className="confirm-title-container">
     <span>This is where our title should go</span>
   </div>
   ```

   This now compiles down to two calls to `React.createElement`, with `span` being passed in as a child to `div`:

   ```
   React.createElement(
     "div",
     { className: "confirm-title-container" },
     React.createElement(
       "span",
       null,
       "This is where our title should go"
     )
   );
   ```

3. This is starting to make sense, but so far our JSX has consisted of only HTML. Let's add some JavaScript now, by declaring a props object literal. Let's also reference the `title` prop inside the `span` using curly braces:

```
const props = {
  title: "React and TypeScript"
};
<div className="confirm-title-container">
  <span>{props.title}</span>
</div>
```

This is more interesting now. It compiles down to this:

```
var props = {
 title: "React and TypeScript"
};
React.createElement(
 "div",
 { className: "confirm-title-container" },
 React.createElement(
 "span",
 null,
 props.title
 )
);
```

The key point is that we can inject JavaScript into HTML by using curly braces.

4. To further illustrate the point, let's empty the `props` object literal, and use a JavaScript ternary inside `span`:

```
const props = {};
<div className="confirm-title-container">
  <span>{props.title ? props.title : "React and
TypeScript"}</span>
</div>
```

We see that the nested call to `React.createElement` uses our ternary as the child of `span`:

```
React.createElement(
  "span",
  null,
  props.title ? props.title : "React and TypeScript"
)
```

So, why do we use the `className` attribute rather than `class`? Well, we now understand that JSX compiles down to JavaScript, and as `class` is a keyword in JavaScript, having a `class` attribute in JSX would clash. So, React uses `className` instead for CSS class references.

Now that we understand a little more about JSX, let's come back to our `Confirm` component.

Component props

At the moment, the title and content text for our `Confirm` component is hardcoded. Let's change these to reference properties (props) that the component takes in.

1. First, we need to define a TypeScript type for our props. We'll use an interface for this preceding the `Confirm` class in `Confirm.tsx`:

```
interface IProps {
   title: string;
   content: string;
}
```

2. We can then reference the `IProps` type in angle brackets, after we reference `React.Component` in the class definition:

```
class Confirm extends React.Component<IProps>
```

React.Component is what is called a generic class. Generic classes allow types used within the class to be passed in. In our case, we have passed in our `IProps` interface. Don't worry if this doesn't make too much sense at the moment—we'll cover generic classes later in the book.

3. We get access to props in our class using `this.props.propName`. In our JSX, we can now reference props instead of hardcoding the title and content:

```
...
<div className="confirm-title-container">
  <span>{this.props.title}</span>
</div>
<div className="confirm-content-container">
  <p>{this.props.content}</p>
</div>
...
```

Note that we now have a TypeScript compilation error when we reference our
`Confirm` component in `App.tsx`. This is because our component now
expects `title` and `content` attributes, as follows:

```
21              <img src={logo} className="App-logo" alt="logo" />
22              <h1 className="App-title">Welcome to React</h1>
23          </header>
24          <p className="App-intro">
25              To get started, edit <code>src/App.tsx</code> and save to reload.
26          </p>
27          <Confirm />
28          </div>
29      );
30      }
31  }
32
33  export default App;
```

```
PROBLEMS ①   OUTPUT   DEBUG CONSOLE   TERMINAL        Filter. Eg: text, **/*.ts !*/node_modules/**  ⚙
⏴ App.tsx confirm\src   ①
   ⊗ [ts] Type '{}' is not assignable to type 'Readonly<IProps>'. Property 'title' is missing in type '{}'. (27, 10)
```

4. Let's add the `title` and `content` attributes:

```
<Confirm
  title="React and TypeScript"
  content="Are you sure you want to learn React and
TypeScript?"
/>
```

The compilation error now goes away, and if we look at the browser, our
component is rendered exactly as it was before we implemented props.

Optional props

Interface props can be optional, as we discovered in Chapter 1, *TypeScript Basics*. So, we
can also use this mechanism to add optional props to a React component.

Let's add some optional props to allow the button captions to be configurable on our
confirmation component:

1. Add some additional optional props called `cancelCaption` and `okCaption` to
   our interface:

```
interface IProps {
  title: string;
```

```
content: string;
cancelCaption?: string;
okCaption?: string;
}
```

 We put a ? before the type annotation to denote that the prop is optional. Note also that we don't get a compilation error in App.tsx, where we reference, Confirm because we are not required to enter these as attributes on Confirm.

2. Let's reference these props in our JSX now, replacing the hardcoded captions:

```
<div className="confirm-buttons-container">
  <button className="confirm-cancel">
{this.props.cancelCaption}
</button>
<button className="confirm-ok">
{this.props.okCaption}
</button>
</div>
```

If we look at the browser now, we have no button captions in our running app:

React and TypeScript

Are you sure you want to learn React and TypeScript?

This is because we haven't supplied these values when we reference Confirm in App.tsx.

In the next section, we'll resolve this issue by adding some default values for cancelCaption and okCaption.

Default prop values

Default values can be added to component props when the component is initialized. These can be implemented using a static object literal called `defaultProps`.

Let's make use of this feature in our `Confirm` component, as follows:

1. Create some default values for `cancelCaption` and `okCaption` in our class:

```
class Confirm extends React.Component<IProps> {
  public static defaultProps = {
    cancelCaption: "Cancel",
    okCaption: "Okay"
  };
  public render() { ... }
}
```

If we look at our running app again, we have button captions once more.

2. Let's finish this section by overriding the defaults, and supplying specific attributes for these captions in `App.tsx`, as follows:

```
<Confirm
  title="React and TypeScript"
  content="Are you sure you want to learn React and TypeScript?"
  cancelCaption="No way"
  okCaption="Yes please!"
/>
```

Our running app should now look like the following:

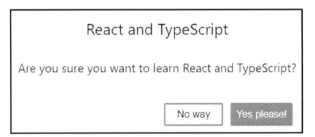

Optional props with default values can make components easier to consume, because the most common configurations can be automatically set up without needing to specify anything.

So, our `Confirm` component is nice and flexible now, but the buttons don't do anything yet. We'll tackle this in the following sections.

Handling class component events

Events exist in many programming languages. They allow us to specify logic to be executed, depending on how a user interacts with our app.

Basic event handlers

All the native JavaScript events are available for us to handle in JSX. JSX allows us to do this with props that call functions. The prop name is derived by prefixing the native event name with `on`, using camel case. So the prop name for the `click` event is `onClick` in JSX.

We can see a list of all the available events with their corresponding types in the `index.d.ts` file in the `node_modules/@types/react` folder.

We need to be able to control what the buttons do in our `Confirm` component. Follow these steps:

1. The first step is handling the `click` events on those buttons. Let's set the `onClick` prop on the **Okay** button, as follows:

   ```
   <button className="confirm-ok"
   onClick={this.handleOkClick}>...</button>
   ```

   So, we're telling the button to call a `handleOkClick` method within our `Confirm` class when it is clicked.

2. Next, let's create the `handleOkClick` method:

   ```
   private handleOkClick() {
     console.log("Ok clicked");
   }
   ```

Switch to the browser with our app running, and click the **Yes please!** button. If we look in the console, we should see **Ok clicked** displayed:

As we can see, it is pretty straightforward to handle events, using mechanisms we are already familiar with. There is actually a problem with our `handleOkClick` method, though. We'll drill into this and resolve the issue in the next section.

The this problem

Our event handler suffers from JavaScript's classic `this` problem. We aren't currently referencing `this` in our event handler, which is why the problem hasn't surfaced yet.

Let's expose the problem with the `handleOkClick` method, so that we can better understand what's happening:

1. Log the component props to the console:

    ```
    private handleOkClick() {
        console.log("Ok clicked", this.props);
    }
    ```

    Now, try clicking the **Yes please!** button again. The following error appears:

```
TypeError: Cannot read property 'props' of undefined                    ×

./src/Confirm.4.tsx.Confirm3.handleOkClick
C:/code/_temp/ts-react-confirm/confirm/src/Confirm.4.tsx:39

  36 |  }
  37 |
  38 |   private handleOkClick() {
> 39 |     console.log("Ok clicked", this.props);
  40 |  }
  41 |
  42 |   private handleCancelClick() {

View compiled
```

The problem is that `this` doesn't reference our class in the event handler—it is `undefined` instead.

One solution is to change the `handleOkClick` method to be an arrow function.

 Arrow function expressions have shorter syntax than function expressions. They also don't create their own `this`—so they are a great solution to the `this` problem.

2. Let's convert our method to an arrow function, as follows:

```
private handleOkClick = () => {
  console.log("Ok clicked", this.props);
};
```

Now try clicking the **Yes please!** button again. We should see props successfully output to the console.

3. Moving on, let's implement a click handler on the **Cancel** button now. First, we need to reference a handler on the **Cancel** button's `onClick` prop:

```
<button className="confirm-cancel"
onClick={this.handleCancelClick}>...</button>
```

4. Now we'll create the `handleCancelClick` arrow function:

```
private handleCancelClick = () => {
  console.log("Cancel clicked", this.props);
};
```

To summarize, in order to avoid the `this` problem, we can use arrow functions to implement event handlers.

Next, we want the consumer of the component to be able to execute some logic when the buttons are clicked. We'll cover how to do this in the next section.

Function props

In the previous section, we saw how props can be set for functions with our `onClick` event handlers. In this section, we'll implement our own function props, so that the consumer of our component can execute some logic when the **Ok** and **Cancel** buttons are pressed.

1. Let's implement these two additional props on our interface. The function will take no parameters, and not return anything. So, the type is `() => void`, as follows:

```
interface IProps {
  title: string;
  content: string;
  cancelCaption?: string;
  okCaption?: string;
  onOkClick: () => void;
  onCancelClick: () => void;
}
```

The props are required, so, we immediately get a compilation error in `App.tsx` when we reference the `Confirm` component. We'll fix this a little later.

2. Next, let's invoke our function props when the buttons are clicked, instead of logging messages to the console:

```
private handleCancelClick = () => {
  this.props.onCancelClick();
};

private handleOkClick = () => {
  this.props.onOkClick();
};
```

3. We'll fix the compilation error now, by implementing arrow function handlers for these props in `App.tsx`. First let's create the arrow function handlers:

```
private handleCancelConfirmClick = () => {
  console.log("Cancel clicked");
};

private handleOkConfirmClick = () => {
  console.log("Ok clicked");
};
```

4. Now we can reference these functions we where consume the `Confirm` component:

```
<Confirm
  ...
  onCancelClick={this.handleCancelConfirmClick}
  onOkClick={this.handleOkConfirmClick}
/>
```

If we go back to our app, we'll see the compilation errors have been resolved. If we click the **Ok** and **Cancel** buttons, we get the message output to the console as expected:

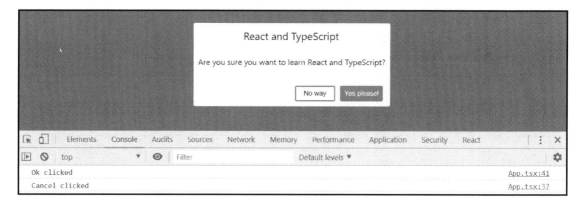

At the moment, our buttons still don't do anything other than log a message to the console. We want the confirmation dialog to close when we click either button. We'll implement this in the next section.

Class component states

State is an object that determines how the component behaves and renders. We need to introduce state into our app, in order to manage whether our confirmation dialog is open or closed.

This particular state is going to live and be managed within the `App` component, and be passed in as a prop to the `Confirm` component.

1. First, create an `open` prop in the `Confirm` component by adding it to its props interface:

```
interface IProps {
  open: boolean;
  title: string;
  content: string;
  cancelCaption?: string;
  okCaption?: string;
  onOkClick: () => void;
  onCancelClick: () => void;
}
```

2. We're going to use the `open` prop in the `render` function to determine whether the dialog is visible or not. The `confirm-visible` CSS class makes the dialog visible.

   So, on the outermost `div`, let's use a JavaScript ternary expression in the `className` attribute to only include `confirm-visible` when the `open` prop is `true`, as follows:

```
public render() {
  return (
    <div
      className={
        this.props.open
          ? "confirm-wrapper confirm-visible"
          : "confirm-wrapper"
      }
    >
      ...
    </div>
  );
}
```

   We now have a compilation error in `App.tsx` because we haven't specified the `open` attribute where we use `Confirm`.

3. Before we start to create and manage state within `App.tsx`, let's simply pass `false` in the `open` attribute in `Confirm`:

```
<Confirm
  open={false}
  title="React and TypeScript"
  content="Are you sure you want to learn React and
TypeScript?"
  cancelCaption="No way"
  okCaption="Yes please!"
  onCancelClick={this.handleCancelConfirmClick}
  onOkClick={this.handleOkConfirmClick}
/>
```

If we look at the app in the browser now, the compilation error will have disappeared, and our confirmation dialog will be closed.

Defining state type

Let's create a state in `App.tsx`, and properly manage whether the confirmation dialog is open or closed:

1. First, let's create an interface for the state above the `App` class:

```
interface IState {
 confirmOpen: boolean;
}
```

2. We then tell the `App` component about the state type, which we can do using the second generic parameter of `React.Component`:

```
class App extends React.Component<{}, IState>
```

We have used `{}` as the props type because there are no props for this component.

Initializing the state

Now that we have specified that our component has a state, we need to initialize it. We initialize component state in the class constructor.

1. Let's create a constructor, and initialize the `confirmOpen` state to be `true`:

```
constructor(props: {}) {
  super(props);
  this.state = {
   confirmOpen: true,
  };
}
```

We call `super` because our class extends `React.Component`.

The state is held in a private prop in a component class. In the constructor, we can set the state to our required object literal, which in our case has `confirmOpen` set to `true`.

2. We can then use this state when we reference the `Confirm` component:

```
<Confirm
  open={this.state.confirmOpen}
  ...
/>
```

If we look at our running app, the confirmation dialog should be open again.

So, a private state prop gives us access to the component state, and we can initialize this in the class constructor.

Changing state

When the confirmation dialog buttons are clicked, we want to close the dialog. So, we want to change the state of `confirmOpen` to be false when the buttons are clicked.

We already have arrow function handlers for the button click events, so perhaps we can change state in there:

1. Let's try to do that in `handleOkConfirmClick`, replacing the `console.log`:

```
private handleOkConfirmClick = () => {
  this.state.confirmOpen = false;
};
```

We get a compilation error, as follows:

```
private handleCancelConfirmClick = () => {
  console.log [ts] Cannot assign to 'confirmOpen' because it is a constant or
};               a read-only property.

private handl (property) confirmOpen: boolean
  this.state.confirmOpen = false;
};
```

The error message is saying that the state is read-only! Why is this so, and how can we change the state?

We need to use a method called `setState` in the component class to change state. This helps ensure we manage state robustly and efficiently. `setState` takes a parameter, which is an object literal containing the state we want to change.

2. Let's change our code to use `setState`:

```
private handleOkConfirmClick = () => {
  this.setState({ confirmOpen: false });
};
```

The compilation error disappears, and if we click **Yes please!** in the running app, the confirmation dialog will now close. We have successfully changed the state.

3. Change the implementation of `handleCancelConfirmClick` to close the dialog as well:

```
private handleCancelConfirmClick = () => {
  this.setState({ confirmOpen: false });
};
```

After we close the confirmation dialog, we have no way to open it.

4. So, let's add a button labeled **Confirm** that does that in `App.tsx`:

```
<button onClick={this.handleConfirmClick}>Confirm</button>
<Confirm ... />
```

5. We need to create the handler that we just referenced:

```
private handleConfirmClick = () => {
  this.setState({ confirmOpen: true });
};
```

We can now click the **Confirm** button to reopen the confirmation dialog when it has been closed.

6. Let's add a piece of text above the **Confirm** button in App.tsx that changes depending on whether the confirmation dialog is canceled or okayed. We'll define an additional state to drive this text:

```
interface IState {
  confirmOpen: boolean;
  confirmMessage: string;
}
```

7. Now, let's initialize the message in the constructor:

```
constructor(props: {}) {
  super(props);
  this.state = {
    confirmMessage: "Please hit the confirm button",
    confirmOpen: true,
  };
}
```

8. The state is now changed when the confirmation dialog is okayed or canceled:

```
private handleOkConfirmClick = () => {
  this.setState({
    confirmMessage: "Cool, carry on reading!",
    confirmOpen: false
  });
};

private handleCancelConfirmClick = () => {
  this.setState({
    confirmMessage: "Take a break, I'm sure you will later
...",
    confirmOpen: false
  });
};
```

9. Finally, we can render the message above the **Confirm** button:

```
<p>{this.state.confirmMessage}</p>
<button onClick={this.handleConfirmClick}>Confirm</button>
<Confirm ... />
```

If we play with the running app now, we'll see the message in our app changing depending on whether we okay or cancel the confirmation dialog.

Although we can set the state prop directly in the constructor when we initialize it, we can't elsewhere in a class component. Instead, state should be changed by calling the `setState` method in the component class.

Class component life cycle methods

Life cycle methods in a class component allow us to run code at particular points in the process. The following is a high-level diagram of the component process, showing when the different methods are invoked:

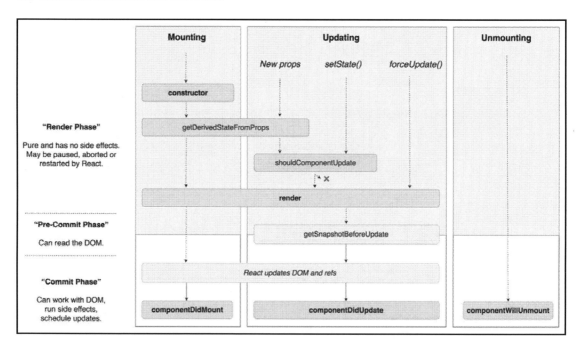

Diagram of modern React life cycle methods, from React documentation

componentDidMount

`componentDidMount` is invoked when a component has been inserted into the DOM. Here are some common use cases for this method:

- Calling a web service to get some data
- Adding event listeners
- Initializing timers
- Initializing third-party libraries

We're going to change the app we have been building to give users a time limit of 10 seconds to confirm whether or not they want to learn React and TypeScript. In order to do this, we'll need to make use of the `componentDidMount` method:

1. Let's start by making the confirmation dialog closed when the app loads in `App.tsx`:

```
constructor(props: {}) {
  super(props);
  this.state = {
    confirmMessage: "Please hit the confirm button",
    confirmOpen: false
  };
}
```

2. We're going to count down the seconds from `10` to `0`, and then hide the **Confirm** button when `0` is reached. Let's add and initialize a state for both of these in `App.tsx`:

```
interface IState {
  confirmOpen: boolean;
  confirmMessage: string;
  confirmVisible: boolean;
  countDown: number;
}

constructor(props: {}) {
  super(props);
  this.state = {
    confirmMessage: "Please hit the confirm button",
    confirmOpen: false,
    confirmVisible: true,
    countDown: 10
  };
}
```

3. We'll use `timer` to count down from `10` to 1 in the `App` class. Let's create a private prop called `timer` just above the constructor:

```
private timer: number = 0;
```

4. Now, let's use the `componentDidMount` method to initialize our `timer`:

```
public componentDidMount() {
  this.timer = window.setInterval(() => this.handleTimerTick(),
1000);
}
```

5. The timer will call a method called `handleTimerTick` every second. Implement this method as follows:

```
private handleTimerTick() {
  this.setState(
    {
      confirmMessage: `Please hit the confirm button ${
        this.state.countDown
      } secs to go`,
      countDown: this.state.countDown - 1
    }
  );
}
```

We are reducing our counter as well, updating the message shown to the user in this method. We need to do some more work here, though: we need to stop the timer, hide the **Confirm** button, and tell the user they are too late!

6. Our natural instinct may be to write something like this:

```
private handleTimerTick() {
  this.setState(
    {
      confirmMessage: `Please hit the confirm button ${
        this.state.countDown
      } secs to go`,
      countDown: this.state.countDown - 1
    }
  );
  if (this.state.countDown <= 0) {
    clearInterval(this.timer);
    this.setState({
      confirmMessage: "Too late to confirm!",
      confirmVisible: false
    });
```

```
        }
    }
```

However, this is incorrect, because the state is updated asynchronously, and so `this.state.countDown` won't have necessarily updated the line after we update it in the `setState` call.

7. Instead, we need to move this code to the callback in `setState`:

```
private handleTimerTick() {
  this.setState(
    {
      confirmMessage: `Please hit the confirm button ${
        this.state.countDown
      } secs to go`,
      countDown: this.state.countDown - 1
    },
    () => {
      if (this.state.countDown <= 0) {
        clearInterval(this.timer);
        this.setState({
          confirmMessage: "Too late to confirm!",
          confirmVisible: false
        });
      }
    }
  );
}
```

8. Let's also stop the timer if the **Confirm**, **Ok**, or **Cancel** buttons are clicked:

```
private handleConfirmClick = () => {
  this.setState({ confirmOpen: true });
  clearInterval(this.timer);
};

private handleCancelConfirmClick = () => {
  this.setState(...);
  clearInterval(this.timer);
};

private handleOkConfirmClick = () => {
  this.setState(...;
  clearInterval(this.timer);
};
```

9. Our final job is to put a condition around the **Confirm** button to only show it if the `confirmVisible` state is `true`:

```
<p>{this.state.confirmMessage}</p>
{this.state.confirmVisible && (
  <button onClick={this.handleConfirmClick}>Confirm</button>
)}
<Confirm ... />
```

 `x && y` allows us to concisely express a condition with a single branch in JSX. Basically, the right operand of `&&` isn't evaluated and rendered if the left operand is falsy.

Now, it's time to give this a try. We'll see the countdown when the app first runs:

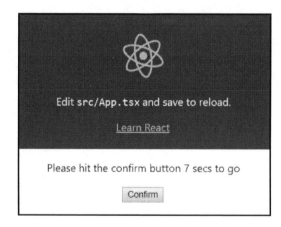

If we don't confirm within ten seconds, it'll be too late:

componentWillUnmount

`componentWillUnmount` is invoked just before the component is removed from the DOM. Here are some common use cases for this method:

- Removing event listeners
- Canceling active network requests
- Removing timers

We are going to use `componentWillUnmount` in our app to make sure our `timer` is stopped and removed. Let's add the following in the `App` class after the `componentDidMount` method:

```
public componentWillUnmount() {
  clearInterval(this.timer);
}
```

getDerivedStateFromProps

`getDerivedStateFromProps` is invoked every time a component is rendered. It can be used to change state when certain props change. This is a static method in a component class that returns the changed state, or null if there are no changes to the state.

Let's have a look at this life cycle method in our app. Add the following at the top of the `App` class:

```
public static getDerivedStateFromProps(props: {}, state: IState) {
  console.log("getDerivedStateFromProps", props, state);
  return null;
}
```

If we look in the console when the app is running, we see that our method is called each time the countdown decrements:

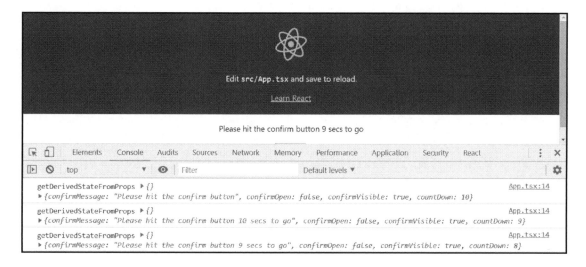

getSnapshotBeforeUpdate and componentDidUpdate

getSnapshotBeforeUpdate is called just before the DOM is updated. The value that is returned from getSnapshotBeforeUpdate is passed on to componentDidUpdate.

componentDidUpdate is called as soon as the DOM is updated. Resizing the window during rendering is an example of when getSnapshotBeforeUpdate can be useful.

Let's have a look at these life cycle methods in our app:

1. Let's add the following near the top of the App class, under the timer variable declaration:

```
private renderCount = 0;
```

2. Now, let's add the life cycle methods:

```
public getSnapshotBeforeUpdate(prevProps: {}, prevState:
IState) {
  this.renderCount += 1;
  console.log("getSnapshotBeforeUpdate", prevProps, prevState,
{
```

```
    renderCount: this.renderCount
  });
  return this.renderCount;
}

public componentDidUpdate(prevProps: {}, prevState: IState,
snapshot: number) {
  console.log("componentDidUpdate", prevProps, prevState,
  snapshot, {
    renderCount: this.renderCount
  });
}
```

Look at the running app:

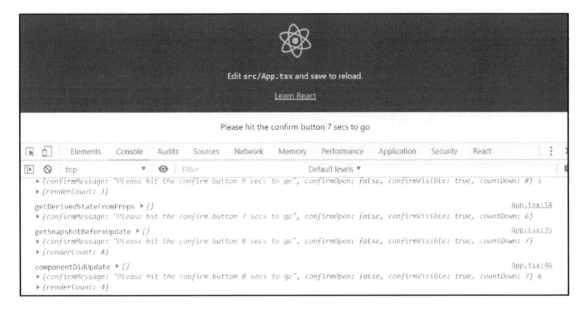

We see the methods being invoked in the order we expect, and
componentDidUpdate successfully taking in the render count from
getSnapshotBeforeUpdate.

shouldComponentUpdate

`shouldComponentUpdate` is invoked just before rendering happens. It returns a Boolean value that determines whether rendering should happen. It can be used to optimize performance, preventing unnecessary render cycles.

1. Let's have a look at this life cycle method in our app by adding the following method:

```
public shouldComponentUpdate(nextProps: {}, nextState: IState)
{
  console.log("shouldComponentUpdate", nextProps, nextState);
  return true;
}
```

If we look at the running app, we see that `shouldComponentUpdate` happens between `getDerivedStateFromProps` and `getSnapshotBeforeUpdate`, as we expect.

2. Let's now prevent rendering by returning `false`:

```
public shouldComponentUpdate(nextProps: {}, nextState: IState)
{
  console.log("shouldComponentUpdate", nextProps, nextState);
  return false;
}
```

We see `getSnapshotBeforeUpdate` and `componentDidUpdate` aren't invoked, because no rendering occurs after the initial render:

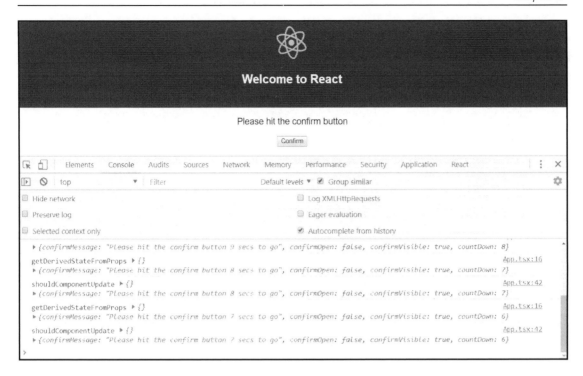

3. Before moving on to the next section, let's allow our component to render again by setting this flag back to `true`:

```
public shouldComponentUpdate(nextProps: {}, nextState: IState)
{
  console.log("shouldComponentUpdate", nextProps, nextState);
  return true;
}
```

`shouldComponentUpdate` can increase performance by stopping unnecessary rendering, but it should be used with care. It can introduce bugs that are hard to pin down. Also, the additional code we need to add to check whether a render should occur could in fact slow the app down.

Deprecated life cycle methods

There are a few life cycle methods that have been deprecated and renamed in React 17. We don't need to use these anymore—`getDerivedStateFromProps` and `getSnapshotBeforeUpdate` essentially replaced them. However, here's a brief description of these methods, in case you come across them in existing codebases:

- `componentWillMount` (now `UNSAFE_componentWillMount`): This is called before the component is added to the DOM during an initial render
- `componentWillReceiveProps` (now `UNSAFE_componentWillReceiveProps`): This is called when the component props change
- `componentWillUpdate` (now `UNSAFE_componentWillUpdate`): This is called just before a component updates

Creating a function component

As the name suggests, a function component is implemented using a JavaScript function. These components are sometimes referred to as *functional stateless components*, which can be a little confusing because they can contain states in more recent versions of React.

Creating a basic function component

Let's refactor our `Confirm` component to be a function component, in order to learn how to implement these:

1. Open `Confirm.tsx` and replace the class signature with the following:

```
const Confirm: React.SFC<IProps> = (props) => {
...
}
```

We define a function component using an arrow function, passing the props type in as a generic parameter.

We'll learn about generic functions later in the book—so don't worry if this doesn't make perfect sense right now.

We use **stateless functional component (SFC)** React.SFC to represent these type of components.

Our component is now throwing several compilation errors. We'll resolve these in the next steps.

2. Function components don't have render methods. Instead, the function itself returns the JSX that should be rendered. So, let's change this part of our function by removing the render signature, and leaving the return statement as it was:

```
return (
  <div
    className={
      this.props.open
        ? "confirm-wrapper confirm-visible"
        : "confirm-wrapper"
    }
  >
    . . .
  </div>
);
```

3. We need to change the event handlers to be arrow function constants, and access props directly rather than through this. We should also move these handlers above the return statement:

```
const handleCancelClick = () => {
  props.onCancelClick();
};

const handleOkClick = () => {
  props.onOkClick();
};

return ( ... )
```

4. We then reference the props and event handlers directly, rather than through `this` in our JSX:

```
<div
  className={
    props.open
      ? "confirm-wrapper confirm-visible"
      : "confirm-wrapper"
  }
>
  <div className="confirm-container">
    <div className="confirm-title-container">
      <span>{props.title}</span>
    </div>
    <div className="confirm-content-container">
      <p>{props.content}</p>
    </div>
    <div className="confirm-buttons-container">
      <button className="confirm-cancel" onClick=
        {handleCancelClick}>
        {props.cancelCaption}
      </button>
      <button className="confirm-ok" onClick={handleOkClick}>
        {props.okCaption}
      </button>
    </div>
  </div>
</div>
```

5. We also have a problem with the static `defaultProps` variable. We move this outside our function, and place it as an object literal under the function, as follows:

```
Confirm.defaultProps = {
  cancelCaption: "Cancel",
  okCaption: "Okay"
}
```

If we look at the running app, all the compilation errors should be resolved, and the app should be working as it was before.

The following code is a template for a function component. Our `Confirm` component should have a structure similar to this now:

```
import * as React from "react";

const ComponentName: React.SFC<IProps> = props => {
  const handler = () => {
    ...
  };

  return (
  <div>Our JSX</div>
  );
};
ComponentName.defaultProps = {
  ...
};

export default ComponentName;
```

So, function components are an alternative way to create components. In the next section, we'll look at how to add state to a function component.

Stateful function components

We've mentioned that function components can have state. In this section, we'll add state to our function `Confirm` component, to force users to click the **Cancel** button twice before closing it, as follows:

1. We'll start by defining and initializing state for the number of times the **Cancel** button is clicked, by adding the highlighted line:

```
const Confirm: React.SFC<IProps> = props => {

  const [cancelClickCount, setCancelClickCount] =
  React.useState(0);

  const handleOkClick = () => {
    props.onOkClick();
  };
  ...
}
```

This line of code looks a little strange, so let's break it down:

- `React.useState` is a React function that lets us create state, passing in a default value as a parameter. In our case, we pass it a default value of 0.
- The `useState` function returns an array containing two elements:
  - The first array element contains the current value of state
  - The second array element contains a function to set state to a different value
- We destructure the array and store the first array element (the state value) in `cancelClickCount`, and the second array element (the function to set state) in `setCancelClickCount`.
- The rest of the function now has access to the cancel click count, via the `cancelClickCount` variable. The function is also able to increment the cancel click **count**, via the `setCancelClickCount` variable.

2. Let's refactor the `handleCancelClick` arrow function to increment `cancelClickCount`, and only invoke the `onCancelClick` prop if the count has reached 2:

```
const handleCancelClick = () => {
  const newCount = cancelClickCount + 1;
  setCancelClickCount(newCount);
  if (newCount >= 2) {
    props.onCancelClick();
  }
};
```

Now, functions to set the piece of state take in the new state as their parameter.

3. Next, we'll change the **Cancel** button caption, to say **Really?** after the first click:

```
<button className="confirm-cancel" onClick={handleCancelClick}>
  {cancelClickCount === 0 ? props.cancelCaption : "Really?"}
</button>
```

So, we access the state value in JSX through the variable we destructured when the state was defined.

If we give this a try in the running app, we should find the **Cancel** button text changes to **Really?** after the first click, and the confirmation dialog closes after the second click.

After we've got our heads around the code needed to define state, accessing and setting state is fairly simple and elegant.

Let's continue to the next section, and look into how we can hook into a function component's life cycle events.

Function component life cycle hooks

We can invoke code to execute at certain points in a function component's life cycle. Let's explore this in our `Confirm` component, starting with when the component is first rendering, as follows:

1. Let's add the highlighted lines of code just beneath where we define state:

```
const [cancelClickCount, setCancelClickCount] =
React.useState(0);

React.useEffect(() => {
  console.log("Confirm first rendering");
}, []);
```

- We use React's `useEffect` function to hook into the component life cycle.
- The function takes in an arrow function, which executes when the component is first rendered.
- The function takes in a second parameter, which determines when our arrow function is called. This parameter is an array of values that, when changed, will cause the arrow function to be invoked. In our case, we pass in an empty array, so our arrow function will never be called after the first render.
- If we now try the running app and open the console, we'll see **Confirm first rendering** only appears once.

2. Let's remove the second parameter into `useEffect` now:

```
React.useEffect(() => {
  console.log("Confirm rendering");
});
```

If we look at the running app and the console, we'll see **Confirm rendering** appear each time `Confirm` is rendered.

3. Let's change this once again to the following:

```
React.useEffect(
  () => {
    console.log("open changed");
```

```
  },
  [props.open]
);
```

If we look at the running app and the console, we'll see **open changed** appear each time the `Confirm` component's `open` prop changes value.

4. What about hooking into when a component is unmounted? Let's try the following:

```
React.useEffect(() => {
  console.log("Confirm first rendering");
  return () => {
    console.log("Confirm unmounted");
  };
}, []);
```

So, our arrow function can return a function that is executed when the component is unmounted.

5. Our `Confirm` component doesn't currently unmount, so, in `App.tsx`, let's make this not render if the countdown reaches `0`:

```
{this.state.countDown > 0 && (
  <Confirm
    ...
  />
)}
```

If we look at the running app and the console, we'll see `Confirm unmounted` appear when the countdown reaches `0`.

So, we can execute logic in function components when they are first rendered, when their props change, and when they are unmounted.

In the next section, we'll look at a method we can use to optimize function component rendering cycles.

This section on hooks is written on React v16.6.0. We will share updated codes when new version releases.

Optimizing function component rendering

Our `Confirm` component is actually being rendered more than it needs to be. In this section, we are going to optimize this so that it only renders when its props change:

1. First, let's add a line at the top of our function component, so that we can see when it renders:

   ```
   console.log("Confirm rendering");
   ```

   If we look at the running app and the console, we'll see that a render occurs every time the `App` component counts down. The countdown is in the `App` component state, and a change to state means the component will be rendered again, along with any child components. This is why, without any optimization, our `Confirm` component renders on each countdown.

2. On to the optimization then. It's actually really simple:

   ```
   const ConfirmMemo = React.memo(Confirm);
   export default ConfirmMemo;
   ```

   So, we wrap our component with a function called `memo` from React. We then export this wrapper function. The `memo` function then only renders the component if its props change.

   If we look at the running app and the console, we'll see that our component no longer renders on each countdown.

So, given how simple this is, shouldn't we just wrap all our function components with `memo`? No! There is a performance cost when `memo` determines whether a component has changed. If the component doesn't actually do any unnecessary rendering, using `memo` would result in the component being slower.

`memo` should be used with care, and only on components that are being rendered more than they need to be.

Given that the features of class components and function components are similar, which type should we be using? There is no straightforward answer, really. If our team is used to object-oriented code, perhaps class-based components will be easier to learn. If our team is used to more functional programming techniques, then function-based components may enable them to be more productive.

Both approaches are great ways to create React components—it's down to you to choose!

Summary

In this chapter we learned a couple of different ways we can create a React and TypeScript project. The more manual way taught us just how many moving parts there are. We'll use `create-react-app` regularly to quickly create our apps in this book.

We learned how all React class components have a `render` method that returns JSX, which tells React what to display. JSX is very flexible and powerful, because JavaScript expressions can be mixed in with HTML.

We learned how components can be configured using props, and how we can add TypeScript types to props, to help prevent mistakes when consuming components.

Next, we learnt how components manage what is rendered and how they behave using state. Like props, state in a React and TypeScript app is strongly typed. We initialize state in the constructor, and change it via a `setState` method.

We also learnt about event handlers, which allow us to react to how users interact with our components. JSX gives us handy `onEventName` attributes for handling events.

Next, we learnt about the various life cycle methods that can be implemented to execute logic at various points in the process. The most commonly used life cycle method is `componentDidMount` , which occurs when a component has just been added to the DOM.

Finally, we learned about function components, which are an alternative approach to implementing components. In recent versions of React, we are able to use state within them, access common life cycle hooks, and even optimize rendering cycles.

In `Chapter 3`, *Getting Started with React and TypeScript*, we will learn about how we can efficiently build React and TypeScript apps that have multiple pages.

Questions

Answer the following questions, based on what we have just learned:

1. During development, what are the TSLint settings for allowing debugger statements and logging to the console?
2. In JSX, how can we display a button with a label from a prop called `buttonLabel` in a class component?
3. How can we make the `buttonLabel` prop optional, and default to **Do It**?

4. In JSX, how can we display this button only if the `doItVisible` state is `true`? (Assume we already have a state type declared containing `doItVisible`, and it has already been initialized in the constructor.)

5. How would we create a click handler for this button?

6. We have a state type declared containing `doItDisabled`. It has also been initialized in the constructor. How would we set this state to disable the **Do it** button after we click it?

7. If the button is clicked when it is in a disabled state, is the click handler still executed?

8. What life cycle method would we use in a class component to add event handlers to a non-React web component living in our React component?

9. Which life cycle method would we use to remove this event handler?

10. We have a function component called `Counter`. It needs to contain a piece of state called `count`, and a function to update it called `setCount`. How can we define this state and default the initial count to 10?

11. In the preceding `Counter` component, we have a `decrement` function that needs to reduce `count` by 1.

```
const decrement = () => {
  // TODO - reduce count by 1
};
```

How can this be implemented?

Further reading

- The official React introduction tutorial is worth going through: `https:// reactjs.org/tutorial/tutorial.html`
- The `create-react-app` documentation is also worth bookmarking: `https:// facebook.github.io/create-react-app/docs/getting-started`

4
Routing with React Router

If our app has multiple pages, we need to manage the navigation between the different pages. React Router is a great library that helps us do just this!

In this chapter, we are going to build a web shop where we can purchase a few tools for React. Our simple shop will have multiple pages that we'll manage using React Router. The shop will look like the following screenshot when we are finished:

In this chapter, we'll learn the following topics:

- Installing React Router with routing types
- Declaring routes
- Creating navigation
- Route parameters
- Handling not found routes
- Implementing page redirects
- Query parameters

- Route prompts
- Nested routes
- Animated transitions
- Lazy loading routes

Technical requirements

We'll use the following technologies in this chapter:

- **Node.js and** npm: TypeScript and React are dependent on these. We can install these from `https://nodejs.org/en/download/`. If we already have these installed, make sure npm is at least at version 5.2.

- **Visual Studio Code**: We'll need an editor to write our React and TypeScript code, which can be installed from `https://code.visualstudio.com/`. We will also need the TSLint (by egamma) and Prettier (by Estben Petersen) extensions installed within Visual Studio Code.

 All the code snippets in this chapter can be found online at `https://github.com/carlrip/LearnReact17WithTypeScript/tree/master/04-ReactRouter`.

Installing React Router with routing types

React Router and its Types are in npm, so we can install them from there.

Before installing React Router, we need to create our React shop project. Let's get ready to do that by choosing an empty folder of our choice and opening Visual Studio Code. To do this, follow these steps:

1. Let's now open a Terminal and enter the following command to create a new React and TypeScript project:

```
npx create-react-app reactshop --typescript
```

Note that the version of React we use needs to be at least version `16.7.0-alpha.0`. We can check this in the `package.json` file. If the version of React in `package.json` is less that `16.7.0-alpha.0`, then we can install this version using the following command:

```
npm install react@16.7.0-alpha.0
npm install react-dom@16.7.0-alpha.0
```

2. After the project is created, let's add TSLint as a development dependency to our project along with some rules that work well with React and Prettier:

```
cd reactshop
npm install tslint tslint-react tslint-config-prettier --save-dev
```

3. Let's now add a `tslint.json` file containing some rules:

```
{
  "extends": ["tslint:recommended", "tslint-react", "tslint-config-prettier"],
  "rules": {
    "ordered-imports": false,
    "object-literal-sort-keys": false,
    "no-debugger": false,
    "no-console": false,
  },
  "linterOptions": {
    "exclude": [
      "config/**/*.js",
      "node_modules/**/*.ts",
      "coverage/lcov-report/*.js"
    ]
  }
}
```

4. Now, let's enter the following command to install React Router into our project:

```
npm install react-router-dom
```

5. Let's also install the TypeScript types for React Router and save them as a development dependency:

```
npm install @types/react-router-dom --save-dev
```

Before going on to the next section, we're going to remove some of the files `create-react-app` created that we don't need:

1. First, let's remove the `App` component. So, let's delete the `App.css`, `App.test.tsx`, and `App.tsx` files. Let's also remove the import reference `"./App"` in `index.tsx`.

2. Let's also remove the service worker by deleting the `serviceWorker.ts` file and removing the references to it in `index.tsx`.

3. In `index.tsx`, let's change the root component from `<App/>` to `<div/>`. Our `index.tsx` file should have the following content in it now:

```
import * as React from 'react';
import * as ReactDOM from 'react-dom';
import './index.css';

ReactDOM.render(
  <div />,
  document.getElementById('root') as HTMLElement
);
```

Declaring routes

We declare the pages in our app using the `BrowserRouter` and `Route` components. `BrowserRouter` is the top-level component and this looks for `Route` components beneath it to determine all the different page paths.

We are going to declare some pages in our app using `BrowserRouter` and `Route` later in this section, but before that we need to create our first two pages. This first page is going to contain the list of our React tools that we are going to sell in our shop. We use the following steps to create our pages:

1. So, let's start by creating the data for our list of tools by creating a `ProductsData.ts` file with the following content:

```
export interface IProduct {
  id: number;
  name: string;
  description: string;
  price: number;
}

export const products: IProduct[] = [
  {
```

```
    description:
      "A collection of navigational components that compose
        declaratively with your app",
    id: 1,
    name: "React Router",
    price: 8
  },
  {
    description: "A library that helps manage state across your
app",
    id: 2,
    name: "React Redux",
    price: 12
  },
  {
    description: "A library that helps you interact with a
GraphQL backend",
    id: 3,
    name: "React Apollo",
    price: 12
  }
];
```

2. Let's create another file called `ProductsPage.tsx` containing the following to import React as well as our data:

```
import * as React from "react";
import { IProduct, products } from "./ProductsData";
```

3. We are going to reference the data in our component state, so let's create an interface for this:

```
interface IState {
  products: IProduct[];
}
```

4. Let's move on to create our class component called `ProductsPage`, initializing the state to an empty array:

```
class ProductsPage extends React.Component<{}, IState> {
  public constructor(props: {}) {
    super(props);
    this.state = {
      products: []
    };
  }
```

```
    }

    export default ProductsPage;
```

5. Let's now implement the `componentDidMount` life cycle method and set the data to the `products` array from `ProductData.ts`:

```
public componentDidMount() {
  this.setState({ products });
}
```

6. Moving on to implementing the `render` method, let's welcome our users and set out the products in a list:

```
public render() {
  return (
    <div className="page-container">
      <p>
        Welcome to React Shop where you can get all your tools
for ReactJS!
      </p>
      <ul className="product-list">
        {this.state.products.map(product => (
          <li key={product.id} className="product-list-item">
            {product.name}
          </li>
        ))}
      </ul>
    </div>
  );
}
```

We have used the `map` function in the `products` array to iterate through the elements and produce a list item tag, `li`, for each product. We need to give each `li` a unique `key` attribute to help React manage any changes to the list items, which in our case is the `id` product.

7. We've referenced some CSS classes, so let's add these to `index.css`:

```
.page-container {
  text-align: center;
  padding: 20px;
  font-size: large;
}

.product-list {
  list-style: none;
```

```
  margin: 0;
  padding: 0;
}

.product-list-item {
  padding: 5px;
}
```

8. Let's implement our second page now, which is going to be an admin panel. So, let's create a file called `AdminPage.tsx` with the following function component inside:

```
import * as React from "react";

const AdminPage: React.SFC = () => {
  return (
    <div className="page-container">
      <h1>Admin Panel</h1>
      <p>You should only be here if you have logged in</p>
    </div>
  );
};

export default AdminPage;
```

9. Now that we have two pages in our shop, we can declare our two routes to them. Let's create a file called `Routes.tsx` with the following content to import `React`, the `BrowserRouter` and `Route` components from React Router, and our two pages:

```
import * as React from "react";
import { BrowserRouter as Router, Route } from "react-router-dom";

import AdminPage from "./AdminPage";
import ProductsPage from "./ProductsPage";
```

We have renamed `BrowserRouter` to `Router` in the import statement to save a few keystrokes.

10. Let's go on to implement a function component containing our two routes:

```
const Routes: React.SFC = () => {
  return (
    <Router>
      <div>
        <Route path="/products" component={ProductsPage} />
```

```
            <Route path="/admin" component={AdminPage} />
        </div>
      </Router>
    );
};

export default Routes;
```

 During rendering, if the `path` in a `Route` component matches the current path, the component will be rendered, and if not, `null` will be rendered. In our example, `ProductPage` will be rendered if the path is `"/products"` and `AdminPage` will be rendered if the path is `"/admin"`.

11. The following is the final step to render our `Routes` as the root component in `index.tsx`:

```
import * as React from "react";
import * as ReactDOM from "react-dom";
import "./index.css";
import Routes from "./Routes";

ReactDOM.render(<Routes />, document.getElementById("root") as
HTMLElement);
```

12. We should now be able to run our app:

    npm start

    The app will probably start on the root page, which will be blank because that path doesn't point to anything.

13. If we change the path to `"/products"`, our product list should render the following:

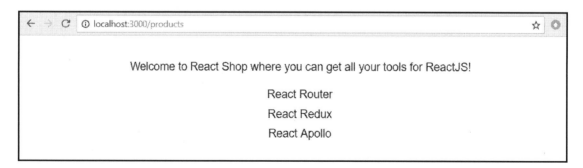

14. If we change the path to `"/admin"`, our admin panel should render the following:

Now that we have successfully created a couple of routes, we really need a navigation component to make our pages a little more discoverable. We will do just that in the next section.

Creating navigation

React Router comes with some nice components for providing navigation. We are going to use these to implement navigation options in the app header.

Using the Link component

We are going to use the `Link` component from React Router to create our navigation options by carrying out the following steps:

1. Let's start by creating a new file called `Header.tsx` with the following imports:

```
import * as React from "react";
import { Link } from "react-router-dom";

import logo from "./logo.svg";
```

2. Let's create two links using the `Link` component in a `Header` function component:

```
const Header: React.SFC = () => {
  return (
    <header className="header">
      <img src={logo} className="header-logo" alt="logo" />
      <h1 className="header-title">React Shop</h1>
      <nav>
```

```
          <Link to="/products" className="header-
          link">Products</Link>
          <Link to="/admin" className="header-link">Admin</Link>
        </nav>
      </header>
    );
};

export default Header;
```

 The `Link` component allows us to define the path where the link navigates to as well as the text to display.

3. We've referenced some CSS classes, so, let's add these to `index.css`:

```css
.header {
  text-align: center;
  background-color: #222;
  height: 160px;
  padding: 20px;
  color: white;
}

.header-logo {
  animation: header-logo-spin infinite 20s linear;
  height: 80px;
}

@keyframes header-logo-spin {
  from {
    transform: rotate(0deg);
  }
  to {
    transform: rotate(360deg);
  }
}

.header-title {
  font-size: 1.5em;
}

.header-link {
  color: #fff;
  text-decoration: none;
  padding: 5px;
}
```

4. Now that our `Header` component is in place, let's `import` into `Routes.tsx`:

```
import Header from "./Header";
```

5. We can then use it in the JSX as follows:

```
<Router>
  <div>
    <Header />
    <Route path="/products" component={ProductsPage} />
    <Route path="/admin" component={AdminPage} />
  </div>
</Router>
```

6. If we examine the running app, it should look like the following screenshot with a nice header and two navigation options to go to our **Products** and **Admin** pages rendered:

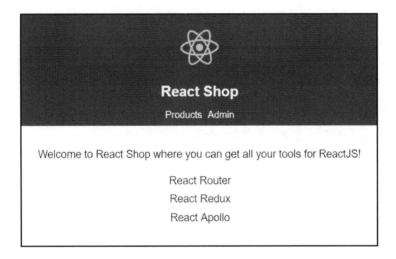

7. Try clicking the navigation options — they work! If we inspect the **Products** and **Admin** elements using the browser **Developer tools**, we see that React Router has rendered them as anchor tags:

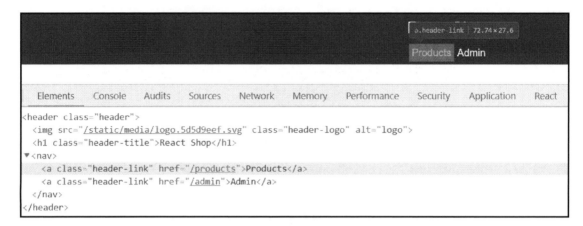

If we look at the **Network** tab in **Developer tools** while clicking the navigation options, we'll see no network request is being made to serve the pages. This shows that React Router is handling the navigation for us in our React app.

Using the NavLink component

React Router providers another component for linking to pages, called `NavLink`. This is actually even more suitable for our requirements. The following steps explain how we can refactor our `Header` component to use `NavLink`:

1. So, let's replace `Link` with `NavLink` in our `Header` component and make some improvements:

```
import * as React from "react";
import { NavLink } from "react-router-dom";

import logo from "./logo.svg";

const Header: React.SFC = () => {
  return (
    <header className="header">
      <img src={logo} className="header-logo" alt="logo" />
      <h1 className="header-title">React Shop</h1>
      <nav>
        <NavLink to="/products" className="header-
```

```
          link">Products</NavLink>
            <NavLink to="/admin" className="header-
            link">Admin</NavLink>
        </nav>
      </header>
    );
  };

  export default Header;
```

At this point, our app looks and behaves exactly the same.

2. NavLink exposes an `activeClassName` attribute that we can use to style the active link. So, let's use this:

```
<NavLink to="/products" className="header-link"
activeClassName="header-link-active">
  Products
</NavLink>
<NavLink to="/admin" className="header-link"
activeClassName="header-link-active">
  Admin
</NavLink>
```

3. Let's add the CSS for `header-link-active` into our `index.css`:

```
.header-link-active {
  border-bottom: #ebebeb solid 2px;
}
```

4. If we switch to the running app now, the active link will be underlined:

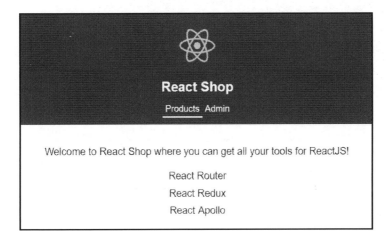

So, `NavLink` is great for the main app navigation where we want to highlight the active link and `Link` is great for all the other links in our app.

Route parameters

A Route parameter is a variable part of the path that can used in the destination component to conditionally render something.

We need to add another page to our shop to show the description and price of each product, along with an option to add it to the basket. We want to be able to navigate to this page using the `"/products/{id}"` path, where `id` is the ID of the product. For example, the path to React Redux would be `"products/2"`. So, the `id` part of the path is a route parameter. We can do all this by following these steps:

1. Let's add this route to `Routes.tsx` in between the two existing routes. The `id` part of the route is going to be a route parameter, which we define with a colon in front of it:

   ```
   <Route path="/products" component={ProductsPage} />
   <Route path="/products/:id" component={ProductPage} />
   <Route path="/admin" component={AdminPage} />
   ```

2. Of course, the `ProductPage` component doesn't exist yet, so, let's create that by first creating a new file called `ProductPage.tsx` with the following imports:

   ```
   import * as React from "react";
   import { RouteComponentProps } from "react-router-dom";
   import { IProduct, products } from "./ProductsData";
   ```

3. The key part here is that we are going to use the `RouteComponentProps` type to access the `id` parameter in the path. Let's define the props type alias for our `ProductPage` component using the `RouteComponentProps` generic type and passing in a type with an `id` property:

   ```
   type Props = RouteComponentProps<{id: string}>;
   ```

   Don't worry if you don't understand the angle brackets in the `type` expression. This denotes a generic type, which we will explore in `Chapter 5`, *Advanced Types*.

Ideally, we'd have specified the id property as a number to match the type in the product data. However, RouteComponentProps only allows us to have Route parameters of type string or undefined.

4. The ProductPage component is going to have state to hold the product that is being rendered and whether it has been added to the basket, so let's define an interface for our state:

```
interface IState {
  product?: IProduct;
  added: boolean;
}
```

5. The product is initially going to be undefined, which is why it is defined as optional. Let's create our ProductPage class and initialize the state so that the product is not in the basket:

```
class ProductPage extends React.Component<Props, IState> {
  public constructor(props: Props) {
    super(props);
    this.state = {
      added: false
    };
  }
}

export default ProductPage;
```

6. When the component is loaded into the DOM, we need to find our product from the product data with the id property from the Route parameter. RouteComponentProps gives us a match object, containing a params object, containing our id route parameter. So, let's implement this:

```
public componentDidMount() {
  if (this.props.match.params.id) {
    const id: number = parseInt(this.props.match.params.id,
10);
    const product = products.filter(p => p.id === id)[0];

    this.setState({ product });
  }
}
```

Remember that the `id` route parameter is a string, which is why we cast it to a number using `parseInt` before comparing it with the product data in the `filter` array.

7. Now that we have our product in our component state, let's move on to the `render` function:

```
public render() {
  const product = this.state.product;
  return (
    <div className="page-container">
      {product ? (
        <React.Fragment>
          <h1>{product.name}</h1>
          <p>{product.description}</p>
          <p className="product-price">
            {new Intl.NumberFormat("en-US", {
              currency: "USD",
              style: "currency"
            }).format(product.price)}
          </p>
          {!this.state.added && (
            <button onClick={this.handleAddClick}>Add to
              basket</button>
          )}
        </React.Fragment>
      ) : (
        <p>Product not found!</p>
      )}
    </div>
  );
}
```

There are a few interesting bits in this JSX:

- On the first line inside the function, we set a `product` variable to the product state to save a few keystrokes because we reference the product a lot in the JSX.
- The ternary inside `div` renders the product if there is one. Otherwise, it informs the user that the product cannot be found.
- We use `React.Fragment` in the true part of the ternary because each part of a ternary can only have a single parent and `React.Fragment` is a mechanism for achieving this, without rendering something like a `div` tag that is not really needed.

- We use `Intl.NumberFormat` to format the product price as currency with a currency symbol.

8. We are also calling the `handleAddClick` method when the **Add to basket** button is clicked. We haven't implemented this yet, so, let's do that now and set the `added` state to `true`:

```
private handleAddClick = () => {
  this.setState({ added: true });
};
```

9. Now that we've implemented the `ProductPage` component, let's go back to `Routes.tsx` and import it:

```
import ProductPage from "./ProductPage";
```

10. Let's go to our running app and type in `"/products/2"` as the path:

Not quite what we want! Both `ProductsPage` and `ProductPage` have rendered because `"/products/2"` matches both `"/products"` and `"/products/:id"`.

11. To resolve this, we can tell the `"/products"` route to only render when there is an exact match:

```
<Route exact={true} path="/products" component={ProductsPage} />
```

12. After we make this change and save `Routes.tsx`, our product page looks much better:

13. We aren't going to make our users type in the specific paths to visit the products! So, we are going to change `ProductsPage` to link to `ProductPage` for each product using the `Link` component. First, let's import `Link` into `ProductsPage` from React Router:

```
import { Link } from "react-router-dom";
```

14. Now, instead of rendering the product name in each list item, we are going to render a `Link` component that goes to our product page:

```
public render() {
  return (
    <div className="page-container">
```

```
<p>
  Welcome to React Shop where you can get all your tools
    for ReactJS!
</p>
<ul className="product-list">
  {this.state.products.map(product => (
    <li key={product.id} className="product-list-item">
      <Link to={`/products/${product.id}`}>{product.name}
      </Link>
    </li>
  ))}
</ul>
</div>
);
}
```

15. Before we take a look a the running app, let's add the following CSS class in our `index.css`:

```
.product-list-item a {
  text-decoration: none;
}
```

Now, if we go to the products list in our app and click on a list item, it takes us to the relevant product page.

Handling not found routes

What if a user enters a path that doesn't exist in our app? For example, if we try to navigate to "`/tools`" we get nothing appearing beneath our header. This makes sense, because React Router didn't find any matching routes, so nothing is rendered. However, if the user does navigate to an invalid path, we want to inform them that the path doesn't exist. The following steps make this happen:

1. So, let's create a new file called `NotFoundPage.tsx` with the following component:

```
import * as React from "react";

const NotFoundPage: React.SFC = () => {
  return (
    <div className="page-container">
      <h1>Sorry, this page cannot be found</h1>
    </div>
  );
```

```
};

export default NotFoundPage;
```

2. Let's import this into our routes in `Routes.tsx`:

```
import NotFoundPage from "./NotFoundPage";
```

3. Let's then add a `Route` component to this with the other routes:

```
<Router>
  <div>
    <Header />
    <Route exact={true} path="/products"
component={ProductsPage}
      />
    <Route path="/products/:id" component={ProductPage} />
    <Route path="/admin" component={AdminPage} />
    <Route component={NotFoundPage} />
  </div>
</Router>
```

However, this is going to render for every path:

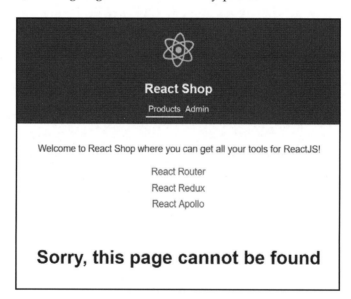

How can we just render `NotFoundPage` when it hasn't found another route? The answer is to wrap the Routes in the `Switch` component in React Router.

4. Let's first import `Switch` into `Routes.tsx`:

```
import { BrowserRouter as Router, Route, Switch } from "react-router-dom";
```

5. Let's now wrap the `Route` components in a `Switch` component:

```
<Switch>
  <Route exact={true} path="/products" component={ProductsPage} />
  <Route path="/products/:id" component={ProductPage} />
  <Route path="/admin" component={AdminPage} />
  <Route component={NotFoundPage} />
</Switch>
```

The `Switch` component renders only the first matching `Route` component. If we look at the running app we see that our problem is resolved. If we enter a path that doesn't exist, we get our nice not found message:

Implementing page redirects

React Router has a component called `Redirect` that we can use to redirect to pages. We use this component in a couple of cases to improve our shop in the following sections.

Simple redirect

If we visit the / route path, we'll notice that we get the **Sorry, this page cannot be found** message. Let's change this to redirect to "/products" when the path is /.

1. First, we need to import the `Redirect` component from React Router into `Routes.tsx`:

```
import { BrowserRouter as Router, Redirect, Route, Switch }
from "react-router-dom";
```

2. We can now use the `Redirect` component to redirect to "/products" when the path is /:

```
<Switch>
  <Redirect exact={true} from="/" to="/products" />
  <Route exact={true} path="/products" component={ProductsPage}
  />
  <Route path="/products/:id" component={ProductPage} />
  <Route path="/admin" component={AdminPage} />
  <Route component={NotFoundPage} />
</Switch>
```

3. We've used the `exact` attribute on `Redirect` so that it only matches / and not "/products/1" and "/admin". If we give this a try and enter / as the path in our running app, it will immediately redirect to "/products".

Conditional redirect

We can use the `Redirect` component to protect pages from unauthorized users. In our shop, we can use this to ensure only logged in users can access our **Admin** page. We do this through the following steps:

1. Let's start by adding a route to a `LoginPage` in `Routes.tsx` after the route to the **Admin** page:

```
<Route path="/login" component={LoginPage} />
```

2. Of course, `LoginPage` doesn't exist at the moment, so, let's create a file called `LoginPage.tsx` and enter the following:

```
import * as React from "react";

const LoginPage: React.SFC = () => {
```

```
    return (
      <div className="page-container">
        <h1>Login</h1>
        <p>You need to login ...</p>
      </div>
    );
};

export default LoginPage;
```

3. We can then go back to Routes.tsx and import LoginPage:

```
import LoginPage from "./LoginPage";
```

4. If we go to the running app and navigate to "/login", we will see our **Login** page:

We are not going to fully implement our **Login** page; the page that we have implemented is enough to demonstrate a conditional redirect.

5. Before we implement the conditional redirect on the "admin" path, we need to add a piece of state for whether a user is logged in or not in Routes.tsx:

```
const Routes: React.SFC = () => {
  const [loggedIn, setLoggedIn] = React.useState(false);
  return (
    <Router>
      ...
    </Router>
  );
};
```

So, we have used a `useState` hook to add a state variable called `loggedIn` and a function to set it called `setLoggedIn`.

6. The final step is to add the following inside the `Route` component with the `"/admin"` path:

```
<Route path="/admin">
  {loggedIn ? <AdminPage /> : <Redirect to="/login"
  />}
</Route>
```

We conditionally render `AdminPage` if the user is logged in, otherwise, we redirect to the `"/login"` path. If we now click the `admin` link in our running app, we get redirected to the **Login** page.

7. If we change the `loggedIn` state to be true when we initialize it, we are able to access our **Admin** page again:

```
const [loggedIn, setLoggedIn] = React.useState(true);
```

Query parameters

A query parameter is part of the URL that allows additional parameters to be passed into a path. For example, `"/products?search=redux"` has a query parameter called `search` with a `redux` value.

Let's implement this example and allow the users of the shop to search for a product:

1. Let's start by adding a variable in the state in `ProductsPage.tsx` called `search`, which is going to hold the search criteria:

```
interface IState {
  products: IProduct[];
  search: string;
}
```

2. Given that we need to access the URL, we need to use `RouteComponentProps` as the props type in `ProductsPage`. Let's first import this:

```
import { RouteComponentProps } from "react-router-dom";
```

3. We can then use this as the `props` type:

```
class ProductsPage extends React.Component<RouteComponentProps,
IState> {
```

4. We can initialize the `search` state to an empty string in `constructor`:

```
public constructor(props: RouteComponentProps) {
  super(props);
  this.state = {
    products: [],
    search: ""
  };
}
```

5. We then need to set the `search` state in `componentDidMount` to the search query parameter. React Router gives us access to all the query parameters in `location.search` within the `props` argument that it passes into the component. We then need to parse that string to get our search query string parameter. We can use the `URLSearchParams` JavaScript function to do this. We are going to use the static `getDerivedStateFromProps` life cycle method to do this, which is called when the component loads and when its `props` parameters change:

```
public static getDerivedStateFromProps(
  props: RouteComponentProps,
  state: IState
) {
  const searchParams = new
URLSearchParams(props.location.search);
  const search = searchParams.get("search") || "";
  return {
    products: state.products,
    search
  };
}
```

6. Unfortunately, `URLSearchParams` hasn't been implemented yet in all browsers, so we can use a polyfill called `url-search-params-polyfill`. Let's install this:

```
npm install url-search-params-polyfill
```

7. Let's import this into `ProductPages.tsx`:

```
import "url-search-params-polyfill";
```

8. We then can use the `search` state in the `render` method by wrapping an `if` statement around the returned list item to only return something when the value of `search` is contained within the product name:

```
<ul className="product-list">
  {this.state.products.map(product => {
    if (
      !this.state.search ||
      (this.state.search &&
        product.name
          .toLowerCase()
          .indexOf(this.state.search.toLowerCase()) > -1)
    ) {
      return (
        <li key={product.id} className="product-list-item">
          <Link to={`/products/${product.id}`}>{product.name}
          </Link>
        </li>
      );
    } else {
      return null;
    }
  })}
</ul>
```

9. If we enter `"/products?search=redux"` as the path in our running app, we will see our products list containing only **React Redux**:

10. We are going to finish implementing this feature by adding a search input in our app header that sets the search query parameter. Let's start this by creating some state in the `Header` component for the search value in `Header.tsx`:

```
const [search, setSearch] = React.useState("");
```

11. We are also going to need to access the query string via React Router and `URLSearchParams`, so let's import `RouteComponentProps`, `withRouter`, and the `URLSearchParams` polyfill:

```
import { NavLink, RouteComponentProps, withRouter} from "react-
router-dom";
import "url-search-params-polyfill";
```

12. Let's add a `props` parameter to our `Header` component:

```
const Header: React.SFC<RouteComponentProps> = props => { ... }
```

13. We can now get the search value from the path query string and set the `search` state to this when the component first renders:

```
const [search, setSearch] = React.useState("");
React.useEffect(() => {
  const searchParams = new
URLSearchParams(props.location.search);
  setSearch(searchParams.get("search") || "");
}, []);
```

14. Let's now add a `search` input in the `render` method for the user to enter their search:

```
public render() {
  return (
    <header className="header">
      <div className="search-container">
        <input
          type="search"
          placeholder="search"
          value={search}
          onChange={handleSearchChange}
          onKeyDown={handleSearchKeydown}
        />
      </div>
      <img src={logo} className="header-logo" alt="logo" />
      <h1 className="header-title">React Shop</h1>
      <nav>
        . . .
```

```
        </nav>
      </header>
    );
  }
```

15. Let's add the `search-container` CSS class that we just referenced to `index.css`:

```
.search-container {
  text-align: right;
  margin-bottom: -25px;
}
```

16. Back in `Header.tsx`, let's add the `handleSearchChange` method, which is referenced in the `render` method and will keep our `search` state up to date with the value being entered:

```
const handleSearchChange = (e:
React.ChangeEvent<HTMLInputElement>) => {
  setSearch(e.currentTarget.value);
};
```

17. We can now implement the `handleSearchKeydown` method, which is referenced in the `render` method. This needs to add the `search` state value to the path query string when the `Enter` key is pressed. We can leverage the `push` method in the `history` prop that `RouteComponentProps` gives us:

```
const handleSearchKeydown = (e:
React.KeyboardEvent<HTMLInputElement>) => {
  if (e.key === "Enter") {
    props.history.push(`/products?search=${search}`);
  }
};
```

18. We need to export the `Header` component wrapped with the `withRouter` higher order component in order for the reference to `this.props.history` to work. So, let's do this and adjust our `export` expression:

```
export default withRouter(Header);
```

19. Let's give this a try in the running app. If we enter `redux` in the search input and press the *Enter* key, the app should navigate to the **Products** page and filter the products to **React Redux**:

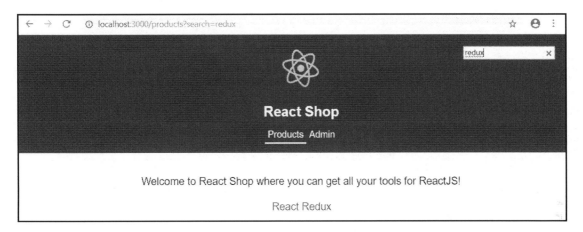

Route prompts

Sometimes, we might want to ask the user to confirm that they want to navigate away from a page. This is useful if the user is in the middle of data entry on a page and presses a navigation link to go to a different page before they have saved the data. The `Prompt` component in React Router allows us to do this, as set out in the following steps:

1. In our app, we are going to prompt users to confirm that they want to navigate away from the **Product** page if they haven't added the product to their basket. First, in `ProductPage.tsx`, let's import the `Prompt` component from React Router:

```
import { Prompt, RouteComponentProps } from "react-router-dom";
```

2. The `Prompt` component invokes a confirmation dialog during navigation when a certain condition is met. We can use the `Prompt` component in our JSX as follows:

```
<div className="page-container">
  <Prompt when={!this.state.added}
message={this.navAwayMessage}
  />
  ...
</div>
```

The `when` attribute allows us to specify an expression for when the dialog should appear. In our case, this is when the product hasn't been added to the basket.

The `message` attribute allows us to specify a function that returns the message to display in the dialog.

3. In our case, we call a `navAwayMessage` method, which we'll implement next:

```
private navAwayMessage = () =>
    "Are you sure you leave without buying this product?";
```

4. Let's give this a try by navigating to the React Router product and then navigating away without clicking the **Add to basket** button:

We are asked to confirm whether we want to navigate away.

Nested routes

A nested route is when a URL is more than one level deep and it renders multiple components. We are going to implement some nested routes in this section in our **Admin** page. Our completed **Admin** page will look like the following screenshot:

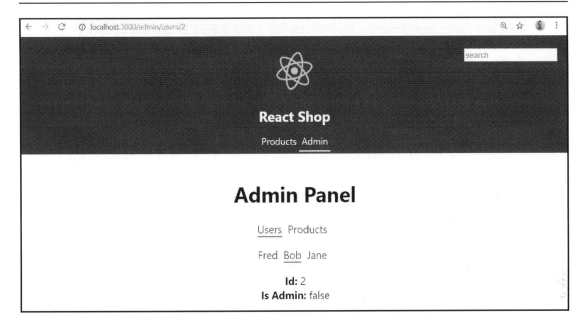

The URL in the preceding screenshot is 3 levels deep which renders the following:

- The top-level menu containing links for **Users** and **Products**.
- A menu containing all the users. This is just **Fred**, **Bob**, and **Jane** is our example.
- Information about the selected user.

1. Let's start by opening `AdminPage.tsx` and add `import` statements for the following from `react-router-dom`:

   ```
   import { NavLink, Route, RouteComponentProps } from "react-
   router-dom";
   ```

   - We'll use the `NavLink` component to render the menus
   - The `Route` component will be used to render the nested routes
   - The `RouteComponentProps` type will be used to get the `id` of a user from the URL

2. We are going to replace the `p` tag with an unordered list containing menu options **Users** and **Products**:

   ```
   <div className="page-container">
     <h1>Admin Panel</h1>
     <ul className="admin-sections>
       <li key="users">
   ```

```
            <NavLink to={`/admin/users`} activeClassName="admin-link-
              active">
              Users
            </NavLink>
          </li>
          <li key="products">
            <NavLink to={`/admin/products`} activeClassName="admin-link-
              active">
              Products
            </NavLink>
          </li>
        </ul>
      </div>
```

We use the `NavLink` component to navigate to the nested route for the two options.

3. Let's add the CSS classes we have just referenced in `index.css`:

```
.admin-sections {
  list-style: none;
  margin: 0px 0px 20px 0px;
  padding: 0;
}

.admin-sections li {
  display: inline-block;
  margin-right: 10px;
}

.admin-sections li a {
  color: #222;
  text-decoration: none;
}

.admin-link-active {
  border-bottom: #6f6e6e solid 2px;
}
```

4. Moving back to `AdminPage.tsx`, let's add two `Route` components beneath the menu we have just added. These will handle the `/admin/users` and `/admin/products` paths we referenced in our menu:

```
<div className="page-container">
  <h1>Admin Panel</h1>
  <ul className="admin-sections">
    ...
```

```
    </ul>
    <Route path="/admin/users" component={AdminUsers} />
    <Route path="/admin/products" component={AdminProducts} />
  </div>
```

5. We have just referenced `AdminUsers` and `AdminProducts` components that don't exist yet. Let's implement the `AdminProducts` component first by entering the following beneath the `AdminPage` component in `AdminPage.tsx`:

```
const AdminProducts: React.SFC = () => {
  return <div>Some options to administer products</div>;
};
```

So, this component just renders a bit of text on the screen.

6. Let's move on to the `AdminUsers` component now which is more complex. We'll start by defining an interface for a user along with some user data beneath the `AdminProducts` component in `AdminPage.tsx`:

```
interface IUser {
  id: number;
  name: string;
  isAdmin: boolean;
}
const adminUsersData: IUser[] = [
  { id: 1, name: "Fred", isAdmin: true },
  { id: 2, name: "Bob", isAdmin: false },
  { id: 3, name: "Jane", isAdmin: true }
];
```

So, we have 3 users in our example.

7. Let's start to implement the `AdminUsers` component then in `AdminPage.tsx`:

```
const AdminUsers: React.SFC = () => {
  return (
    <div>
      <ul className="admin-sections">
        {adminUsersData.map(user => (
          <li>
            <NavLink
              to={`/admin/users/${user.id}`}
              activeClassName="admin-link-active"
            >
              {user.name}
            </NavLink>
          </li>
```

```
            ))}
        </ul>
      </div>
    );
  };
```

The component renders a link containing each user's name. The link is to a nested path which will eventually show details about the user.

8. So, we need to define another route that will call a component to render details about a user. We can do this by using another `Route` component:

```
<div>
  <ul className="admin-sections">
    ...
  </ul>
  <Route path="/admin/users/:id" component={AdminUser} />
</div>
```

9. The path we have just defined routes to an `AdminUser` component we haven't defined yet. So, let's make a start on this beneath the `AdminUsers` component:

```
const AdminUser: React.SFC<RouteComponentProps<{ id: string }>> =
props => {
  return null;
};
```

We use `RouteComponentProps` to get the `id` from the URL path and make this available in the props.

10. We can now use the `id` from the path to get the user from our `adminUsersData` array:

```
const AdminUser: React.SFC<RouteComponentProps<{ id: string }>> =
props => {
  let user: IUser;
  if (props.match.params.id) {
    const id: number = parseInt(props.match.params.id, 10);
    user = adminUsersData.filter(u => u.id === id)[0];
  } else {
    return null;
  }
  return null;
};
```

11. Now that we have the `user` object, we can render the information within it.

```
const AdminUser: React.SFC<RouteComponentProps<{ id: string }>> =
props => {
  let user: IUser;
  if (props.match.params.id) {
    const id: number = parseInt(props.match.params.id, 10);
    user = adminUsersData.filter(u => u.id === id)[0];
  } else {
    return null;
  }
  return (
    <div>
      <div>
        <b>Id: </b>
        <span>{user.id.toString()}</span>
      </div>
      <div>
        <b>Is Admin: </b>
        <span>{user.isAdmin.toString()}</span>
      </div>
    </div>
  );
};
```

12. If we go to the running app, go to the **Admin** page and click on the **Products** menu item, it will look like below:

13. If we click on the **Users** menu item, we'll see the 3 users that we can click on to get more information about a user. This will look like the first screenshot in this section.

So, in order to implement nested routes, we create the necessary links using `NavLink` or `Link` components and route those links to the component to render the content using a `Route` component. We already knew about these components before this section, so, we just needed to learn how to use these in the context of nested routes.

Animated transitions

In this section, we are going to add a bit of animation when users navigate to different pages. We do this using the TransitionGroup and CSSTransition components from the react-transition-group npm package, as shown in the following steps:

1. So, let's first install this package with its TypeScript types:

   ```
   npm install react-transition-group
   npm install @types/react-transition-group --save-dev
   ```

   TransitionGroup keeps track of all its children inside its local state and calculates when children are entering or exiting. CSSTransition takes whether children are leaving or exiting from TransitionGroup and applies CSS classes to the children based on that status.
   So, TransitionGroup and CSSTransition can wrap our routes and invoke CSS classes that we can create to animate pages in and out.

2. So, let's import these components into Routes.tsx:

   ```
   import { CSSTransition, TransitionGroup } from "react-transition-group";
   ```

3. We also need to import RouteComponentProps from React Router:

   ```
   import { Redirect, Route, RouteComponentProps, Switch} from "react-router-dom";
   ```

4. Let's use RouteComponentProps as the Route component props type:

   ```
   const Routes: React.SFC<RouteComponentProps> = props => {
     ...
   }
   ```

5. Let's add the CSSTransition and TransitionGroup components to the JSX around the Switch component:

   ```
   <TransitionGroup>
     <CSSTransition
       key={props.location.key}
       timeout={500}
       classNames="animate"
     >
     <Switch>
       ...
       </Switch>
   ```

```
    </CSSTransition>
  </TransitionGroup>
```

`TransitionGroup` requires children to have a unique key for it to determine what is exiting and entering. So, we have specified a `key` attribute on `CSSTransition` to be the `location.key` property from `RouteComponentProps`. We have specified that the transition is going to run for up to half a second via the `timeout` attribute. We have also specified the CSS classes that are going to be invoked with an `animate` prefix via the `classNames` attribute.

6. So, let's add these CSS classes in `index.css`:

```
.animate-enter {
  opacity: 0;
  z-index: 1;
}
.animate-enter-active {
  opacity: 1;
  transition: opacity 450ms ease-in;
}
.animate-exit {
  display: none;
}
```

`CSSTransition` is going to invoke these CSS classes when its key changes. The CSS classes initially hide the element being transitioned and gradually ease the element's opacity so that it shows.

7. If we go to `index.tsx`, we get a compilation error where we reference the `Routes` component because it is expecting us to pass props such as `history` from the router:

```
ReactDOM.render(<Routes />, document.getElementById("root") as HTMLElement);
                  [ts]
                  Type '{}' is not assignable to type 'Readonly<RouteComponentPro
                  ps<{}, StaticContext, any>>'.
                    Property 'history' is missing in type '{}'.

                  (alias) class Routes
                  import Routes
```

Unfortunately, we can't use the `withRouter` higher order component because this would be outside the `Router` component. To resolve this, we can add a new component called `RoutesWrap`, which doesn't take in any props and wraps our existing `Routes` component. The `Router` will move up to `RoutesWrap` and will contain a `Route` component that always renders our `Routes` component.

8. So, let's add this `RoutesWrap` component to `Routes.tsx` and export `RoutesWrap` instead of `Routes`:

```
const RoutesWrap: React.SFC = () => {
  return (
    <Router>
      <Route component={Routes} />
    </Router>
  );
};

class Routes extends React.Component<RouteComponentProps,
IState> {
  ...
}

export default RoutesWrap;
```

The compilation error goes away, which is great.

9. Let's now remove `Router` from our `Routes` component, leaving the `div` tag as its root:

```
public render() {
  return (
    <div>
      <Header />
      <TransitionGroup>
        ...
      </TransitionGroup>
    </div>
  );
}
```

If we go to the running app and navigate to the different pages, you'll see a nice fade animation as the page comes into view.

Lazy loading routes

At the moment, all the JavaScript for our app is loaded when the app first loads. This includes the **Admin** page that users don't use that often. It would be great if the `AdminPage` component wasn't loaded when the app loads and instead loaded on demand. This is exactly what we are going to do in this section. This is called "lazy loading" components. The following steps allows us to load things on demand:

1. First, we are going to import the `Suspense` component from React, which we are going to use a little later:

   ```
   import { Suspense } from "react";
   ```

2. Now, we are going to import the `AdminPage` component differently:

   ```
   const AdminPage = React.lazy(() => import("./AdminPage"));
   ```

   We use a React function called `lazy` which takes in a function that returns a dynamic import, which in turn is assigned to our `AdminPage` component variable.

3. After we have done this, we may get a linting error: **A dynamic import call in ES5/ES3 requires the 'Promise' constructor. Make sure you have a declaration for the 'Promise' constructor or include 'ES2015' in your `--lib` option.** So, in `tsconfig.json`, let's add the `lib` compiler option:

   ```
   "compilerOptions": {
     "lib": ["es6", "dom"],
     ...
   }
   ```

4. The next part is to wrap the `Suspense` component around the `AdminPage` component:

   ```
   <Route path="/admin">
     {loggedIn ? (
       <Suspense fallback={<div className="page-
   container">Loading...</div>}>
         <AdminPage />
       </Suspense>
     ) : (
       <Redirect to="/login" />
     )}
   </Route>
   ```

The `Suspense` component shows a `div` tag containing
Loading... whilst `AdminPage` is being loaded.

5. Let's try this in the running app. Let's open the browser developer tools and go to
   the **Network** tab. In our app, let's go to the **Products** page and refresh the
   browser. Let's then clear the content in the **Network** tab in the developer tools. If
   we then go to the **Admin** page in our app and look at the content in the **Network**
   tab, we'll see the *chunk* of JavaScript for the `AdminPage` component dynamically
   loaded:

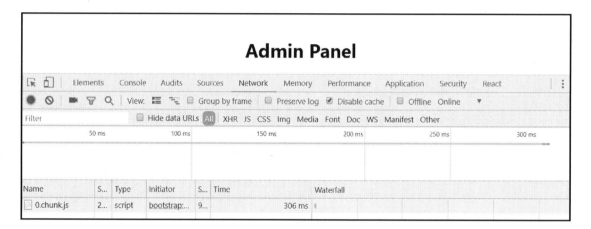

6. The `AdminPage` component loads really fast, so we never really see the **Loading**
   ... `div` tag. So, let's slow the connection down in the browser developer tools:

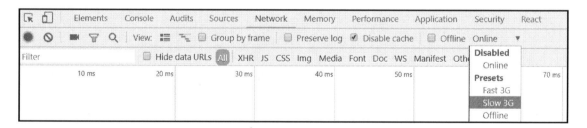

7. If we then refresh the browser, and go to the **Admin** page again, we'll see **Loading ...**:

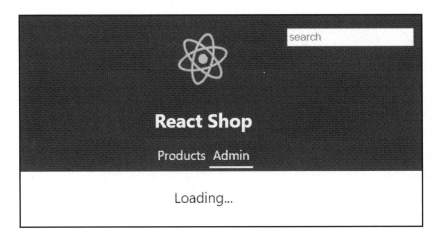

In this example, the `AdminPage` component isn't that big so this approach doesn't really positively impact performance. However, loading larger components on demand can really help performance, particularly on slow connections.

Summary

React Router gives us a comprehensive set of components for managing the navigation between pages in our app. We learned that the top-level component is `Router`, which looks for `Route` components beneath it where we define what components should be rendered for certain paths.

The `Link` component allows us to link to different pages with an app. We learned that the `NavLink` component is like `Link`, but it includes the ability to style it depending on whether it is the active path or not. So, `NavLink` is perfect for the main navigation element in an app and `Link` is great for other links that appear on pages.

`RouteComponentProps` is a type that gives us access to route parameters and query parameters. We discovered that React Router doesn't parse query parameters for us, but can use the native JavaScript `URLSearchParams` interface to do this for us.

The `Redirect` component redirects to a path under certain conditions. We found that this is perfect for protecting pages that only privileged users can access.

The `Prompt` component allows us to ask the user to confirm they want to leave a page under a certain condition. We used this on the **Product** page to double-check whether users wanted to buy the product. Another common use case for this component is confirming navigation away from a data entry page when the inputted data hasn't been saved.

We learnt about how nested routes can provide users with deep links into very specific parts of our app. We simply define the relevant links using `Link` or `NavLink` and `Route` components to handle those links.

We improved our app experience with page transitions using the `TransitionGroup` and `CSSTransition` components from the `react-transition-group` npm package. We wrapped these components around our `Route` components that define the app paths and added CSS classes to do the animation we want when pages exit and enter into view.

We learnt that the React `lazy` function along with its `Suspense` component can be used on large components that are rarely used by users to load them on demand. This helps performance for the startup time of our app.

Questions

Let's test our knowledge on React Router with the following questions:

1. We have the following `Route` component that shows a list of customers:

   ```
   <Route path="/customers" component={CustomersPage} />
   ```

   Will the `CustomersPage` component render when the page is `"/customers"`?

2. Will the `CustomersPage` component render when the page is `"/customers/24322"`?

3. We only want the `CustomersPage` component to render when the path is `"/customers"`. How can we change the attributes on `Route` to achieve this?

4. What would be the `Route` component that could handle the `"/customers/24322"` path be? It should put `"24322"` in a route parameter called `customerId`.

5. How can we catch paths that don't exist so that we can inform the user?

6. How would we implement a `search` query parameter in `CustomersPage`? So, `"/customers/?search=Cool Company"` would show customers with the name `"Cool Company"`.

7. After a while, we decide to change the `"customer"` paths to `"clients"`. How can we implement this so that users can still use the existing `"customer"` paths but have the paths automatically redirect to the new `"client"` paths?

Further reading

- The React Router documentation at the following link is worth going through: `https://reacttraining.com/react-router`

- The `react-transition-group` documentation is also worth looking at to gain further knowledge on transitioning components: `https://reactcommunity.org/react-transition-group/`

5
Advanced Types

We've already learned about a fair amount of the type system in TypeScript. In this chapter, we'll continue on this journey, this time diving into some of the more advanced types and concepts that will help us later in the book to create reusable strongly type React components.

We'll learn about how we can combine existing types to create union type. We'll find out in `Chapter 8`, *React Redux*, that these types are fundamental to creating strongly typed React Redux code.

We briefly covered type guards in `Chapter 2`, *What is New in TypeScript 3*, when we learned about the `unknown` type. We look at these in more detail in this chapter.

Generics are a TypeScript feature that many libraries use to allow consumers to create strongly typed apps with their library. React itself uses it in class components to allow us to create strongly typed props and states in the component. We cover generics in detail in this chapter.

Overload signatures is a nice feature that allows us to have a single function taking different combinations of parameters. We'll learn how to use these in this chapter.

Lookup and mapped types allow us to dynamically create new types from existing types. We learn all about these at the end of this chapter.

In this chapter, we'll learn about the following topics:

- Union types
- Type guards
- Generics
- Overload signatures
- Lookup and mapped types

Technical requirements

We'll use the following technologies in this chapter:

- **TypeScript playground**: This is a website at `http://www.typescriptlang.org/play` that allows us to play and understand the features in TypeScript without installing it. We'll use this the majority of the time in this chapter.
- **Visual Studio Code**: We'll need an editor to write our React and TypeScript code that can be installed from the `https://code.visualstudio.com/` website. We will also need the **TSLint** (by egamma) and **Prettier** (by Esben Petersen) extensions installed within Visual Studio Code.

All the code snippets in this chapter can be found online at: `https://github.com/carlrip/LearnReact17WithTypeScript/tree/master/05-AdvancedTypes`.

Union types

As the name suggests, union types are types that we can combine together to form a new type. Unions are commonly used with string literal types, which we'll cover in the first section. Unions can be used in a pattern called discriminated union, which we can use when creating generic and reusable React components.

String literal types

A variable of a string literal type can only be assigned the exact string value specified in the string literal type.

In the TypeScript playground, let's go through an example:

1. Let's create a string literal type called `Control` that can only be set to the `"Textbox"` string:

```
type Control = "Textbox";
```

2. Let's now create a variable called `notes` with our `Control` type and set this to
   `"Textbox"`:

   ```
   let notes: Control;
   notes = "Textbox";
   ```

   As we would expect, the TypeScript compiler is happy with this.

3. Now let's set our variable to a different value:

   ```
   notes = "DropDown";
   ```

   We get the compilation error **Type '"DropDown"' is not assignable to type
   '"Textbox"'**:

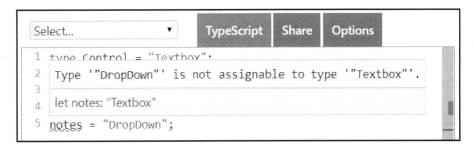

4. As with all other types in TypeScript, `null` and `undefined` are valid values as
   well:

   ```
   notes = null;
   notes = undefined;
   ```

String literal types aren't that useful on their own. However, they become extremely useful
when used in a union type, which we'll look at in the next section.

String literal union types

A string literal union type is where we combine multiple string literal types together.

Let's continue from the previous example and go through this.

1. Let's enhance our `Control` type to be a union of string literals:

   ```
   type Control = "Textbox" | "DropDown"
   ```

   We combine types in a union type using `|`.

2. Setting our `notes` variable to either `"Textbox"` or `"DropDown"` is now perfectly valid:

```
let notes: Control;
notes = "Textbox";
notes = "DropDown";
```

3. Let's extend our `Control` type to include more string literals:

```
type Control = "Textbox" | "DropDown" | "DatePicker" |
"NumberSlider";
```

4. We can now set our `notes` variable to any of these values:

```
notes = "DatePicker";
notes = "NumberSlider";
```

If we think about it, this is really useful. We could have declared the `notes` variable as a `string`, but declaring it with the specific string literals it can contain makes it super type-safe.

Discriminated union pattern

The discriminated union pattern allows us to handle the logic for different union types.

Let's go through an example:

1. Let's first create three interfaces to represent a textbox, a date picker, and a number slider:

```
interface ITextbox {
  control: "Textbox";
  value: string;
  multiline: boolean;
}

interface IDatePicker {
  control: "DatePicker";
  value: Date;
}

interface INumberSlider {
  control: "NumberSlider";
  value: number;
}
```

They all have a property called `control`, which will be the discriminant in the pattern.

2. Let's move on to combine these interfaces into a union type called `Field`:

```
type Field = ITextbox | IDatePicker | INumberSlider;
```

So, we can create union types from any types, and not just string literals. In this case, we have created a union type from three interfaces.

3. Let's now create a function to initialize the value in the `Field` type:

```
function intializeValue(field: Field) {
  switch (field.control) {
    case "Textbox":
      field.value = "";
      break;
    case "DatePicker":
      field.value = new Date();
      break;
    case "NumberSlider":
      field.value = 0;
      break;
    default:
      const shouldNotReach: never = field;
  }
}
```

The value we need to set depends on the discriminant property, `control`. So, we have used a `switch` statement to branch on this property.

The `default` branch in the `switch` statement is where things get interesting. This branch should never be reached, so we have put a statement with the `never` type in that branch. We'll see the value of doing this after the next steps.

4. Let's pretend time has passed and we have a new requirement for checkbox fields. Let's implement an interface for this:

```
interface ICheckbox {
  control: "Checkbox";
  value: boolean;
}
```

5. Let's also add this to the union `Field` type:

```
type Field = ITextbox | IDatePicker | INumberSlider | ICheckbox;
```

We'll immediately see that our `initializeValue` function throws a compilation error on the `never` declaration:

```
24  function intializeValue(field: Field) {
25    switch (field.control) {
26      case "Textbox":
27        field.value = "";
28        break;
29      case "DatePicker":
30        field.value = new Date();
31        break;
32      case "NumberSlider":
33        field. Type 'ICheckbox' is not assignable to type 'never'.
34        break;  const shouldNotReach: never
35      default:
36        const shouldNotReach: never = field;
37    }
38  }
```

This is very valuable because the `never` statement ensures we don't forget to add a branch of code for the new checkbox requirement.

6. So, let's go and implement this additional branch for the `"Checkbox"` field:

```
function intializeValue(field: Field) {
  switch (field.control) {
    case "Textbox":
      field.value = "";
      break;
    case "DatePicker":
      field.value = new Date();
      break;
    case "NumberSlider":
      field.value = 0;
      break;
    case "Checkbox":
      field.value = false;
      break;
    default:
      const shouldNotReach: never = field;
  }
}
```

So, union types allow us to combine any types together to form another type. This allows us to create stricter types, particularly when working with strings. The discriminated union pattern allows us to have branches of logic for different types in the union, and the `never` type helps us catch all the changes that need to happen when we add a new type into the union type.

Type guards

Type guards allow us to narrow down the specific type of an object within a conditional branch of code. They are useful when working with union types, when we need to implement a branch of code that deals with a specific type in the union.

We already worked with a type guard in the last section when we implemented the `intializeValue` function. The `switch` statement on the discriminant property `control` allowed us to set the value on each type in the union.

There are other ways we can implement type guards. The following sections go through different ways.

Using the typeof keyword

The `typeof` keyword is a JavaScript keyword that returns a string that represents the type. So, we can use this in a condition to narrow down the type.

Let's go through an example:

1. We have a union type that can be a string or an array of strings:

   ```
   type StringOrStringArray = string | string[];
   ```

2. We need to implement a function called `first` that takes in a parameter of type `StringOrStringArray` **and returns a** `string`:

   ```
   function first(stringOrArray: StringOrStringArray): string {
   }
   ```

3. The function needs to return the first character if `stringOrArray` is a string; otherwise, it should return the first array element:

```
function first(stringOrArray: StringOrStringArray): string {
  if (typeof stringOrArray === "string") {
    return stringOrArray.substr(0, 1);
  } else {
    return stringOrArray[0];
  }
}
```

If we hover over `stringOrArray` in the first branch, we see that the type has been successfully narrowed to `string`:

```
1 type StringOrStringArray = string | string[];
2 function fi                          stringArray): string {
3   if (typeo (parameter) stringOrArray: string ) {
4     return stringOrArray.substr(0, 1);
5   } else {
6     return stringOrArray[0];
7   }
8 }
```

If we hover over `stringOrArray` in the second branch, we see that the type has been successfully narrowed to `string[]`:

```
1 type StringOrStringArray = string | string[];
2 function first(stringOrArray: StringOrStringArray): string {
3   if (typeof stringOrArray === "string") {
4     return
5   } else {   (parameter) stringOrArray: string[]
6     return stringOrArray[0];
7   }
8 }
```

4. To check our function works, we can add the following:

```
console.log(first("The"));
console.log(first(["The", "cat"]));
```

If we run the program, **T** and **The** will be output to the console.

The `typeof` keyword can only be used with JavaScript types, though. To illustrate that point, let's create an enhanced version of our function:

1. We'll call our function `firstEnhanced`. We want to make the second branch specifically deal with the `string[]` type and mark the third branch as a place that should never be reached. Let's give this a try:

```
function firstEnhanced(stringOrArray: StringOrStringArray): string
{
  if (typeof stringOrArray === "string") {
    return stringOrArray.substr(0, 1);
  } else if (typeof stringOrArray === "string[]") {
    return stringOrArray[0];
  } else {
    const shouldNotReach: never = stringOrArray;
  }
}
```

The TypeScript compiler isn't happy with the second branch:

```
 1  type StringOr  This condition will always return 'false' since the types '"str
 2  function firs  ing" | "number" | "boolean" | "symbol" | "undefined" | "object"
 3    if (typeof   | "function"' and '"string[]"' have no overlap.
 4      return st
 5    } else if (typeof stringOrArray === "string[]") {
 6      return stringOrArray[0];
 7    } else {
 8      const shouldNotReach: never = stringOrArray;
 9    }
10  }
```

The message gives us a clue as to what is going on. The JavaScript `typeof` keyword works with JavaScript types, which are `string`, `number`, `boolean`, `symbol`, `undefined`, `object`, and `function`; hence the union type in the error message combining these types. So, `typeof` in our second branch will actually return `"object"`.

2. Let's implement this properly:

```
function firstEnhanced(stringOrArray: StringOrStringArray): string
{
  if (typeof stringOrArray === "string") {
    return stringOrArray.substr(0, 1);
  } else if (typeof stringOrArray === "object") {
    return stringOrArray[0];
  } else {
```

```
        const shouldNotReach: never = stringOrArray;
    }
}
```

The TypeScript compiler is now happy again.

So, `typeof` is great for branching on JavaScript types but not ideal for TypeScript specific types. Let's find out how we can bridge this gap in the following sections.

Using the instanceof keyword

The `instanceof` keyword is another JavaScript keyword. It checks whether an object has a particular constructor function. It is typically used to determine whether an object is an instance of a class.

Let's go through an example:

1. We have two classes representing `Person` and `Company`:

    ```
    class Person {
      id: number;
      firstName: string;
      surname: string;
    }

    class Company {
      id: number;
      name: string;
    }
    ```

2. We also have a union type combining both of these classes:

    ```
    type PersonOrCompany = Person | Company;
    ```

3. We now need to write a function that takes in a `Person` or `Company` and outputs their name to the console:

    ```
    function logName(personOrCompany: PersonOrCompany) {
      if (personOrCompany instanceof Person) {
        console.log(`${personOrCompany.firstName}
    ${personOrCompany.surname}`);
      } else {
        console.log(personOrCompany.name);
      }
    }
    ```

When using `instanceof`, we have the variable we are checking before it and the constructor name (the class name) after it.

If we hover over `personOrCompany` in the first branch, we get the `Person` type:

```
14  function logName(pe
15    if (personOrCompa  (parameter) personOrCompany: Person
16      console.log(`${personOrCompany.firstName} ${personOrCompany.surname}`);
17    } else {
18      console.log(personOrCompany.name);
19    }
20  }
```

If we hover over `personOrCompany` in the second branch, we get the `Company` type:

```
14  function logName(personOrCompany: PersonOrCompany) {
15    if (personOrCompany instanceof Person) {
16      console.log(`                          sonOrCompany.surname}`);
17    } else {     (parameter) personOrCompany: Company
18      console.log(personOrCompany.name);
19    }
20  }
```

So, `instanceof` is great for narrowing down the type if we are dealing with classes. However, there are lots of TypeScript types we use that aren't JavaScript types or based on classes. So, what do we do in these situations? Let's find out in the following sections.

Using the in keyword

The `in` keyword is another JavaScript keyword that can be used to check whether a property is in an object.

Let's implement the example from the last section using the `in` keyword:

1. Instead of classes for the `Person` and `Company` structures, we have interfaces this time:

```
interface IPerson {
  id: number;
  firstName: string;
  surname: string;
```

```
  }

interface ICompany {
  id: number;
  name: string;
}
```

2. We again create a union type from the `Person` and `Company` structures:

```
type PersonOrCompany = IPerson | ICompany;
```

3. Finally, let's implement our function using the `in` keyword:

```
function logName(personOrCompany: PersonOrCompany) {
 if ("firstName" in personOrCompany) {
  console.log(`${personOrCompany.firstName}
${personOrCompany.surname}`);
 } else {
  console.log(personOrCompany.name);
 }
}
```

We put the property name in double quotes before the `in` keyword, followed by the object to check.

If we hover over `personOrCompany` in the first branch, we get the `IPerson` type. If we hover over `personOrCompany` in the second branch, we get the `ICompany` type.

So, the `in` keyword is pretty flexible. It can be used with any object to narrow down its type by checking if a property exists.

There is one final type guard we will go through in the next section.

Using a user-defined type guard

In situations where we can't use the other type guards, we can create our own. We can do this by creating a function with the return type as type predicate. We actually used a user-defined type guard earlier in the book when we went through the `unknown` type.

Let's implement the example from the last two sections using our own type guard function:

1. We have the same interfaces and union type:

```
interface IPerson {
  id: number;
  firstName: string;
  surname: string;
}

interface ICompany {
  id: number;
  name: string;
}

type PersonOrCompany = IPerson | ICompany;
```

2. So, let's implement the type guard function that returns whether the object is of type IPerson:

```
function isPerson(personOrCompany: PersonOrCompany):
personOrCompany is IPerson {
  return "firstName" in personOrCompany;
}
```

The type predicate personOrCompany is IPerson helps the TypeScript compiler narrow down the type. To confirm this, hovering over personOrCompany in the first branch should give the IPerson type. If we then hover over personOrCompany in the second branch, we should get the ICompany type.

Creating a user-defined type guard is a little more work than the other methods, but it gives us lots of flexibility to deal with cases if the other methods don't work.

Generics

Generics can be applied to a function or a whole class. It's a mechanism for allowing the consumers, own type to be used with the generic function or class. The following sections go through examples of both of these.

Generic functions

Let's go through an example of a generic function. We are going to create a wrapper function around the `fetch` JavaScript function for getting data from a web service:

1. Let's start by creating the `function` signature:

   ```
   function getData<T>(url: string): Promise<T> {

   }
   ```

   We place a `T` in angled brackets after the function name to denote that it is a generic function. We can actually use any letter, but `T` is commonly used. We then use `T` in the signature where the type is generic. In our example, the generic bit is the return type, so we are returning `Promise<T>`.

   If we wanted to use an arrow function, this would be:

   ```
   const getData = <T>(url: string): Promise<T> => {
   };
   ```

2. Let's now implement our function:

   ```
   function getData<T>(url: string): Promise<T> {
     return fetch(url).then(response => {
       if (!response.ok) {
         throw new Error(response.statusText);
       }
       return response.json();
     });
   }
   ```

3. Finally, let's consume the function:

   ```
   interface IPerson {
     id: number;
     name: string;
   }

   getData<IPerson>("/people/1").then(person => console.log(person));
   ```

   We pass the type we want to use in the function in angle brackets after the function name. In our case, it is `IPerson`.

If we hover over `person` in the `then` callback, we see that `person` is correctly typed to `IPerson`:

```
12
13                                              (parameter) person: IPerson
14  getData<IPerson>("/people/1").then(person => console.log(person));
15
```

So, as the name suggests, a generic function is a function that works with a generic type. An alternative implementation for the previous example would be to use `any` as the return type, but that wouldn't be type-safe.

Generic classes

We can make a whole class generic. Let's dive into an example of a generic class that stores data in a list:

1. Let's define our class first without any content:

   ```
   class List<T> {

   }
   ```

   We mark the class as generic by putting `<T>` after the class name.

2. Inside the class, let's create a `private` property for the data in the list:

   ```
   private data: T[] = [];
   ```

   We refer to the generic type using `T`. In our example, our `data` property is an array of whatever type the class has been declared with.

3. Let's now add a `public` method to get all the data in the list:

   ```
   public getList(): T[] {
     return this.data;
   }
   ```

   We reference the generic array as the return type with `T[]`.

4. Let's implement a method for adding an item to the list:

```
public add(item: T) {
  this.data.push(item);
}
```

We reference the data item being passed in with the generic type T. The implementation simply uses the arrays `push` method to add the item to our `private` array.

5. Let's also implement a method for removing an item from the list:

```
public remove(item: T) {
  this.data = this.data.filter((dataItem: T) => {
    return !this.equals(item, dataItem);
  });
}
private equals(obj1: T, obj2: T) {
  return Object.keys(obj1).every(key => {
    return obj1[key] === obj2[key];
  });
}
```

We again reference the data item being passed in with the generic type T. The implementation uses the arrays `filter` method to filter the item out of our private array. The filter predicate uses a `private` method that checks whether two objects are equal.

6. So, now that we've implemented our generic list class, let's create a type and some data in preparation for consuming it:

```
interface IPerson {
  id: number;
  name: string;
}
const billy: IPerson = { id: 1, name: "Billy" };
```

7. Let's now create an instance of our generic class:

```
const people = new List<IPerson>();
```

We put the type we want to use with the class after the class name in angled brackets.

8. We can now interact with the class by adding and removing `billy`:

```
people.add(billy);
people.remove(billy);
```

9. Let's try to use a different type with our list instance:

```
people.add({name: "Sally"});
```

We get a compilation error, as we would expect:

```
31
32      Argument of type '{ name: string; }' is not assignable to param
33      eter of type 'IPerson'.
34          Property 'id' is missing in type '{ name: string; }'.
35 people.add({name: "Sally"});
36
```

10. Let's save all the items in our list instance to a variable:

```
const items = people.getList();
```

If we hover over the `items` variable, we see that the type has been correctly inferred to `IPerson[]`:

```
30
31          const items: IPerson[]
32 const items = people.getList();
33
```

So, a generic class allows us to use the class with different types but still maintain strong typing.

We actually used generic classes earlier in the book where we implemented React class components with props and state:

```
interface IProps { ... }
interface IState { ... }
class App extends React.Component<IProps, IState> {
  ...
}
```

Here, the `React.Component` class has two generic parameters for the props and state.

So, generics are a really important concept that we'll use heavily in this book to create strongly typed React components.

Overload signatures

Overload signatures allow a function to be called with different signatures. This feature can be used nicely to streamline a set of functions that a library offers to consumers. Wouldn't it be nice for a library that contained `condenseString` public functions and `condenseArray` to be streamlined so that it just contained a single public `condense` function? We'll do just this in this section:

1. We have a function that removes spaces from a string:

   ```
   function condenseString(string: string): string {
     return string.split(" ").join("");
   }
   ```

2. We have another function that removes spaces from array items:

   ```
   function condenseArray(array: string[]): string[] {
     return array.map(item => item.split(" ").join(""));
   }
   ```

3. We now want to combine these two functions into a single function. We can do this as follows using union types:

   ```
   function condense(stringOrArray: string | string[]): string |
   string[] {
     return typeof stringOrArray === "string"
       ? stringOrArray.split(" ").join("")
       : stringOrArray.map(item => item.split(" ").join(""));
   }
   ```

4. Let's consume our unified function:

   ```
   const condensedText = condense("the cat sat on the mat");
   ```

   As we enter the function parameter, IntelliSense reminds us that we need to enter a string or an array of strings:

   ```
   24
   25                                    condense(stringOrArray: string | string[]):
   26                                    string | string[]
   27  const condensedText = condense("The c")
   28  console.log("condensedText", condensedText);
   29
   ```

If we hover over the `condensedText` variable, we see that the inferred type is the union type:

```
25
26          const condensedText: string | string[]
27  const condensedText = condense("The c")
28  console.log("condensedText", condensedText);
```

5. It's time to add two signature overloads to improve the consumption of our function:

```
function condense(string: string): string;
function condense(array: string[]): string[];
function condense(stringOrArray: string | string[]): string |
string[] { ... }
```

We add function overload signatures before the main function signature. We've added an overload for when we work with a string, and a second overload for when we work with an array of strings.

6. Let's consume our overloaded function:

```
const moreCondensedText = condense("The cat sat on the mat");
```

We get improved IntelliSense now as we type the parameter. We also get up and down arrows to scroll through the two different signatures:

```
28                                    ^   condense(string: string): string
29                                   1/2
                                      ˅
30  const moreCondensedText = condense("The")
31
```

If we hover over the `moreCondensedText` variable, we see that we get better type inference:

```
28
29          const moreCondensedText: string
30  const moreCondensedText = condense("The")
31
```

So, overload signatures improve the experience for developers consuming our functions. They can give improved IntelliSense and type inference.

Lookup and mapped types

The `keyof` is a keyword in TypeScript that creates a union type of all the properties in an object. The type that is created is called a lookup type. This allows us to create types dynamically, based on the properties of an existing type. It's a useful feature that we can use to create generic but strongly typed code against varying data.

Let's go through an example:

1. We have the following `IPerson` interface:

   ```
   interface IPerson {
     id: number;
     name: string;
   }
   ```

2. Let's create a lookup type on this interface using `keyof`:

   ```
   type PersonProps = keyof IPerson;
   ```

   If we hover over the `PersonProps` type, we see that a union type containing `"id"` and `"name"` has been created:

   ```
   1 interface IPerson {
   2   id: number;
   3   name: string;
   4 }
   5
   6        type PersonProps = "id" | "name"
   7 type PersonProps = keyof IPerson;
   ```

3. Let's add a new property to `IPerson`:

   ```
   interface IPerson {
     id: number;
     name: string;
     age: number
   }
   ```

If we hover over the `PersonProps` type again, we see that the type has been automatically extended to include `"age"`:

```
1  interface IPerson {
2    id: number;
3    name: string;
4    age: number;
5  }
6
7        type PersonProps = "id" | "name" | "age"
8  type PersonProps = keyof IPerson;
```

So, the `PersonProps` type is a lookup type because it looks up the literals it needs to contain.

Let's create something useful now with a lookup type:

1. We're going to create a `Field` class that contains the field name, a label, and a default value:

```
class Field {
  name: string;
  label: string;
  defaultValue: any;
}
```

2. This is a start, but we can make `name` more strongly typed by making our class generic:

```
class Field<T, K extends keyof T> {
  name: K;
  label: string;
  defaultValue: any;
}
```

We have created two generic parameters on the class. The first one is for the type of the object containing the field, and the second one is for the property name within the object.

3. It will probably make more sense if we create an instance of the class. Let's do just that using `IPerson` from the last example and passing `"id"` in as the field name:

```
const idField: Field<IPerson, "id"> = new Field();
```

4. Let's try and reference a property that doesn't exist in IPerson:

```
const addressField: Field<IPerson, "address"> = new Field();
```

We get a compilation error, as we would expect:

```
                                      Type '"address"' does not satisfy the constraint
                                      '"id" | "name" | "age"'.
const addressField: Field<IPerson, "address"> = new Field();
```

Catching problems like this is the benefit of the lookup type, rather than using a string type.

5. Let's move our attention to the defaultValue property in our Field class. This is not type-safe at the moment. For example, we can set idField to a string:

```
idField.defaultValue = "2";
```

6. Let's resolve this and make defaultValue type-safe:

```
class Field<T, K extends keyof T> {
  name: K;
  label: string;
  defaultValue: T[K];
}
```

We are looking up the type using T[K]. For idField, this will resolve to the type of the id property in IPerson, which is number.

The line of code that sets idField.defaultValue now throws a compilation error, as we would expect:

```
14
15    Type '"2"' is not assignable to type 'number'.
16
17    (property) Field<IPerson, "id">.defaultValue: number      );
18   idField.defaultValue = "2";
```

7. Let's change `"2"` to `2`:

```
idField.defaultValue = 2;
```

The compilation error disappears.

So, lookup types can be useful when creating generic components for variable data types.

Let's move on to mapped types now. Again, these let us create new types from an existing type's properties. However, mapped types allow us to specifically define the properties in the new type by mapping them from the existing property.

Let's go through an example:

1. First, let's create a type that we will map from in the next step:

```
interface IPerson {
  id: number;
  name: string;
}
```

2. Now let's create a new version of the `interface` where all the properties are `readonly` using mapped type:

```
type ReadonlyPerson = { readonly [P in keyof IPerson]: IPerson[P]
};
```

The important bit that creates the map is `[P in keyof IPerson]`. This iterates through all the properties in `IPerson` and assigns each one to `P` to create the type. So, the type that is generated in the previous example is the following:

```
type ReadonlyPerson = {
  readonly id: number
  readonly name: string
};
```

3. Let try this out to see if our type really is `readonly`:

```
let billy: ReadonlyPerson = {
  id: 1,
  name: "Billy"
};
billy.name = "Sally";
```

As we expect, a compilation error is thrown where we try to set the `readonly` property to a new value:

```
 6  type ReadonlyPerson = { readonly [P in keyof IPerson]: IPerson[P] };
 7
 8  let bi Cannot assign to 'name' because it is a constant or a read-only
 9    id:    property.
10    name
11  };       (property) name: string
12  billy.name = "Sally";
```

So our mapped type worked! A more generic version of this mapped type is actually in TypeScript as a standard type, and is `Readonly<T>`.

4. Let's use the standard `readonly` type now:

```
let sally: Readonly<IPerson> = {
   id: 1,
   name: "sally"
};
```

5. Let's try changing the values in our `readonly`:

```
Sally.name = "Billy";
```

A compilation error is thrown, as we would expect:

```
13
14  let sa Cannot assign to 'name' because it is a constant or a read-only
15    id:    property.
16    name
17  };       (property) name: string
18  sally.name = "Billy";
```

If we were in Visual Studio Code and used the **Go to Definition** option on the `Readonly` type, we would get the following:

```
type Readonly<T> = {
    readonly [P in keyof T]: T[P];
};
```

This is very similar to our `ReadonlyPerson` type, but `IPerson` has been substituted with generic type `T`.

Let's have a go at creating our own generic mapped type now:

1. We are going to create a mapped type that makes all the properties of an existing type of type `string`:

```
type Stringify<T> = { [P in keyof T]: string };
```

2. Let's try to consume our mapped type:

```
let tim: Stringify<IPerson> = {
 id: "1",
 name: "Tim"
};
```

3. Let's try to set `id` to a number:

```
tim.id = 1
```

The expected compilation error is thrown:

```
24  type Stringify<T> = { [P in keyof T]: string };
25  let tim: Stringify<IPerson> = {
26    id: "1"
27  Type '1' is not assignable to type 'string'.
28
29  (property) id: string
30  tim.id = 1
```

So, mapped types are useful in situations when we need a new type that is based on an existing type. Along with `Readonly<T>`, there are quite a few standard mapped types in TypeScript, such as `Partial<T>`, which creates a mapped type making all the properties optional.

Summary

We've learned some of the more advanced types in TypeScript in this chapter, starting with union types. Union types are extremely useful, allowing us to create new types by unioning existing types together. We discovered that unioning together string literals allow us to create a type that is more specific and type-safe than a regular `string`.

We explored various ways of implementing type guards. Type guards are useful to help the compiler narrow down a union type in branches of logic. They are also useful when working with the `unknown` type to tell the compiler what the type is in branches of logic.

Generics, as the name suggests, allow us to create generic types. Having covered this topic in detail, the type-safety for props and state in React components makes a lot more sense now. We will continue to use generic classes and functions heavily in the rest of the book.

We learned that overload signatures allow us to have a function that has different parameters and return types. We can now use this feature to good effect to streamline public functions we expose in a library.

We learned about how we can dynamically create new types from existing type properties using both lookup and mapped types. We are now aware that there are lots of useful standard TypeScript mapped types such as `Readonly<T>` and `Partial<T>`.

Learning about all these features is great preparation for the next chapter, where we'll dive into some common patterns when working with React components.

Questions

Let's have a go at some questions on advanced types:

1. We have an `interface` that represents a course result, as follows:

```
interface ICourseMark {
  courseName: string;
  grade: string;
}
```

We can use this `interface` as follows:

```
const geography: ICourseMark = {
  courseName: "Geography",
  grade: "B"
}
```

The grades can only be A, B, C, or D. How can we create a stronger typed version of the `grade` property in this interface?

2. We have the following functions that validate that numbers and strings are populated with a value:

```
function isNumberPopulated(field: number): boolean {
  return field !== null && field !== undefined;
}

function isStringPopulated(field: string): boolean {
  return field !== null && field !== undefined && field !== "";
}
```

How can we combine these into a single function called `isPopulated` with signature overloads?

3. How can we implement a more flexible version of the `isPopulated` function with generics?

4. We have the follow `type` alias of stages:

```
type Stages = {
  pending: 'Pending',
  started: 'Started',
  completed: 'Completed',
};
```

5. How can we programmatically turn this into the `'Pending'` | `'Started'` | `'Completed'` union type?

6. We have the following union type:

```
type Grade = 'gold' | 'silver' | 'bronze';
```

How can we programmatically create the following type:

```
type GradeMap = {
  gold: string;
  silver: string;
  bronze: string
};
```

Further reading

The TypeScript documentation has a great section on advanced types that is worth looking at:

```
https://www.typescriptlang.org/docs/handbook/advanced-types.html
```

6
Component Patterns

In this chapter, we will continue with the React shop we were building previously. We'll build a reusable tab component as well as a reusable loading indicator component that will both be used on the product page in our shop. The chapter will start by splitting the product page into a container and a presentational component before working on the tab component, leveraging the compound component and render props patterns. We'll then move on to implement a loading indicator component using the higher-order component pattern.

In this chapter, we'll learn about the following topics:

- Container and presentational components
- Compound components
- Render props pattern
- Higher-order components

Technical requirements

We'll use the following technologies in this chapter:

- **Node.js and** `npm`: TypeScript and React are dependent on these. We can install these from: `https://nodejs.org/en/download/`. If we already have these installed, make sure `npm` is at least version 5.2.
- **Visual Studio Code**: We'll need an editor to write our React and TypeScript code, which can be installed from `https://code.visualstudio.com/`. We will also need the TSLint (by egamma) and Prettier (by Estben Petersen) extensions installed within Visual Studio Code.
- **React shop**: We'll start from the project we began in the chapter where we looked at React Router. This is available on GitHub at: `https://github.com/carlrip/LearnReact17WithTypeScript/tree/master/04-ReactRouter`.

All the code snippets in this chapter can be found online at: `https://github.com/carlrip/LearnReact17WithTypeScript/tree/master/06-ComponentPatterns`.

Container and presentational components

Splitting pages up into container and presentational components makes the presentational component easier to reuse. The container component is responsible for how things work, fetching any data from a web API and managing state. The presentational component is responsible for how things look. Presentational components receive data via their properties and also have property event handlers so that their container can manage the user interactions.

We are going use this pattern in our React shop to split the product page into container and presentational components. The `ProductPage` component will be the container and we'll introduce a new component called `Product` that will be the presentational component:

1. Let's start by opening our shop project in Visual Studio Code and entering the following command in a terminal to start the app:

   npm start

2. If we navigate to a product, let's remind ourselves what the product page looks like:

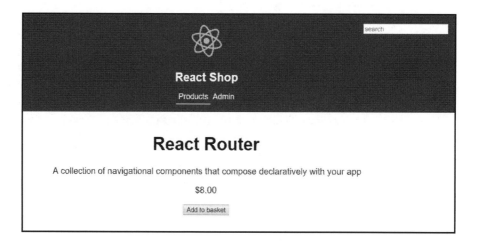

3. Let's create a new file called `Product.tsx` that will contain our presentational component with the following content:

```
import * as React from "react";

const Product: React.SFC<{}> = props => {
  return <React.Fragment>TODO</React.Fragment>;
};

export default Product;
```

Our presentational component is a function component.

4. Presentational components receive data via props and also delegate event handling via props. So, let's create props for the product data item, whether it has been added to the basket, and the handler for adding it to the basket:

```
import * as React from "react";
import { IProduct } from "./ProductsData";

interface IProps {
  product: IProduct;
  inBasket: boolean;
  onAddToBasket: () => void;
}
const Product: React.SFC<IProps> = props => {
  return <React.Fragment>TODO</React.Fragment>;
};

export default Product;
```

5. If we look at `ProductsPage.tsx`, we are going to copy the JSX for when there is a product that is the `React.Fragment` section. We then paste this into the return statement for our `Product` component:

```
const Product: React.SFC<IProps> = props => {
  return (
    <React.Fragment>
      <h1>{product.name}</h1>
      <p>{product.description}</p>
      <p className="product-price">
        {new Intl.NumberFormat("en-US", {
          currency: "USD",
          style: "currency"
        }).format(product.price)}
      </p>
      {!this.state.added && (
```

```
            <button onClick={this.handleAddClick}>Add to
    basket</button>
        )}
      </React.Fragment>
    );
};
```

We have a few reference issues now to resolve.

6. Let's define a product variable above the return statement to resolve the issue with the product reference in the JSX:

```
const product = props.product;
return (
    ...
)
```

7. Whether the product is in the basket is passed in via the `inBasket` prop now. So, let's change the conditional around the **Add to Basket** button to use this prop:

```
{!props.inBasket && (
    <button onClick={this.handleAddClick}>Add to basket</button>
)}
```

8. The final reference issue we need to resolve is with the handler for clicking the **Add to Basket** button. Let's first create a handler that simply calls the `onAddToBasket` prop:

```
const product = props.product;

const handleAddClick = () => {
    props.onAddToBasket();
};

return (
    ...
);
```

9. We can remove the `this` reference where we reference this handler in the JSX:

```
{!props.inBasket && (
    <button onClick={handleAddClick}>Add to basket</button>
)}
```

That's our `Product` presentational component complete for the time being. So, let's reference our `Product` component in our `ProductPage` component.

10. First, let's import our `Product` component into `ProductPage.tsx`:

```
import Product from "./Product";
```

11. Now, let's replace the section we copied in the JSX with our `Product` component:

```
return (
 <div className="page-container">
    <Prompt when={!this.state.added} message={this.navAwayMessage}
 />
    {product ? (
      <Product
        product={product}
        inBasket={this.state.added}
        onAddToBasket={this.handleAddClick}
      />
    ) : (<p>Product not found!</p>)}
 </div>
);
```

We pass the product, whether the product has been added to basket, and the handler for adding to the basket together as props to the `Product` component.

If we look at the shop again and go to the product page, it will look exactly the same.

So, we just implemented our first container and presentational components. Container components are great as the top-level component within a page, fetching data from a web API, and managing all the state within the page. Presentational components just focus on what needs to be rendered to the screen. A benefit of this pattern is that presentational components can be used elsewhere in the app more easily. For example, our `Product` component could fairly easily be used on other pages that we create in our shop. Another benefit of this pattern is that presentational components are generally easier to unit-test. In our example, our `Product` component is a pure function and so unit-testing this is simply a case of checking that the output is correct for different inputs because there are no side-effects. We'll cover unit testing in detail later in the book.

We'll continue to enhance our product page in the next section by adding reviews to it and adding tabs to separate the product description from the reviews.

Compound components

Compound components are a set of components that work together. We are going to use this pattern to create a reusable tab component for use on the product page to separate reviews the product descriptions.

Adding reviews to a product

Before we create our `Tabs` compound component, let's add reviews to the product page:

1. First, we need to add an interface for the review data structure in `ProductsData.ts`:

    ```
    export interface IReview {
      comment: string;
      reviewer: string;
    }
    ```

2. We can now add reviews to our product interface :

    ```
    export interface IProduct {
      ...
      reviews: IReview[];
    }
    ```

3. We can now add reviews to our product data array:

    ```
    const products: IProduct[] = [
      {
        id: 1,
        ...
        reviews: [
          {
            comment: "Excellent! This does everything I want",
            reviewer: "Billy"
          },
          { comment: "The best router I've ever worked with", reviewer:
          "Sally" }
        ]
      },
      {
        id: 2,
        ..
        reviews: [
          {
    ```

```
            comment: "I've found this really useful in a large app I'm
            working on",
            reviewer: "Billy"
          },
          {
            comment: "A bit confusing at first but simple when you get
            used to it",
            reviewer: "Sally"
          }
        ]
      },
      {
        id: 3,
        ..
        reviews: [
          {
            comment: "I'll never work with a REST API again!",
            reviewer: "Billy"
          },
          {
            comment: "It makes working with GraphQL backends a breeze",
            reviewer: "Sally"
          }
        ]
      }
    ];
```

So, we add a `reviews` property to each product that is an array of reviews. Each review is an object containing `comment` and `reviewer` properties as defined by the `IReview` interface.

4. With our data in place, let's add the reviews to our `Product` component after the description:

```
<p>{product.description}</p>
<div>
  <ul className="product-reviews">
    {product.reviews.map(review => (
      <li key={review.reviewer} className="product-reviews-item">
        <i>"{review.comment}"</i> - {review.reviewer}
      </li>
    ))}
  </ul>
</div>
<p className="product-price">
  ...
</p>
```

So, we are using the `map` function on the `reviews` array to display `comment` and `reviewer` in a list.

5. We have referenced some new CSS classes, so let's add these into `index.css`:

```
.product-reviews {
  list-style: none;
  padding: 0px;
}
.product-reviews .product-reviews-item {
  display: block;
  padding: 8px 0px;
}
```

If we look at the running app and go to a product, we'll now see the reviews:

Now that we have added the reviews, we can work on our `Tabs` component in the next section.

Creating a basic tab component

Our job now is to separate the description from the reviews using a tab component that we are going to build. We are going to create a simple tab component first and refactor this into the compound component pattern in the next section.

It's time to start on our tab component:

1. First, let's create a file called `Tabs.tsx` for our tab component with the following content in it as a skeleton class component:

```
import * as React from "react";

interface IProps {}
interface IState {}
class Tabs extends React.Component<IProps, IState> {
  public constructor(props: IProps) {
    super(props);
    this.state = {};
  }
  public render() {
    return;
  }
}

export default Tabs;
```

   We have chosen to create a class-based component because our component will have to track state for whichever tab heading is active.

2. So, let's complete the interface for our state by adding a property that will give the active heading name:

```
interface IState {
  activeHeading: string;
}
```

3. Our component will take in the tab headings and display them as properties. So, let's complete our interface for this:

```
interface IProps {
  headings: string[];
}
```

So, our component can take in an array of heading names in a `headings` prop.

4. Let's create the initial value for the `activeHeading` state in the constructor now:

```
public constructor(props: IProps) {
  super(props);
  this.state = {
    activeHeading:
      this.props.headings && this.props.headings.length > 0
        ? this.props.headings[0]
        : ""
  };
}
```

So, the active heading will initially be set to the first element in the `headings` array. The ternary ensures our component doesn't produce an error if no tabs have been passed to it by the consumer.

5. Moving on to the render method now, let's render our tabs in a list by mapping over the `headings` prop:

```
public render() {
  return (
    <ul className="tabs">
      {this.props.headings.map(heading => (
        <li className={heading === this.state.activeHeading ?
        "active" : ""}
        >
          {heading}
        </li>
      ))}
    </ul>
  );
}
```

We have referenced some CSS classes including `active`, which is set using a ternary based on whether it is the active tab heading being rendered or not.

6. Let's add these CSS classes to `index.css` now:

```css
.tabs {
  list-style: none;
  padding: 0;
}
.tabs li {
  display: inline-block;
  padding: 5px;
  margin: 0px 5px 0px 5px;
  cursor: pointer;
}
.tabs li:focus {
  outline: none;
}
.tabs li.active {
  border-bottom: #222 solid 2px;
}
```

Before we can see what our tab component looks like, we need to consume it.

7. So, let's add this on the `Product` component by first importing the `Tabs` component:

```
import Tabs from "./Tabs";
```

8. We can now add the `Tabs` component in between the product name and description:

```
<h1>{product.name}</h1>
<Tabs headings={["Description", "Reviews"]} />
<p>{product.description}</p>
```

We pass the `Tabs` component the two tab headings we want to display, which are **Description** and **Reviews**.

Let's see what this looks like:

That's a good start. The first tab is underlined from the `active` CSS style just as we wanted. If we click on the **Reviews** tab nothing happens, though.

9. So, let's reference the click handler back in `Tabs.tsx` for each tab:

```
<li
  onClick={this.handleTabClick}
  className={heading === this.state.activeHeading ? "active" : ""}
>
  {heading}
</li>
```

10. Let's implement the click handler as well now:

```
private handleTabClick = (e: React.MouseEvent<HTMLLIElement>) => {
  const li = e.target as HTMLLIElement;
  const heading: string = li.textContent ? li.textContent : "";
  this.setState({ activeHeading: heading });
};
```

We first extract the heading from the `textContent` of `li`. We then set the `activeHeading` state to this. This will cause React to re-render the component with the clicked tab shown as being active.

Notice that we help the TypeScript compiler declare the `li` variable as `HTMLLIElement` using the `as` keyword. Without doing this, the compiler wouldn't be happy with us accessing the `textContent` property within it.

If we go to the running app again, we can now click on our tabs and see the active state changing.

At the moment, our tabs component just renders some tabs that can be clicked on. It doesn't tie into any content yet. We'll actually not tie in our headings to content until the next section on the render props pattern. However, now it's time to explore the compound component pattern and enhance our tab headings a little more in the next section.

Leveraging the compound component pattern

Our tab headings can only be strings at the moment. What if we want to allow the consumer of the component to define richer content in the headings? For example, a consumer might want to put an icon in front of a tab heading or make a heading bold. So, the consuming JSX could look something like this:

```
<Tabs>
  <Tabs.Tab name="Description" initialActive={true}>
    <b>Description</b>
  </Tabs.Tab>
  <Tabs.Tab name="Reviews">
    Reviews
  </Tabs.Tab>
</Tabs>
```

In the previous example, `Tabs` and `Tabs.Tab` are compound components:

- `Tabs` is the component that renders the `Tabs.Tab` components within it. It also manages the state for whichever tab is active.
- `Tabs.Tab` renders a single heading. It takes a unique tab name as a property, which allows the active tab to be managed. It also takes in a `boolean` property called `initialActive` that sets that tab to be active when first loaded. The heading that is rendered is the content within the `Tabs.Tab` tag. So, the first tab will render **Description** in bold.

So, let's refactor our basic tabs component into a compound component that can be used similarly to the previous example:

1. Our `Tabs` component no longer takes in any properties, so, let's remove the `IProps` interface. We can remove the constructor because we no longer need to initialize the state from the props. Let's also change the name of our state property from `activeHeading` to `activeName` as well:

   ```
   interface IState {
     activeName: string;
   }
   class Tabs extends React.Component<{}, IState> {
     public render() {
       ...
     }
     ...
   }
   ```

2. We are going to work on the `Tab` component within `Tabs`, first. So, let's create an interface for its properties:

   ```
   interface ITabProps {
     name: string;
     initialActive?: boolean;
   }
   ```

   - The `name` property is a unique name for the tab. This will be used later to help us manage the active tab.
   - The `initialActive` property specifies whether the tab is active when the component first loads.

3. Let's add the following `Tab` function component inside our `Tabs` class component now:

   ```
   class Tabs extends React.Component<IProps, IState> {
     public static Tab: React.SFC<ITabProps> = props => <li>TODO -
   render the nodes child nodes</li>;

     public render() {...}
     ...
   }
   ```

This is the start of the component that will render each tab. The `Tab` component is defined as a static property on the `Tabs` component. This means `Tab` lives on the actual `Tabs` class and not in its instances. So, we must remember we don't have access to any `Tabs` instance members (for instance, `this`). However, we can reference `Tab` in JSX using `Tabs.Tab` now, which was one of our requirements.

At the moment, `Tab` is just rendering `li` with a note reminding us that we need to somehow render the child nodes of the component. Remember that we want the consuming markup for our `Tabs` component to be as follows:

```
<Tabs.Tab name="Description" initialActive={true}>
  <b>Description</b>
/Tabs.Tab>
```

4. So, our render function needs to somehow render `<b> Description </b>` inside our `li` tag. How do we do this? The answer is via a special property called `children`:

```
public static Tab: React.SFC<ITabProps> = props =>
<li>{props.children}</li>;
```

React component properties can be of any type, including React nodes. The `children` property is a special property that React gives a component that contains the component's child nodes. We render a component's child nodes in JSX by referencing the `children` property in curly brackets.

Our `Tab` component is not finished, but we'll leave it like this for the time being. We now need to move on to the `Tabs` component.

5. The `render` method in the `Tabs` class is simply going to render its child nodes now. Let's replace this method with the following:

```
public render() {
  return (
    <ul className="tabs">{this.props.children}</ul>
  );
}
```

We again use the magical `children` property to render the child nodes within `Tabs`.

We are progressing well with our compound `Tabs` and `Tab` components but our project no longer compiles because we have the tab click handler, `handleTabClick`, that is not referenced anymore. We need to somehow reference it from the `Tab` component when a tab heading is clicked, but remember `Tab` doesn't have access to members of `Tabs`. So, how can we do this? We'll find the answer to this problem in the next section.

Sharing state with React context

React context allows state to be shared between components. It works really well with compound components. We are going to use it in our `Tabs` and `Tab` components to share state between them:

1. Our first task is to create an interface for the context we are going to use in `Tabs.tsx` at the top of the file just beneath the import statements:

   ```
   interface ITabsContext {
     activeName?: string;
     handleTabClick?: (name: string) => void;
   }
   ```

   So, our context will contain the active tab name as well as a reference to a tab click handler. These are the two bits of state that need to be shared between the components.

2. Next, let's create the context underneath the `ITabsContext` interface:

   ```
   const TabsContext = React.createContext<ITabsContext>({});
   ```

   We've used the `createContext` function in React to create our context, which is a generic function that creates a context of a generic type, which in our case in `ITabsContext`.

   We are required to pass the default context value as the parameter value to `createContext` but that doesn't make sense in our case, so we just pass an empty `{}` object to keep the TypeScript compiler happy. This is why both the properties in `ITabsContext` are optional.

3. It's time to use this context now in our compound components. The first thing we need to do is to define the context provider in the `Tabs render` method:

   ```
   public render() {
     return (
       <TabsContext.Provider
   ```

```
    value={{
      activeName: this.state ? this.state.activeName : "",
      handleTabClick: this.handleTabClick
    }}
  >
    <ul className="tabs">{this.props.children}</ul>
  </TabsContext.Provider>
  );
}
```

There are a few things going on here, so let's break this down:

- The constant for our context we declared earlier, `TabsContext`, is available in JSX as a `<TabsContext />` component.
- The context provider fills the context with values. Given that `Tabs` manages the state and event handling, it makes sense for the provider to be referenced there.
- We reference the provider using `<TabsContext.Provider />`.
- The provider takes in a property called `value` for the context value. We set this to an object containing the active tab name and the tab click event handler.

4. We need to adjust the tab click handler slightly because the click isn't going to be handled directly in `Tabs` anymore. So, we simply need to take in the active tab name as a parameter and then set the active tab name state within the method:

```
private handleTabClick = (name: string) => {
  this.setState({ activeName: name });
};
```

5. Now that we have fed the context some data, it's time to consume this in the `Tab` component:

```
public static Tab: React.SFC<ITabProps> = props => (
  <TabsContext.Consumer>
    {(context: ITabsContext) => {
      const activeName = context.activeName
        ? context.activeName
        : props.initialActive
          ? props.name
          : "";
      const handleTabClick = (e: React.MouseEvent<HTMLLIElement>)
=>
        {
          if (context.handleTabClick) {
```

```
        context.handleTabClick(props.name);
      }
    };
    return (
      <li
        onClick={handleTabClick}
        className={props.name === activeName ? "active" : ""}
      >
        {props.children}
      </li>
    );
  }}
</TabsContext.Consumer>
);
```

This again looks a little daunting, so let's break it down:

- We can consume a context via a `Consumer` component within the context component. So, this is `<TabsContext.Consumer />` in our case.
- The child for `Consumer` needs to be a function that has a parameter for the context value and returns some JSX. `Consumer` will then render the JSX we return.

Don't worry if this is still a little confusing. We'll cover this pattern in a lot more detail later when we cover children props and render props.

- This context function gives us everything we need to render the tab. We have access to the state from the `context` argument as well as access to the `Tab` component `props` object.
- The first line of the function determines the active tab name by using what is in the context. If the active tab in the context is an empty string, we use the current tab name if it has been defined as the initial active tab.
- The second line of the function creates a tab click handler that calls the context tab click handler if it has been specified.
- The return statement is as it was before, but we've been able to add a reference to the tab click handler and the class name now.

So, that's it for our tabs compound component. The syntax for React context may seem a little strange at first, but when you get used to it, it is really simple and elegant.

Before we can give this a try, we need to consume our compound component in our `Product` component. Let's replace our previous consumption of the `Tabs` component with the following highlighted JSX:

```
<React.Fragment>
  <h1>{product.name}</h1>

  <Tabs>
    <Tabs.Tab name="Description" initialActive={true}>
      <b>Description</b>
    </Tabs.Tab>
    <Tabs.Tab name="Reviews">Reviews</Tabs.Tab>
  </Tabs>

  <p>{product.description}</p>
  ...
</React.Fragment>
```

This is exactly the JSX we wanted to achieve when we started to build the compound tabs component. If we go to the running app and browse to the product page, our tabs component works perfectly, with the description tab in bold:

So, compound components are great for components that rely on each other. The `<Tabs.Tab />` syntax really *calls out the fact* that `Tab` needs to be used with `Tabs`.

React context works really well with compound components allowing the components, in the compound to easily share state. The state can even include functions such as event handlers.

Allowing the consumer to specify the content to be rendered in sections of a component gives the consumer a great deal of flexibility. Specifying this custom content as a child of a component is intuitive and feels natural. We'll continue with this approach in the following section where we'll complete our tabs component.

Render props pattern

We used a form of the render props pattern in the previous section where we leveraged the `children` prop. We used this to allow a consumer of our `Tab` component to render custom content for the tab heading. This is great, but what if we want to allow the consumer to render custom content in different sections of the component? In our `Tabs` component, we haven't allowed the consumer to render the content of the tab yet. We definitely want the consumer to be able to specify custom content for this, but how do we do this now that we've already used the `children` prop for the heading?

The answer is simple but not obvious at first. The answer is that, because props can be anything, they can be a function that renders content – just like the special `children` prop. These types of prop are called render props. We can have as many render props as we like, giving us the flexibility to allow multiple sections of a component to be rendered by the consumer.

We actually used a render prop in the last section when we used React context. The way we consumed the context was via a render prop.

Next, we'll complete our `Tabs` component by leveraging the render props pattern.

Completing Tabs with render props

We are going to complete our Tabs component now by using the render props pattern. Before we implement our first render prop, let's think about how we want the consumer to consume our `Tabs` component when it has been completed. The following JSX is how we would ideally consume the `Tabs` component from the `Product` component:

```
<Tabs>
  <Tabs.Tab
    name="Description"
    initialActive={true}
    heading={() => <b>Description</b>}
  >
    <p>{product.description}</p>
  </Tabs.Tab>

  <Tabs.Tab
    name="Reviews"
    heading={() => "Reviews"}
  >
    <ul className="product-reviews">
      {product.reviews.map(review => (
        <li key={review.reviewer}>
          <i>"{review.comment}"</i> - {review.reviewer}
        </li>
      ))}
    </ul>
  </Tabs.Tab>
</Tabs>
```

Let's go through the steps of the key parts in this:

- We are still using compound components. Render props work perfectly fine with these components.
- The heading for each tab is no longer defined in the child of the `Tab` component. Instead, we use a `heading` render prop where we can still render a simple string or richer content.
- The tab content is then specified as the child of the `Tab` component.

Using render prop for tab headings

So, let's change the implementation of the tab headings to use a render prop:

1. In `Tabs.tsx`, let's start by adding a new property in the tab props interface for the heading:

    ```
    interface ITabProps {
      name: string;
      initialActive?: boolean;
      heading: () => string | JSX.Element;
    }
    ```

    This property is a function with no parameters that returns a `string` or some JSX. This is the definition of our render prop.

2. Changing the implementation is very straightforward. We simply replace the call to the `children` prop function with our new render prop function in the return statement in the `Tab` component:

    ```
    return (
      <li
        onClick={handleTabClick}
        className={props.name === activeName ? "active" : ""}
      >
        {props.heading()}
      </li>
    );
    ```

3. Let's switch the consumption of `Tabs` in `Product.tsx` to the following:

    ```
    <Tabs>
      <Tabs.Tab
        name="Description"
        initialActive={true}
        heading={() => <b>Description</b>}
      />
      <Tabs.Tab name="Reviews" heading={() => "Reviews"} />
    </Tabs>
    ```

We may get a TSLint warning: **Lambdas are forbidden in JSX attributes due to their rendering performance impact.** It is useful to know that lambdas can be problematic so that we can keep this in mind for when we do experience a performance problem. However, we are going to switch this rule off in `tslint.json` by specifying `"jsx-no-lambda"` as `false`:

```
{
   "extends": ["tslint:recommended", "tslint-react", "tslint-config-
prettier"],
   "rules": {
      ...
      "jsx-no-lambda": false
   },
   ...
}
```

 If we want to be super performance-conscious, instead of using a lambda function we can reference a method within the component.

After we have saved the new TSLint settings, the compiler complaint will hopefully go away. Note that we may need to kill the **Terminal** and `npm start` the app again for the compiler complaint to go away.

If we try using the product page in our app, it will behave just as it did before.

So, implementing the render prop pattern is very simple. The most time-consuming thing with this pattern is understanding what it can do and how it works. Once we've got to grips with it, it is an excellent pattern we can use to provide rendering flexibility to consumers of our components.

We have just one more section to go now before our `Tab` component is complete.

Using children prop for tab content

The finish line is in sight now for our `Tab` component. The final task is to allow consumers to render tab content. We'll use the `children` prop to do this:

1. Firstly, in `Tabs.tsx`, let's change the `handleTabClick` property in our context interface to include the content to render:

```
interface ITabsContext {
   activeName: string;
```

```
      handleTabClick?: (name: string, content: React.ReactNode) =>
   void;
   }
```

2. We are also going to hold the active content in state along with the active tab name. So, let's add this to the state interface for `Tabs`:

```
interface IState {
  activeName: string;
  activeContent: React.ReactNode;
}
```

3. Let's now change the tab click handler in `Tabs` to set the state for the active content along with the active tab name:

```
private handleTabClick = (name: string, content: React.ReactNode)
=> {
  this.setState({ activeName: name, activeContent: content });
};
```

4. In the `Tab` component, let's call the tab click handler with the additional parameter for the tab content by passing the `children` prop:

```
const handleTabClick = (e: React.MouseEvent<HTMLLIElement>) => {
  if (context.handleTabClick) {
    context.handleTabClick(props.name, props.children);
  }
};
```

5. Now let's render the active content from our state in the `Tabs render` method under where we render the tab headings:

```
<TabsContext.Provider ...
>
  <ul className="tabs">{this.props.children}</ul>
  <div>{this.state && this.state.activeContent}</div>
</TabsContext.Provider>
```

6. Let's change how we consume the `Tabs` component in the `Product` component:

```
<h1>{product.name}</h1>

<Tabs>
  <Tabs.Tab
    name="Description"
    initialActive={true}
    heading={() => <b>Description</b>}
  >
```

```
          <p>{product.description}</p>
        </Tabs.Tab>

        <Tabs.Tab name="Reviews" heading={() => "Reviews"}>
          <ul className="product-reviews">
            {product.reviews.map(review => (
              <li key={review.reviewer}>
                <i>"{review.comment}"</i> - {review.reviewer}
              </li>
          ))}
          </ul>
        </Tabs.Tab>
      </Tabs>

<p className="product-price">
...
</p>
```

The tab content is now nested within each `Tab` component exactly how we wanted.

Let's give this a try. If we go to the product page we notice an issue:

The content isn't being rendered when the page first loads. If we click on the **Reviews** tab or the **Description** tab, the content then loads.

7. The problem is that we don't have any code to render the content when the tabs initially load. So, let's resolve this in the `Tab` component by adding the highlighted lines:

```
public static Tab: React.SFC<ITabProps> = props => (
 <TabsContext.Consumer>
 {(context: ITabsContext) => {
  if (!context.activeName && props.initialActive) {
   if (context.handleTabClick) {
    context.handleTabClick(props.name, props.children);
    return null;
   }
  }
 const activeName = context.activeName
 ? context.activeName
 : props.initialActive
 ? props.name
 : "";
 ...
 }}
 </TabsContext.Consumer>
);
```

The highlighted lines invoke the tab click handler if there is no active tab in the context and the tab is flagged as initially active. In this case, we return null because invoking the tab click will set the state for the active tab, which will cause another rendering cycle.

Our tabs component should now be complete. Let's check by going to the product page:

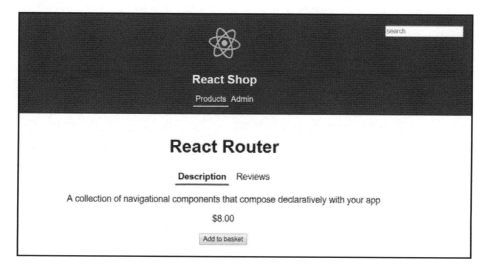

The content renders as we expect. If we click on the **Reviews** tab, this renders fine as well:

So, the render props and children props patterns are great for allowing consumers to render custom content. The syntax may look a little tricky at first, but when you understand it, it makes perfect sense and is really elegant.

In the next section, we'll look at the final pattern in this chapter.

Higher-order components

A **higher-order component (HOC)** is a functional component that takes in a component as a parameter and returns an enhanced version of that component. That may not make a lot of sense, so we're going to go through an example in this section. Our example creates a HOC called `withLoader` that can be applied to any component in order to add a loading spinner when the component is busy. We are going to use this in our React shop (that we worked on in the last section) in the product page whilst data is being fetched. It will look like the following when we have finished:

Adding asynchronous data fetching

At the moment, the data fetching in our shop is instantaneous because all the data is local. So, before working on the withLoader component, let's refactor the data fetching functions to include a delay and be asynchronous as well. This will better simulate a real data fetching function that gets the data using a web API:

1. In ProductData.ts, let's add the following arrow function that can be used to get a product:

```
export const getProduct = async (id: number): Promise<IProduct |
null> => {
  await wait(1000);
  const foundProducts = products.filter(customer => customer.id ===
id);
  return foundProducts.length === 0 ? null : foundProducts[0];
};
```

The function takes in the product ID and uses the filter function in the products array to find the product and then returns it.

The function is prefixed with the async keyword because it is asynchronous.

2. The function also calls a function called wait asynchronously with the await keyword in front of it. So, let's create the wait function:

```
const wait = (ms: number): Promise<void> => {
  return new Promise(resolve => setTimeout(resolve, ms));
};
```

This function uses the standard JavaScript setTimeout function to wait for the number of milliseconds we specify in the function parameter. The function returns a Promise that is resolved when setTimeout completes.

 Don't worry if the async and await keywords along with promises don't make much sense at the moment. We'll look at these in detail later in the book.

So, we have a function that now fetches a product asynchronously taking at least 1 second. Let's plug this into our product page. The ProductPage component is a container component responsible for fetching data, so let's plug this in here.

3. First, let's import the `getProduct` function into `ProductPage`:

```
import { getProduct, IProduct } from "./ProductsData";
```

4. Let's add a property called `loading` to the state of `ProductPage` to indicate whether the data is loading or not:

```
interface IState {
  product?: IProduct;
  added: boolean;
  loading: boolean;
}
```

5. Let's also initialize this state to `true` in the constructor:

```
public constructor(props: Props) {
  super(props);
  this.state = {
    added: false,
    loading: true
  };
}
```

6. Now, we can use the `getProduct` function when the `ProductPage` component loads:

```
public async componentDidMount() {
  if (this.props.match.params.id) {
    const id: number = parseInt(this.props.match.params.id, 10);
    const product = await getProduct(id);
    if (product !== null) {
      this.setState({ product, loading: false });
    }
  }
}
```

We call `getProduct` asynchronously using the `await` keyword. In order to do this, we need to mark the `componentDidMount` lifecycle method as asynchronous with the `async` keyword. After we've got the product, we set it in the state and reset the `loading` flag to `false`.

7. If our shop isn't running, let's run this:

```
npm start
```

If we go to the product page, we see that it takes roughly 1 second for the product to load now. You may notice **Product not found!** being displayed whilst the product loads. This is because the product is not set on the initial render. We'll ignore this for the time being because our `withLoader` HOC will resolve this issue.

So, now that we are getting data asynchronously and roughly taking 1 second, we are ready to implement our `withLoader` HOC and use it on the product page. We'll do just this in the next section.

Implementing the withLoader HOC

We're going to create a loader spinner component called `withLoader` that can be used with any component to indicate that the component is busy doing something:

1. Let's start by creating a new file called `withLoader.tsx` with the following content:

```
import * as React from "react";

interface IProps {
  loading: boolean;
}

const withLoader = <P extends object>(
  Component: React.ComponentType<P>
): React.SFC<P & IProps> => ({ loading, ...props }: IProps) =>
  // TODO - return a loading spinner if loading is true otherwise
  return the component passed in

export default withLoader;
```

There are a few things going on here, so let's break this down:

- `withLoader` is a function that that takes in a component of type `P`.
- `withLoader` calls a function component.

- The properties for the function component are defined as `P & IProps`, which is an intersection type.

 An intersection type combines multiple types into one. So `X`, and `Y`, and `Z` combine all the properties and methods of `X`, `Y`, and `Z` together into a new type.

- So, the properties for the SFC include all the properties from the component passed in along with a `loading boolean` property that we defined.
- The props are destructured into a `loading` variable and a `props` variable containing all the other properties using a rest parameter.

2. So, the remaining work we have to do is return our loading spinner if `loading` is `true`, otherwise we just need to return the component passed in. We can do this using a ternary expression highlighted in the following code:

```
const withLoader = <P extends object>(
  Component: React.ComponentType<P>
): React.SFC<P & IProps> => ({ loading, ...props }: IProps) =>
  loading ? (
    <div className="loader-overlay">
      <div className="loader-circle-wrap">
        <div className="loader-circle" />
      </div>
    </div>
  ) : (
    <Component {...props} />
  );
```

The component passed in is returned in the second ternary branch. We use the spread syntax to spread the properties in the `props` variable into the component.

The loading spinner is returned in the first ternary branch.

3. The loading spinner references some CSS classes, so let's add these into `index.css`:

```
.loader-overlay {
  position: fixed;
  top: 0;
  left: 0;
  width: 100%;
  height: 100%;
  background-color: Black;
```

```
      opacity: 0.3;
      z-index: 10004;
    }
    .loader-circle-wrap {
      position: fixed;
      top: 0;
      right: 0;
      bottom: 0;
      left: 0;
      height: 100px;
      width: 100px;
      margin: auto;
    }
    .loader-circle {
      border: 4px solid #ffffff;
      border-top: 4px solid #899091;
      border-radius: 50%;
      width: 100px;
      height: 100px;
      animation: loader-circle-spin 0.7s linear infinite;
    }
```

The `loader-overlay` class creates a black see-through overlay over the whole page. The `loader-circle-wrap` class creates a `100px` by `100px` square in the center of the overlay. The `loader-circle` class creates the spinning circle.

Our `withLoader` HOC is now complete.

For reference, a class-based version of `withLoader` is shown in the following code block:

```
const withLoader = <P extends object>(Component: React.ComponentType<P>) =>
  class WithLoader extends React.Component<P & IProps> {
    public render() {
      const { loading, ...props } = this.props as IProps;
      return loading ? (
        <div className="loader-overlay">
          <div className="loader-circle-wrap">
            <div className="loader-circle" />
          </div>
        </div>
      ) : (
        <Component {...props} />
      );
    }
  };
```

We are going to stick with the SFC version, though, because it doesn't contain any state or need access to any lifecycle methods.

In the next section, we'll consume our `withLoader` component in the product page in our shop app.

Consuming the withLoader HOC

Consuming a HOC is very simple. We simply wrap the HOC around the component that we want to enhance. The easiest place to do this is in the export statement.

Let's add the `withLoader` HOC we created in the previous section to our product page:

1. So, we are going to wrap the `Product` component with `withLoader`. First, let's import `withLoader` into `Product.tsx`:

   ```
   import withLoader from "./withLoader";
   ```

2. Now we can wrap `withLoader` around `Product` in the export statement:

   ```
   export default withLoader(Product);
   ```

   We now get a compilation error in the `ProductPage` component because it expects to pass `Product` a loading property.

3. So, let's pass the loading property from the loading state where we reference `Product` in `ProductPage`:

   ```
   <Product
     loading={this.state.loading}
     product={product}
     inBasket={this.state.added}
     onAddToBasket={this.handleAddClick}
   />
   ```

4. Whilst still in `ProductPage.tsx`, we should revise the condition that renders the `Product` component. We now want to render `Product` if the product is still being loaded. This will then render the loading spinner:

   ```
   {product || this.state.loading ? (
     <Product
       loading={this.state.loading}
       product={product}
       inBasket={this.state.added}
       onAddToBasket={this.handleAddClick}
   ```

```
      />
  ) : (
    <p>Product not found!</p>
  )}
```

This gives us another compilation error, though, because the `product` property within the `Product` component doesn't expect to be `undefined`. However, it will be `undefined` when the product is being loaded.

5. So, let's make this property optional in `IProps` for the `Product` component:

```
interface IProps {
  product?: IProduct;
  inBasket: boolean;
  onAddToBasket: () => void;
}
```

This then gives further compilation errors in the JSX in the `Product` component where we reference the `product` property because it now will be `undefined` during the loading of the data.

6. A simple resolution to this is to render `null` if we don't have a product. The `withLoader` HOC that wraps `Product` will render a loading spinner in this case, anyway. So, we are just keeping the TypeScript compiler happy here:

```
const handleAddClick = () => {
  props.onAddToBasket();
};
if (!product) {
  return null;
}
return (
  <React.Fragment>
    ...
  </React.Fragment>
);
```

Now that the TypeScript compiler is happy, if we go to the product page in our shop it will display our loading spinner before rendering the product:

So, HOCs are great for enhancing components where the enhancement is something that can be applied to many components. Our loader spinner is a common use case for a HOC. Another very common usage of the HOC pattern is when using React Router. We used the React Router `withRouter` HOC previously in this book to access parameters for a path.

Summary

In this chapter, we learned about container components and how they can be used to manage state and what presentational components need to do. Presentational components can then focus on what they need to look like. This allows presentational components to be more easily reused in multiple places and unit-tested.

We learned that compound components are components that rely on each other. Declaring compound children as static members on the parent class make it clear to a consumer that the components should be used together. React context is a convenient way for compound components to share their state.

We learned about the special children prop that can be used to access and render a component's children. We then learned that we can create our own render props to give consumers great flexibility for custom-rendering sections of a component.

In the last section, we learned about higher-order components and how they can be used to implement common enhancements to components. We already consumed the React Router higher-order component when gaining access to a paths parameters earlier in the book.

In the next chapter, we'll learn how we create forms in React. Towards the end of the next chapter, we'll use some of these patterns that we have learned in this chapter in order to deal with forms in a generic way.

Questions

Let's put what we have learned about component patterns to the test with some questions:

1. What special property does React give us to access a component's, children?
2. How many components can share state with React context?
3. When consuming the React context, what pattern does it use to allow us to render our content with the context?
4. How many render props can we have in a component?
5. How many children props do we have in a component?
6. We only used `withLoader` on the product page. We use the following function in `ProductData.ts` to get all the products:

```
export const getProducts = async (): Promise<IProduct[]> => {
  await wait(1000);
  return products;
};
```

   Can you use this to implement a loader spinner on the products page by consuming the `withLoader` HOC?

7. Is it possible to create a loader spinner using the children props pattern? The consuming JSX would be something like the following:

```
<Loader loading={this.state.loading}>
  <div>
    The content for my component ...
  </div>
</Loader>
```

   If so, have a go at implementing it.

Further reading

- React context is explained in detail in the React documentation at the following link: `https://reactjs.org/docs/context.html`
- Higher-order components are detailed in the React documentation at the following link: `https://reactjs.org/docs/higher-order-components.html`
- The render props pattern is explained in the React documentation at the following link: `https://reactjs.org/docs/render-props.html`

7
Working with Forms

Forms are extremely common in the apps we build. In this chapter, we'll learn how to build forms using controlled components in React and TypeScript. We'll build a **Contact Us** form for the React shop we have been working on in other chapters as our learning exercise.

We'll quickly discover that there is a fair amount of boilerplate code involved in creating forms, so we'll look at building a generic form component to reduce the boilerplate code. Client-side validation is critical to the user experience of the forms we build, so we'll also cover this topic in a fair amount of depth.

Finally, form submission is a critical consideration. We'll cover how to handle submission errors, as well as success.

In this chapter, we'll discuss the following topics:

- Creating a form with controlled components
- Reducing boilerplate code with generic components
- Validating forms
- Form submission

Technical requirements

We'll use the following technologies in this chapter:

- **Node.js** and `npm`: TypeScript and React are dependent on these. Install them from the following link: `https://nodejs.org/en/download/`. If you already have these installed, make sure `npm` is at least version 5.2.
- **Visual Studio Code**: We'll need an editor to write our React and TypeScript code, which can be installed from `https://code.visualstudio.com/`. We'll also need the TSLint extension (by egamma) and the Prettier extension (by Estben Petersen).

- **React shop**: We'll start with the React shop project we finished in `Chapter 6`, *Component Patterns*. This is available on GitHub at `https://github.com/` `carlrip/LearnReact17WithTypeScript/tree/master/06-ComponentPatterns`.

In order to restore code from a previous chapter, the `LearnReact17WithTypeScript` repository at `https://github.com/` `carlrip/LearnReact17WithTypeScript` can be downloaded. The relevant folder can then be opened in Visual Studio Code and then `npm install` can be entered in the terminal to do the restore. All the code snippets in this chapter can be found online at `https://github.com/carlrip/` `LearnReact17WithTypeScript/tree/master/07-WorkingWithForms`.

Creating a form with controlled components

Forms are a common part of most apps. In React, the standard way to create a form is with what is called *controlled components*. A controlled component has its value synchronized with state in React. This will make more sense when we've implemented our first controlled component.

We are going to extend the React shop we have been building to include a **Contact Us** form. This will be implemented using controlled components.

Adding a Contact Us page

Before we start work on our form, we need a page to host the form in. The page will be a container component, and our form will be a presentational component. We also need to create a navigation option that takes us to our new page.

We'll write the following codes before starting to implement our form:

1. If you haven't already, open the React shop project in Visual Studio Code. Create a new file called `ContactUsPage.tsx` in the `src` folder, containing the following code:

```
import * as React from "react";

class ContactUsPage extends React.Component {
  public render() {
    return (
      <div className="page-container">
        <h1>Contact Us</h1>
```

```
      <p>
        If you enter your details we'll get back to you as soon as
        we can.
      </p>
    </div>
  );
  }
}
```

```
export default ContactUsPage;
```

This component will eventually contain state, so, we have created a class-based component. This simply renders a heading with some instructions at the moment. Eventually, it will reference our form.

2. Let's now add this page to the available routes. Open `Routes.tsx`, and import our page:

```
import ContactUsPage from "./ContactUsPage";
```

3. In the `render` method for the `Routes` component, we can now add a new route to our page just above the `admin` route:

```
<Switch>
  <Redirect exact={true} from="/" to="/products" />
  <Route path="/products/:id" component={ProductPage} />
  <Route exact={true} path="/products" component={ProductsPage} />
  <Route path="/contactus" component={ContactUsPage} />
  <Route path="/admin">
    ...
  </Route>
  <Route path="/login" component={LoginPage} />
  <Route component={NotFoundPage} />
</Switch>
```

4. Open `Header.tsx` now, which contains all the navigation options. Let's add a `NavLink` to our new page just above the admin link:

```
<nav>
  <NavLink to="/products" className="header-link"
activeClassName="header-link-active">
    Products
  </NavLink>
  <NavLink to="/contactus" className="header-link"
activeClassName="header-link-active">
    Contact Us
  </NavLink>
```

```
    <NavLink to="/admin" className="header-link"
activeClassName="header-link-active">
        Admin
    </NavLink>
</nav>
```

5. Run the project in your development server, by entering the following in the terminal:

npm start

You should see a new navigation option that takes us to our new page:

Now that we have our new page, we are ready to implement our first controlled input in a form. We'll do this in the following section.

Creating controlled inputs

In this section, we'll start to create our form containing our first controlled input:

1. Create a new file called ContactUs.tsx in the src folder containing the following code:

```
import * as React from "react";

const ContactUs: React.SFC = () => {
  return (
    <form className="form" noValidate={true}>
      <div className="form-group">
```

```
        <label htmlFor="name">Your name</label>
        <input type="text" id="name" />
      </div>
    </form>
  );
};

export default ContactUs;
```

This is a function component that renders a form containing a label and an input for the user's name.

2. We have referenced some CSS classes, so let's add these to the bottom of index.css:

```
.form {
  width: 300px;
  margin: 0px auto 0px auto;
}

.form-group {
  display: flex;
  flex-direction: column;
  margin-bottom: 20px;
}

.form-group label {
  align-self: flex-start;
  font-size: 16px;
  margin-bottom: 3px;
}

.form-group input, select, textarea {
  font-family: Arial;
  font-size: 16px;
  padding: 5px;
  border: lightgray solid 1px;
  border-radius: 5px;
}
```

The form-group class wraps each field in our form, displaying the label above the input with nice spacing.

3. Let's reference our form from our page now. Go to `ContactUsPage.tsx` and import our component:

```
import ContactUs from "./ContactUs";
```

4. We can then reference our component in the `render` method at the bottom of the `div` container:

```
<div className="page-container">
  <h1>Contact Us</h1>
  <p>If you enter your details we'll get back to you as soon as we
can.</p>
  <ContactUs />
</div>
```

If we look at the running app and go to the **Contact Us** page, we'll see our name field rendered:

We can enter our name into this field, but nothing will happen yet. We want the entered name to be stored in the `ContactUsPage` container component state. This is because `ContactUsPage` will eventually manage the form submission.

5. Let's add a state type to `ContactUsPage`:

```
interface IState {
  name: string;
  email: string;
  reason: string;
  notes: string;
}

class ContactUsPage extends React.Component<{}, IState> { ... }
```

As well as the person's name, we are going to capture their email address, reason for contacting the shop, and any additional notes.

6. Let's also initialize the state in a constructor:

```
public constructor(props: {}) {
  super(props);
  this.state = {
    email: "",
    name: "",
    notes: "",
    reason: ""
  };
}
```

7. We now need to get the name value from the state in `ContactUsPage` into the `ContactUs` component. This will allow us to display the value in the input. We can do this by first creating props in the `ContactUs` component:

```
interface IProps {
  name: string;
  email: string;
  reason: string;
  notes: string;
}

const ContactUs: React.SFC<IProps> = props => { ... }
```

We have created props for all the data we are going to eventually capture in our form.

8. Now, we can bind the name input value to the `name` prop:

```
<div className="form-group">
  <label htmlFor="name">Your name</label>
  <input type="text" id="name" value={props.name} />
</div>
```

9. We can now pass these from the state in `ContactUsPage`:

```
<ContactUs
  name={this.state.name}
  email={this.state.email}
  reason={this.state.reason}
  notes={this.state.notes}
/>
```

Let's go to the running app and go to our **Contact Us** page. Try typing something into the name input.

Nothing seems to happen... something is preventing us from entering the value.

We have just set the input value to some React state, so React is now controlling the value of the input. This is why we no longer appear to be able to type into it.

We are part-way through creating our first controlled input. However, controlled inputs aren't much use if users can't enter anything into them. So, how can we make our input editable again?

The answer is that we need to listen to changes to the input value, and update the state accordingly. React will then render the new input value from the state.

10. Let's listen to changes to the input via the `onChange` prop:

```
<input type="text" id="name" value={props.name}
onChange={handleNameChange} />
```

11. Let's create the handler we have just referenced as well:

```
const ContactUs: React.SFC<IProps> = props => {
  const handleNameChange = (e: React.ChangeEvent<HTMLInputElement>)
=> {
    props.onNameChange(e.currentTarget.value);
  };
  return ( ... );
};
```

Note that we've used the generic `React.ChangeEvent` command with the type of the element we are handling (`HTMLInputElement`).

The `currentTarget` prop in the event argument gives us a reference to the element that the event handler is attached to. The `value` property within this gives us the latest value of the input.

12. The handler references an `onNameChange` function prop that we haven't defined yet. So, let's add this to our interface, along with similar props for the other fields:

```
interface IProps {
  name: string;
  onNameChange: (name: string) => void;
  email: string;
  onEmailChange: (email: string) => void;
  reason: string;
  onReasonChange: (reason: string) => void;
  notes: string;
  onNotesChange: (notes: string) => void;
}
```

13. We can now pass these props from `ContactUsPage` into `ContactUs`:

```
<ContactUs
  name={this.state.name}
  onNameChange={this.handleNameChange}
  email={this.state.email}
  onEmailChange={this.handleEmailChange}
  reason={this.state.reason}
  onReasonChange={this.handleReasonChange}
  notes={this.state.notes}
  onNotesChange={this.handleNotesChange}
/>
```

14. Let's create the change handlers we've just referenced in `ContactUsPage` that set the relevant state:

```
private handleNameChange = (name: string) => {
  this.setState({ name });
};
private handleEmailChange = (email: string) => {
  this.setState({ email });
};
private handleReasonChange = (reason: string) => {
  this.setState({ reason });
};
```

```
private handleNotesChange = (notes: string) => {
  this.setState({ notes });
};
```

If we now go to the **Contact Us** page in the running app and enter something into the name, this time the input behaves as expected.

15. Let's add fields for email, reason, and notes in our `render` method for `ContactUs`:

```
<form className="form" noValidate={true} onSubmit={handleSubmit}>
  <div className="form-group">
    <label htmlFor="name">Your name</label>
    <input type="text" id="name" value={props.name}
onChange={handleNameChange} />
  </div>

  <div className="form-group">
   <label htmlFor="email">Your email address</label>
   <input type="email" id="email" value={props.email}
onChange={handleEmailChange} />
   </div>

  <div className="form-group">
    <label htmlFor="reason">Reason you need to contact us</label>
    <select id="reason" value={props.reason}
onChange={handleReasonChange}>
      <option value="Marketing">Marketing</option>
      <option value="Support">Support</option>
      <option value="Feedback">Feedback</option>
      <option value="Jobs">Jobs</option>
      <option value="Other">Other</option>
    </select>
  </div>

  <div className="form-group">
    <label htmlFor="notes">Additional notes</label>
    <textarea id="notes" value={props.notes}
onChange={handleNotesChange} />
  </div>
</form>
```

For each field, we render a `label` and the appropriate editor inside a `div` container, with a `form-group` class to space our fields out nicely.

All the editors reference handlers for handling changes to their value. All the editors also have their value set from the appropriate `ContactUs` prop. So, all the field editors have controlled components.

Let's have a closer look at the `select` editor. We set the value in the `select` tag using a `value` attribute. However, this doesn't exist in the native `select` tag. Usually, we have to include a `selected` attribute in the relevant `option` tag within the `select` tag:

```
<select id="reason">
  <option value="Marketing">Marketing</option>
  <option value="Support" selected>Support</option>
  <option value="Feedback">Feedback</option>
  <option value="Jobs">Jobs</option>
  <option value="Other">Other</option>
</select>
```

React adds the `value` prop to the `select` tag, and manages the `selected` attribute on the `option` tag for us, behind the scenes. This allows us to consistently manage `input`, `textarea`, and `selected` in our code.

16. Let's now create the change handlers for these fields that call the function props we created earlier:

```
const handleEmailChange = (e: React.ChangeEvent<HTMLInputElement>)
=> {
  props.onEmailChange(e.currentTarget.value);
};
const handleReasonChange = (e:
React.ChangeEvent<HTMLSelectElement>) => {
  props.onReasonChange(e.currentTarget.value);
};
const handleNotesChange = (e:
React.ChangeEvent<HTMLTextAreaElement>) => {
  props.onNotesChange(e.currentTarget.value);
};
```

This completes our basic **Contact Us** form, using various controlled form elements. We haven't implemented any validation or submitted the form yet. We'll get to these later in the chapter.

We're already noticing lots of similar code for each field for getting changes to fields into state. In the next section, we are going to start work on a generic form component and switch to using this for our **Contact Us** form.

Reducing boilerplate code with generic components

Generic form components will help reduce the amount of code required to implement a form. We are going to do just this in this section, refactoring what we did in the last section for our `ContactUs` component.

Let's think about how we would ideally consume the generic components to produce the new version of the `ContactUs` component. It could be something like the following JSX:

```
<Form
  defaultValues={{ name: "", email: "", reason: "Support", notes: "" }}
>
  <Form.Field name="name" label="Your name" />
  <Form.Field name="email" label="Your email address" type="Email" />
  <Form.Field name="reason" label="Reason you need to contact us"
type="Select" options={["Marketing", "Support", "Feedback", "Jobs",
"Other"]} />
  <Form.Field name="notes" label="Additional notes" type="TextArea" />
</Form>
```

In this example, there are two generic compound components: `Form` and `Field`. Here are some key points:

- The `Form` component is the container for the compound, managing the state and the interactions.
- We pass default values in for the fields in a `defaultValues` prop on the `Form` component.
- The `Field` component renders the label and an editor for each field.
- Each field has a `name` prop that will determine the property name in the state that the field value is stored under.
- Each field has a `label` prop that specifies the text to display in each field label.
- The specific field editor is specified using a `type` prop. The default editor is a text-based `input`.
- If the editor type is `Select`, then we can specify the options that appear in this using an `options` prop.

The JSX to render the new `ContactUs` component is much shorter than the original version, and arguably easier to read. The state management and event handlers are hidden away and encapsulated within the `Form` component.

Creating a basic form component

It's time to start work on our generic Form component:

1. Let's start by creating a new file in the src folder called Form.tsx, containing the following content:

```
import * as React from "react";

interface IFormProps {}

interface IState {}

export class Form extends React.Component<IFormProps, IState> {
  constructor(props: IFormProps) {}
  public render() {}
}
```

Form is a class-based component because it needs to manage state. We have named the props interface IFormProps because later on we'll need an interface for field props.

2. Let's add a defaultValues prop to the IFormProps interface. This will hold the default value for every field in the form:

```
export interface IValues {
  [key: string]: any;
}

interface IFormProps {
  defaultValues: IValues;
}
```

We use an additional interface called IValues for the default value type. This is an indexable key/value type that has a string type key and an any type value. The key will be the field name, and the value will be the field value.

So, the value for the defaultValues prop could be this:

```
{ name: "", email: "", reason: "Support", notes: "" }
```

3. Let's move on to the state in `Form` now. We are going to store the field values in a state property called `values`:

```
interface IState {
  values: IValues;
}
```

Note that this is the same type as the `defaultValues` prop, which is `IValues`.

4. We are going to initialize the state with the default values in the constructor now:

```
constructor(props: IFormProps) {
  super(props);
  this.state = {
    values: props.defaultValues
  };
}
```

5. The final bit we are going to do in this section is to start implementing the `render` method in the `Form` component:

```
public render() {
 return (
 <form className="form" noValidate={true}>
 {this.props.children}
 </form>
 );
}
```

We render the child components in a `form` tag, using the magical `children` prop we used in the last chapter.

This leads us nicely to the `Field` component, which we'll implement in the next section.

Adding a basic Field component

The `Field` component needs to render a label and an editor. It will live in a static property called `Field` inside the `Form` component. Consumers can then reference this component using `Form.Field`:

1. Let's start by creating an interface for the field props in `Form.tsx` just above `IFormProps`:

```
interface IFieldProps {
  name: string;
```

```
    label: string;
    type?: "Text" | "Email" | "Select" | "TextArea";
    options?: string[];
  }
```

- The `name` prop is the name of the field.
- The `label` prop is the text to display in the field label.
- The `type` prop is the type of editor to display. We have used a union type for this prop, containing the available types we are going to support. Note that we have defined this as an optional prop, so we'll need to define a default value for this a little later.
- The `options` prop, which is only applicable to the `Select` editor type, is also optional. This defines the list of options to display in the drop-down in a `string` array.

2. Now, let's add a skeleton static `Field` property in `Form` for the `Field` component:

```
public static Field: React.SFC<IFieldProps> = props => {
  return ();
};
```

3. Before we forget, let's add that default for the field `type` prop. We define this as follows, outside and underneath the `Form` class:

```
Form.Field.defaultProps = {
  type: "Text"
};
```

So, the default `type` will be a text-based input.

4. Now, let's have a go at rendering the field:

```
public static Field: React.SFC<IFieldProps> = props => {
  const { name, label, type, options } = props;
  return (
    <div className="form-group">
      <label htmlFor={name}>{label}</label>
      <input type={type.toLowerCase()} id={name} />
    </div>
  );
}
```

- We start by destructuring `name`, `label`, `type`, and `options` from the props object.

- The field is wrapped in a `div` container, which spaces the fields out vertically, using the `form-group` class we already implemented in `index.css`.
- The `label` is then rendered just before the `input` inside the `div` container, with the `htmlFor` attribute of the label referencing the `id` of the `input`.

This is a good start, but not all the different field editors are inputs. In fact, this will only work for types `Text` and `Email`.

5. So, let's adjust this slightly and wrap a conditional expression around the input:

```
<label htmlFor={name}>{label}</label>
{(type === "Text" || type === "Email") && (
  <input type={type.toLowerCase()} id={name} />
)}
```

6. Next, let's deal with the `TextArea` type by adding the highlighted JSX:

```
{(type === "Text" || type === "Email") ... }

{type === "TextArea" && (
  <textarea id={name} />
)}
```

7. We can now render the final editor we are going to support, as follows:

```
{type === "TextArea" ... }

{type === "Select" && (
  <select>
    {options &&
      options.map(option => (
        <option key={option} value={option}>
          {option}
        </option>
      ))}
  </select>
)}
```

We render a `select` tag, containing the options specified by using the map function in the `options` array prop. Note that we give each option a unique `key` attribute to keep React happy when detecting any changes to the options.

We now have basic `Form` and `Field` components in play, which is great. However, the implementation is still pretty useless because we are not managing the field values yet in state. Let's cover that in the next section.

Sharing state with React context

The state for field values lives in the `Form` component. However, the values are rendered and changed with the `Field` component. The `Field` component doesn't have access to the state within `Form`, because the state lives in the `Form` instance and `Field` doesn't.

This is very similar to the compound `Tabs` component we implemented in the last chapter. We shared state between the components in the `Tabs` compound using React context.

We are going to use the same approach for our `Forms` component in this section:

1. Let's start by creating an interface for the form context in `Form.tsx`:

   ```
   interface IFormContext {
     values: IValues;
   }
   ```

   The context just contains values that have the same type, `IValues`, as in our state.

2. Let's create the context component now just under `IFormContext` using `React.createContext`:

   ```
   const FormContext = React.createContext<IFormContext>({
     values: {}
   });
   ```

   We keep the TypeScript compiler happy by setting the initial context value to an empty literal value.

3. In the `render` method in `Form`, create the context value containing the values from the state:

   ```
   public render() {
     const context: IFormContext = {
       values: this.state.values
     };
     return ( ... )
   }
   ```

4. Wrap the context provider around the `form` tag in the `render` method's JSX:

   ```
   <FormContext.Provider value={context}>
     <form ... >
       ...
     </form>
   </FormContext.Provider>
   ```

5. We can now consume the context in the `Field` SFC:

```
<FormContext.Consumer>
  {context => (
    <div className="form-group">
    </div>
  )}
</FormContext.Consumer>
```

6. Now that we have access to the context, let's render the values from it in all three editors:

```
<div className="form-group">
  <label htmlFor={name}>{label}</label>
  {(type === "Text" || type === "Email") && (
    <input type={type.toLowerCase()} id={name}
value={context.values[name]} />
  )}

  {type === "TextArea" && (
    <textarea id={name} value={context.values[name]} />
  )}

  {type === "Select" && (
    <select value={context.values[name]}>
    ...
    </select>
  )}
</div>
```

The TypeScript compiler is now happy with our `Form` and `Field` components. So, we could start work on the new `ContactUs` implementation.

However, users will not be able to enter anything into our form yet, because we are not handling changes and passing new values to state. We now need to implement change handlers.

7. Let's start by creating a `setValue` method in the `Form` class:

```
private setValue = (fieldName: string, value: any) => {
  const newValues = { ...this.state.values, [fieldName]: value };
  this.setState({ values: newValues });
};
```

Here are the key points in this method:

- This method takes in the field name and new value as parameters.
- The new state for the `values` object is created using a new object called `newValues`, which spreads the old values from the state and then adds the new field name and value.
- The new values are then set in the state.

8. We then create a reference to this method in the form context so that the `Field` component can access it. Let's add this to the form context interface first:

```
interface IFormContext {
  values: IValues;
  setValue?: (fieldName: string, value: any) => void;
}
```

We set the property as optional to keep the TypeScript compiler happy when the form context component is created.

9. We can then create a reference to the `setValue` method in `Form` when the context value is created:

```
const context: IFormContext = {
  setValue: this.setValue,
  values: this.state.values
};
```

10. We now have access to invoke this method from the `Field` component. In `Field`, just after we destructure the `props` object, let's create a change handler that will invoke the `setValue` method:

```
const { name, label, type, options } = props;

const handleChange = (
  e:
    | React.ChangeEvent<HTMLInputElement>
    | React.ChangeEvent<HTMLTextAreaElement>
    | React.ChangeEvent<HTMLSelectElement>,
  context: IFormContext
) => {
  if (context.setValue) {
    context.setValue(props.name, e.currentTarget.value);
  }
};
```

Let's look at the key points in this method:

- The TypeScript change event type is `ChangeEvent<T>`, where `T` is the type of the element that is being handled.
- The handler's first parameter, `e`, is the React change event handler parameter. We union all the different change handler types for our different editors, so that we can handle all changes in a single function.
- The handler's second parameter is the form context.
- We need a conditional statement to check that the `setValue` method is not `undefined`, to keep the TypeScript compiler happy.
- We can then call the `setValue` method with the field name and new value.

11. We can then reference this change handler in the `input` tag, as follows:

```
<input
  type={type.toLowerCase()}
  id={name}
  value={context.values[name]}
  onChange={e => handleChange(e, context)}
/>
```

Note that we use a lamda function so that we can pass in the context value to `handleChange`.

12. We can do the same in the `textarea` tag:

```
<textarea
  id={name}
  value={context.values[name]}
  onChange={e => handleChange(e, context)}
/>
```

13. We can also do this in the `select` tag:

```
<select
 value={context.values[name]}
 onChange={e => handleChange(e, context)}
>
 ...
</select>
```

So, our `Form` and `Field` components are now nicely working together, rendering fields and managing their values. In the next section, we'll give our generic components a try by implementing a new `ContactUs` component.

Implementing our new ContactUs component

In this section, we are going to implement a new `ContactUs` component using our `Form` and `Field` components:

1. Let's start by removing the props interface from `ContactUs.tsx`.

2. The content within the `ContactUs` SFC will be very different to the original version. Let's start by removing the content so that it looks as follows:

```
const ContactUs: React.SFC = () => {
  return ();
};
```

3. Let's import our `Form` component into `ContactUs.tsx`:

```
import { Form } from "./Form";
```

4. We can now reference the `Form` component, passing some default values:

```
return (
  <Form
    defaultValues={{ name: "", email: "", reason: "Support", notes:
"" }}
  >
  </Form>
);
```

5. Let's add the `name` field:

```
<Form
  defaultValues={{ name: "", email: "", reason: "Support", notes:
"" }}
>
  <Form.Field name="name" label="Your name" />
</Form>
```

Note we haven't passed the `type` prop because this will default to a text-based input, which is just what we require.

6. Let's add the `email`, `reason`, and `notes` fields now:

```
<Form
  defaultValues={{ name: "", email: "", reason: "Support", notes:
"" }}
>
  <Form.Field name="name" label="Your name" />
  <Form.Field name="email" label="Your email address" type="Email"
```

```
  />
  <Form.Field
    name="reason"
    label="Reason you need to contact us"
    type="Select"
    options={["Marketing", "Support", "Feedback", "Jobs", "Other"]}
  />
  <Form.Field name="notes" label="Additional notes" type="TextArea"
/>
</Form>
```

7. The `ContactUsPage` is going to be much simpler now. It won't contain any state because that is managed within the `Form` component now. We also don't need to pass any props to the `ContactUs` component:

```
class ContactUsPage extends React.Component<{}, {}> {
  public render() {
    return (
      <div className="page-container">
        <h1>Contact Us</h1>
        <p>
           If you enter your details we'll get back to you as soon
as we can.
        </p>
        <ContactUs />
      </div>
    );
  }
}
```

If we go to the running app and go to the **Contact Us** page, it renders as required and accepts the values we enter.

Our generic form component is progressing nicely, and we have consumed it to implement the `ContactUs` component as we had hoped. In the next section, we are going to improve our generic component even further by adding validation.

Validating forms

Including validation on a form improves the user experience, by giving them immediate feedback on whether the information entered is valid. In this section, we are going to add validation to our `Form` component and then consume it in our `ContactUs` component.

The validation rules we are going to implement in the `ContactUs` component are these:

- The name and email fields should be populated
- The name field should be at least two characters

We are going to execute validation rules when the field editor loses focus.

In the next section, we'll add a prop to the `Form` component that allows consumers to specify validation rules.

Adding a validation rules prop to form

Let's think about how we would want to specify validation rules to a form. We need to be able to specify one or more rules for a field. Some rules could have a parameter, such as a minimum length. It would be nice if we could specify the rules, as in the example that follows:

```
<Form
  ...
  validationRules={{
    email: { validator: required },
    name: [{ validator: required }, { validator: minLength, arg: 3 }]
  }}
>
  ...
</Form>
```

Let's have a go at implementing the `validationRules` prop on the `Form` component:

1. Start by defining a type for the `Validator` function in `Form.tsx`:

```
export type Validator = (
  fieldName: string,
  values: IValues,
  args?: any
) => string;
```

A `Validator` function will take in the field name, the values for the whole form, and an optional argument specific to the function. A string containing the validation error message will be returned. If the field is valid, a blank string will be returned.

2. Let's use this type to create a `Validator` function to check that a field called `required` under the `Validator` type is populated:

```
export const required: Validator = (
  fieldName: string,
  values: IValues,
  args?: any
): string =>
  values[fieldName] === undefined ||
  values[fieldName] === null ||
  values[fieldName] === ""
    ? "This must be populated"
    : "";
```

We export the function so that it can be used in our `ContactUs` implementation later. The function checks whether the field value is `undefined`, `null`, or an empty string and if so, it returns a **This must be populated** validation error message.

If the field value isn't `undefined`, `null`, or an empty string, then an empty string is returned to indicate the value is valid.

3. Similarly, let's create a `Validator` function for checking that a field input is over a minimum length:

```
export const minLength: Validator = (
  fieldName: string,
  values: IValues,
  length: number
): string =>
  values[fieldName] && values[fieldName].length < length
    ? `This must be at least ${length} characters`
    : "";
```

The function checks whether the length of the field value is less than the length argument, and if so it returns a validation error message. Otherwise, an empty string is returned to indicate the value is valid.

4. Now, let's add the ability to pass validation rules via a prop to the `Form` component:

```
interface IValidation {
  validator: Validator;
  arg?: any;
}
```

```
interface IValidationProp {
  [key: string]: IValidation | IValidation[];
}

interface IFormProps {
  defaultValues: IValues;
  validationRules: IValidationProp;
}
```

- The `validationRules` prop is an indexable key/value type, where the key is the field name and the value is one or more validation rules of type `IValidation`.
- A validation rule contains the validation function of type `Validator`, and an argument to pass into the validation function.

5. With the new `validationRules` prop in place, let's add this to the `ContactUs` component. Import the validator functions first:

```
import { Form, minLength, required } from "./Form";
```

6. Now, let's add the validation rules to the `ContactUs` component JSX:

```
<Form
  defaultValues={{ name: "", email: "", reason: "Support", notes:
"" }}
  validationRules={{
    email: { validator: required },
    name: [{ validator: required }, { validator: minLength, arg: 2
}]
  }}
>
  ...
</Form>
```

Now, our form is valid if the name and email are populated, and the name is at least two characters long.

That's the `validationRules` prop complete. In the next section, we'll track the validation error messages in preparation for rendering them on the page.

Tracking validation error messages

We need to track the validation error messages in state as the user completes the form and fields become valid or invalid. Later on, we'll be able to render the error messages to the screen.

The `Form` component is responsible for managing all the form states, so we'll add the error message state to there, as follows:

1. Let's add the validation error message state to the form state interface:

```
interface IErrors {
  [key: string]: string[];
}

interface IState {
  values: IValues;
  errors: IErrors;
}
```

   The `errors` state is an indexable key/value type where the key is the field name and the value is an array of validation error messages.

2. Let's initialize the `errors` state in the constructor:

```
constructor(props: IFormProps) {
  super(props);
  const errors: IErrors = {};
  Object.keys(props.defaultValues).forEach(fieldName => {
    errors[fieldName] = [];
  });
  this.state = {
    errors,
    values: props.defaultValues
  };
}
```

   The `defaultValues` prop contains all the field names in its keys. We iterate through the `defaultValues` keys, setting the appropriate `errors` key to an empty array. As a result, when the `Form` component initializes, none of the fields contain any validation error messages, which is exactly what we want.

3. The `Field` component is eventually going to render the validation error messages, so we need to add these to the form context. Let's start by adding these to the form context interface:

```
interface IFormContext {
  errors: IErrors;
  values: IValues;
  setValue?: (fieldName: string, value: any) => void;
}
```

4. Let's add an `errors` empty literal as the default value when the context is created. This is to keep the TypeScript compiler happy:

```
const FormContext = React.createContext<IFormContext>({
  errors: {},
  values: {}
});
```

5. We can now include the errors in the context value:

```
public render() {
  const context: IFormContext = {
    errors: this.state.errors,
    setValue: this.setValue,
    values: this.state.values
  };
  return (
    ...
  );
}
```

Now, the validation errors are in the form state, and also in the form context for the `Field` component to access. In the next section, we'll create a method that is going to invoke the validation rules.

Invoking validation rules

So far, we can define validation rules, and have state to track validation error messages, but nothing is invoking the rules yet. This is what we are going to implement in this section:

1. We need to create a method within the `Form` component that is going to validate a field, calling the specified validator function. Let's create a method called `validate` that takes in the field name and its value. The method will return an array of validation error messages:

```
private validate = (
  fieldName: string,
  value: any
): string[] => {
};
```

2. Let's get the validation rules for the field and initialize an `errors` array. We'll collect all the errors in the `errors` array as the validators are executed. We'll also return the array of `errors` after all the validators have been executed:

```
private validate = (
  fieldName: string,
  value: any
): string[] => {
  const rules = this.props.validationRules[fieldName];
  const errors: string[] = [];

  // TODO - execute all the validators

  return errors;
}
```

3. The rules can be an `IValidation` array or just a single `IValidation`. Let's check for this and call the `validator` function if we just have a single validation rule:

```
const errors: string[] = [];
if (Array.isArray(rules)) {
  // TODO - execute all the validators in the array of rules
} else {
  if (rules) {
    const error = rules.validator(fieldName, this.state.values,
rules.arg);
    if (error) {
      errors.push(error);
    }
  }
}
return errors;
```

4. Let's now deal with the branch of code for when there are multiple validation rules. We can use the `forEach` function on the rules array to iterate through the rules and execute the `validator` function:

```
if (Array.isArray(rules)) {
  rules.forEach(rule => {
    const error = rule.validator(
      fieldName,
      this.state.values,
      rule.arg
    );
    if (error) {
      errors.push(error);
```

```
    }
  });
} else {
  ...
}
return errors;
```

5. The final bit of code we need to implement in the `validate` method is to set the new `errors` form state:

```
if (Array.isArray(rules)) {
  ...
} else {
  ...
}
const newErrors = { ...this.state.errors, [fieldName]: errors };
this.setState({ errors: newErrors });
return errors;
```

We spread the old errors state into a new object, and then add the new errors for the field.

6. The `Field` component needs to call into this `validate` method. We are going to add a reference to this method to the form context. Let's add it to the `IFormContext` interface first:

```
interface IFormContext {
  values: IValues;
  errors: IErrors;
  setValue?: (fieldName: string, value: any) => void;
  validate?: (fieldName: string, value: any) => void;
}
```

7. We can now add it to the context value in the `render` method in `Form`:

```
public render() {
  const context: IFormContext = {
    errors: this.state.errors,
    setValue: this.setValue,
    validate: this.validate,
    values: this.state.values
  };
  return (
    ...
  );
}
```

Our form validation is coming along nicely, and we now have a method we can call to invoke all the rules for a field. However, this method isn't being called from anywhere yet as the user fills out the form. We'll do that in the next section.

Triggering validation rule execution from field

When the user fills in the form, we want the validation rules to trigger when a field loses focus. We'll implement this in this section:

1. Let's create a function that is going to handle the `blur` event for all three of the different editors:

```
const handleChange = (
  ...
};

const handleBlur = (
  e:
    | React.FocusEvent<HTMLInputElement>
    | React.FocusEvent<HTMLTextAreaElement>
    | React.FocusEvent<HTMLSelectElement>,
  context: IFormContext
) => {
  if (context.validate) {
    context.validate(props.name, e.currentTarget.value);
  }
};

return ( ... )
```

- The TypeScript blur event type is `FocusEvent<T>`, where `T` is the type of the element that is being handled.
- The handler's first parameter, e, is the React blur event handler parameter. We union all the different handler types for our different editors, so that we can handle all the blur events in a single function.
- The handler's second parameter is the form context.
- We need a conditional statement to check that the `validate` method is not `undefined`, to keep the TypeScript compiler happy.
- We can then call the `validate` method with the field name and new value we need to validate.

2. We can now reference this handler in the `Field` JSX for the text and email editor:

```
{(type === "Text" || type === "Email") && (
  <input
    type={type.toLowerCase()}
    id={name}
    value={context.values[name]}
    onChange={e => handleChange(e, context)}
    onBlur={e => handleBlur(e, context)}
  />
)}
```

We set the `onBlur` prop to a lamda expression that calls our `handleBlur` function, passing in the blur argument as well as the context value.

3. Let's reference the handler in the other two editors now:

```
{type === "TextArea" && (
  <textarea
    id={name}
    value={context.values[name]}
    onChange={e => handleChange(e, context)}
    onBlur={e => handleBlur(e, context)}
  />
)}
{type === "Select" && (
  <select
    value={context.values[name]}
    onChange={e => handleChange(e, context)}
    onBlur={e => handleBlur(e, context)}
  >
    ...
  </select>
)}
```

Our field is now executing validation rules when it loses focus. There's one more task to do before we can give our **Contact Us** page a try, which we'll do in the next section.

Rendering validation error messages

In this section, we are going to render the validation error messages in the `Field` component:

1. Let's display all errors in a `span` with the `form-error` CSS class we have already implemented. We display these at the bottom of the `div` container of the `form-group`:

```
<div className="form-group">
  <label htmlFor={name}>{label}</label>
  {(type === "Text" || type === "Email") && (
    ...
  )}
  {type === "TextArea" && (
    ...
  )}
  {type === "Select" && (
    ...
  )}
  {context.errors[name] &&
    context.errors[name].length > 0 &&
    context.errors[name].map(error => (
      <span key={error} className="form-error">
        {error}
      </span>
    ))}
</div>
```

So, we first check that we have errors for the field name, and then use the `map` function in the `errors` array to render a `span` for each error.

2. We have referenced a CSS `form-error` class, so let's add this to `index.css`:

```
.form-error {
  font-size: 13px;
  color: red;
  margin: 3px auto 0px 0px;
}
```

It's time to give the **Contact Us** page a try. If our app isn't started, start it using `npm start` and go to the **Contact Us** page. If we tab through the name and email fields, the required validation rule triggers and error messages are displayed:

Contact Us

If you enter your details we'll get back to you as soon as we can.

Your name

This must be populated

Your email address

This must be populated

Reason you need to contact us

Support ▾

Additional notes

Submit

This is just what we want. If we go back to the name field and try to enter just a single character before tabbing away, the minimum length validation error triggers, as we would expect:

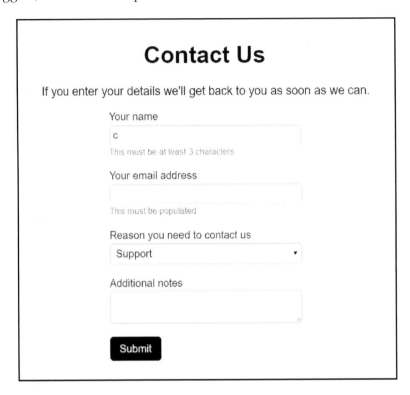

Our generic form component is nearly complete now. Our final task is to submit the form, which we'll do in the next section.

Form submission

Submitting the form is the final part of the form implementation. The consumer of the Form component will handle the actual submission, which will probably result in a call to a web API. Our Form component will simply call a function in the consumer code when the form is submitted.

Adding a submit button to the form

In this section, we are going to add a submit button to our `Form` component:

1. Let's add a submit button to the `Form` JSX, wrapped in a `div` container within `form-group`:

```
<FormContext.Provider value={context}>
  <form className="form" noValidate={true}>
    {this.props.children}
    <div className="form-group">
      <button type="submit">Submit</button>
    </div>
  </form>
</FormContext.Provider>
```

2. Style the button with the following CSS in `index.css`:

```
.form-group button {
  font-size: 16px;
  padding: 8px 5px;
  width: 80px;
  border: black solid 1px;
  border-radius: 5px;
  background-color: black;
  color: white;
}
.form-group button:disabled {
  border: gray solid 1px;
  background-color: gray;
  cursor: not-allowed;
}
```

We now have a black submit button on our form that is gray when disabled.

Adding a onSubmit form prop

In our `Form` component, we need a new prop that allows a consumer to specify the `submit` function to be called. We'll do this in this section:

1. Let's start by creating a new prop function called `onSubmit` in the `Form` props interface:

```
export interface ISubmitResult {
  success: boolean;
```

```
    errors?: IErrors;
}

interface IFormProps {
  defaultValues: IValues;
  validationRules: IValidationProp;
  onSubmit: (values: IValues) => Promise<ISubmitResult>;
}
```

The function will take in the field values and asynchronously return whether the submission was successful, with any validation errors that occurred on the server.

2. We are going to track whether the form is being submitted or not in the Form state. We are also going to track whether the form has successfully been submitted in the Form state:

```
interface IState {
  values: IValues;
  errors: IErrors;
  submitting: boolean;
  submitted: boolean;
}
```

3. Let's initialize those state values in the constructor:

```
constructor(props: IFormProps) {
  ...
  this.state = {
    errors,
    submitted: false,
    submitting: false,
    values: props.defaultValues
  };
}
```

4. We can now disable the submit button if the form is being submitted, or has successfully been submitted:

```
<button
  type="submit"
  disabled={this.state.submitting || this.state.submitted}
>
  Submit
</button>
```

5. Let's reference a submit handler in the `form` tag:

```
<form className="form" noValidate={true}
onSubmit={this.handleSubmit}>
  ...
</form>
```

6. We can now start to implement the submit handler we just referenced:

```
private handleSubmit = async (e: React.FormEvent<HTMLFormElement>)
=> {
  e.preventDefault();
};
```

We call `preventDefault` in the submit event argument to stop the browser automatically posting the form.

7. We need to make sure all the fields are valid before starting the form submission process. Let's reference and create a `validateForm` function that does this:

```
private validateForm(): boolean {
  const errors: IErrors = {};
  let haveError: boolean = false;
  Object.keys(this.props.defaultValues).map(fieldName => {
    errors[fieldName] = this.validate(
      fieldName,
      this.state.values[fieldName]
    );
    if (errors[fieldName].length > 0) {
      haveError = true;
    }
  });
  this.setState({ errors });
  return !haveError;
}

private handleSubmit = async (e: React.FormEvent<HTMLFormElement>)
=> {
  e.preventDefault();
  if (this.validateForm()) {
  }
};
```

The `validateForm` function iterates through the fields, calling the `validate` function that has already been implemented. The state is updated with the latest validation errors, and we return whether there are any errors or not in any of the fields.

8. Let's implement the rest of the submit handler now:

```
private handleSubmit = async (e: React.FormEvent<HTMLFormElement>)
=> {
  e.preventDefault();
  if (this.validateForm()) {
    this.setState({ submitting: true });
    const result = await this.props.onSubmit(this.state.values);
    this.setState({
      errors: result.errors || {},
      submitted: result.success,
      submitting: false
    });
  }
};
```

If the form is valid, we start by setting the `submitting` state to `true`. We then call the `onSubmit` prop function asynchronously. When the `onSubmit` prop function has finished, we set any validation errors from the function in the state along with whether the submission was successful. We also set in the state the fact that the submission process has finished.

Now, our `Form` component has an `onSubmit` function prop. In the next section, we'll consume this in our **Contact Us** page.

Consuming the onSubmit form prop

In this section, we'll consume the `onSubmit` form prop in the `ContactUs` component. The `ContactUs` component won't manage the submission—it will simply delegate to the `ContactUsPage` component to handle the submission:

1. Let's start by importing `ISubmitResult` and `IValues`, and creating a props interface in the `ContactUs` component for the `onSubmit` function:

```
import { Form, ISubmitResult, IValues, minLength, required } from
"./Form";

interface IProps {
  onSubmit: (values: IValues) => Promise<ISubmitResult>;
```

```
    }

    const ContactUs: React.SFC<IProps> = props => { ... }
```

2. Create a `handleSubmit` function that will invoke the `onSubmit` prop:

```
    const ContactUs: React.SFC<IProps> = props => {
      const handleSubmit = async (values: IValues):
    Promise<ISubmitResult> => {
        const result = await props.onSubmit(values);
        return result;
      };
      return ( ... );
    };
```

The `onSubmit` prop is asynchronous, so we need to prefix our function with `async` and prefix the `onSubmit` call with `await`.

3. Bind this submit handler in the form `onSubmit` prop in the JSX:

```
    return (
      <Form ... onSubmit={handleSubmit}>
        ...
      </Form>
    );
```

4. Let's move on to the `ContactUsPage` component now. Let's start by creating the submit handler:

```
    private handleSubmit = async (values: IValues):
    Promise<ISubmitResult> => {
      await wait(1000); // simulate asynchronous web API call
      return {
        errors: {
          email: ["Some is wrong with this"]
        },
        success: false
      };
    };
```

In practice, this will probably call a web API. In our example, we wait asynchronously for one second and return a validation error with the `email` field.

5. Let's create the `wait` function we just referenced:

```
const wait = (ms: number): Promise<void> => {
 return new Promise(resolve => setTimeout(resolve, ms));
};
```

6. Let's wire up the `handleSubmit` method to the `ContactUs onSubmit` prop now:

```
<ContactUs onSubmit={this.handleSubmit} />
```

7. We have referenced `IValues` and `ISubmitResult`, so let's import these:

```
import { ISubmitResult, IValues } from "./Form";
```

If we go to the **Contact Us** page in the running app, fill out the form, and click the **Submit** button, we are informed that there is a problem with the email field, as we would expect:

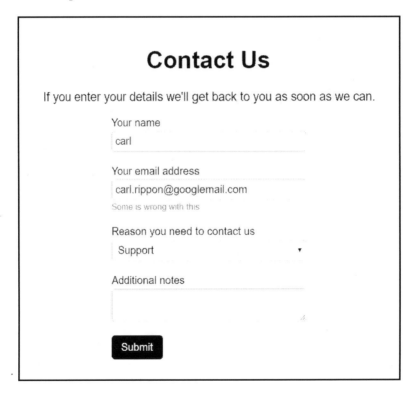

8. Let's change the submit handler in `ContactUsPage` to return a successful result:

```
private handleSubmit = async (values: IValues):
Promise<ISubmitResult> => {
  await wait(1000); // simulate asynchronous web API call
  return {
 success: true
 };
};
```

Now, if we go to the **Contact Us** page in the running app again, fill out the form, and click the **Submit** button, the submission goes through fine and the **Submit** button is disabled:

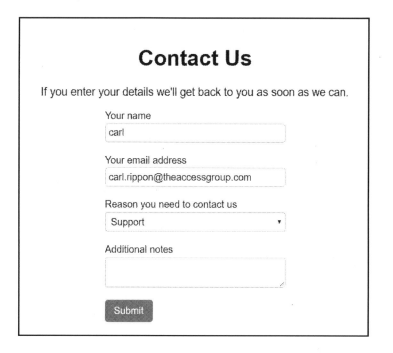

So, that's our **Contact Us** page complete, together with our generic `Form` and `Field` components.

Summary

In this chapter, we discussed controlled components, which are React's recommended method for handling form data entry. With controlled components, we let React control input values via component state.

We looked at building generic `Form` and `Field` components containing state and change handlers, so that we don't need to implement individual state and change handlers for every field in every form in our apps.

We then created some standard validation functions, and added the ability to add validation rules within the generic `Form` component and render validation errors automatically in the `Field` component.

Finally, we added the ability to handle form submission when consuming the generic `Form` component. Our **Contact Us** page was changed to use the generic `Form` and `Field` components.

Our generic components only deal with very simple forms. Not surprisingly, there are a fair number of well-established form libraries already out in the wild. A popular choice is Formik, which is similar in some ways to what we have just built but much more powerful.

If you are building an app that contains lots of forms, it is well worth either building a generic form as we have just done or using an established library such as Formik to speed up the development process.

Questions

Check whether all that information about forms in React and TypeScript has stuck by trying the following implementations:

1. Extend our generic `Field` component to include a number editor, using the native number input.
2. Implement an urgency field on the **Contact Us** form to indicate how urgent a response is. The field should be numeric.
3. Implement a new validator function in the generic `Form` component, which validates whether a number falls between two other numbers.

4. Implement a validation rule on the urgency field to ensure the input is a number between 1 and 10.

5. Our validation triggers when a user clicks in and out of a field without typing anything. How can we trigger validation when a field loses focus, but only when it has been changed?

Further reading

The following links are good sources of further information on forms in React:

- There is a section in the React documentation on forms at `https://reactjs.org/docs/forms.html`.
- The Formik library is well worth looking into. This can be found at `https://github.com/jaredpalmer/formik`.

8
React Redux

So far in this book, we have managed state within our React components. We've also used React context when state needs to be shared between different components. This approach works well for many applications. React Redux helps us to robustly handle complex state scenarios. It shines when user interactions result in several changes to state, perhaps some that are conditional, and particularly when the interaction results in web service calls. It's also great when there is lots of shared state across the application.

We are going to continue building our React shop in this chapter, adding React Redux to help us manage our state interactions. We'll eventually add a basket summary component in the header of our shop, which informs the user of how many items are in their basket. Redux will help us update this component when items are added to the basket.

In the final section of the chapter, we'll explorer a Redux-like method for managing complex state within a component. This is a middle ground between managing state in a Redux store and just within a component using `setState` or `useState`.

In this chapter, we'll learn the following topics:

- Principles and key concepts
- Installing Redux
- Creating reducers
- Creating actions
- Creating a store
- Connecting our React App to the store
- Managing state with useReducer

Technical requirements

We'll use the following technologies in this chapter:

- **Node.js and** `npm`: TypeScript and React are dependent on these. We can install these from `https://nodejs.org/en/download/`. If we already have these installed, make sure `npm` is at least at version 5.2.

- **Visual Studio Code**: We'll need an editor to write our React and TypeScript code, which can be installed from `https://code.visualstudio.com/`. We will also need the TSLint (by egamma) and Prettier (by Estben Petersen) extensions installed within Visual Studio Code.
- **React shop**: We'll start from the React shop project we finished in the last chapter. This is available on GitHub at `https://github.com/carlrip/LearnReact17WithTypeScript/tree/master/07-WorkingWithForms/04-FormSubmission`.

> In order to restore code from a previous chapter, the `LearnReact17WithTypeScript` repository at `https://github.com/carlrip/LearnReact17WithTypeScript` can be downloaded. The relevant folder can then be opened in Visual Studio Code and then `npm install` can be entered in the terminal to do the restore. All the code snippets in this chapter can be found online at `https://github.com/carlrip/LearnReact17WithTypeScript/tree/master/08-ReactRedux%EF%BB%BF`.

Principles and key concepts

In this section, we'll start by going through the three principles in Redux and then dive into the core concepts.

Principles

Let's take a look at the three principles of Redux:

- **Single source of truth**: This means that the whole application state is stored in a single object. In a real app, this object is likely to contain a complex tree of nested objects.
- **State is read-only**: This means that state can't be directly changed. This is a bit like saying we can't directly change the state within a component. In Redux, the only way to change state is to dispatch what's called an action.
- **Changes are made with pure functions**: The functions that are responsible for changing the state are called reducers.

In the following sections, we'll dive into actions and reducers a little more along with the thing that manages them which is what is called a store.

Key concepts

The whole state of the application lives inside what is called a **store**. The state is stored in a JavaScript object like the one following:

```
{
  products: [{ id: 1, name: "Table", ...}, {...}, ...],
  productsLoading: false,
  currentProduct: { id: 2, xname: "Chair", ... },
  basket: [{ product: { id: 2, xname: "Chair" }, quantity: 1 }],
};
```

In this example, the single object contains these:

- An array of products
- Whether the products are being fetched from a web API
- The current product the user is looking at
- The items in the users basket

The state won't contain any functions or setters or any getters. It's a simple JavaScript object. The store also orchestrates all the moving parts in Redux. This includes pushing actions though reducers to update state.

So, the first thing that needs to happen in order to update state in a store is to dispatch an **action**. An action is another simple JavaScript object like the one following:

```
{
  type: "PRODUCTS/LOADING"
}
```

The `type` property determines the type of action that needs to be performed. This is an important and required part of the action. The reducer won't know how to change the state without the `type` in the action object. In the previous example, the action doesn't contain anything else other than the `type` property. This is because the reducer doesn't need any more information in order to make the change to state for this type of action.

The following example is another action:

```
{
  type: "PRODUCTS/GETSINGLE",
  product: { id: 1, name: "Table", ...}
}
```

This time, an additional bit of information is included in the action in a `product` property. This additional information is needed by the reducer to make the change to state for this type of action.

So, reducers are pure functions that make the actual state changes.

 A pure function always returns the same result for a given set of parameters. So, these functions don't depend on any state outside the scope of the function that isn't passed into the function. Pure functions also don't change any state outside the scope of the function.

The following is an example of a reducer:

```
export const productsReducer = (state = initialProductState, action) => {
  switch (action.type) {
    case "PRODUCTS/LOADING": {
      return {
        ...state,
        productsLoading: true
      };
    }
    case "PRODUCTS/GETSINGLE": {
      return {
        ...state,
        currentProduct: action.product,
        productsLoading: false
```

```
    };
  }
  default:
}
  return state || initialProductState;
};
```

Here is something about reducers:

- Reducers take in two parameters for the current state and the action that is being performed
- The state argument defaults to an initial state object for when the reducer is called for the very first time
- A switch statement is used on the action type and creates a new state object appropriately for each action type in each of its branches
- To create the new state, we spread the current state into a new object and then overwrite it with properties that have changed
- The new state is returned from the reducer

You'll notice that the actions and reducer we have just seen didn't have TypeScript types. Obviously, we'll include the necessary types when we implement these in the following sections.

So, now that we have started to get an understanding of what Redux is, it's time to put this into practice in our React shop.

Installing Redux

Before we can use Redux, we need to install it along with the TypeScript types. We will also install an additional library called redux-thunk, which we need in order to implement asynchronous actions:

1. If we haven't already, let's open our React shop project in Visual Studio Code from where we left off in the last chapter. So, let's install the core Redux library via npm in the terminal:

   npm install redux

   Note that the core Redux library contains TypeScript types within it. So, there is no need for an additional install for these.

2. Let's now install the React-specific bits for Redux. These bits allow us to connect our React components to the Redux store. Let's install these via npm:

    ```
    npm install react-redux
    ```

3. Let's also install the TypeScript types for react-redux:

    ```
    npm install --save-dev @types/react-redux
    ```

4. Let's install redux-thunk as well:

    ```
    npm install redux-thunk
    ```

5. Lastly, we can install the TypeScript types for redux-thunk:

    ```
    npm install --save-dev @types/redux-thunk
    ```

With all the Redux bits now installed, we can add Redux to the React shop we have been working on in the next section.

Creating actions

We are going to extend the React shop we have been building in previous chapters and add Redux to manage the state on the Products page. In this section, we'll create actions to start the process of getting the products into the page. There will be one action to get the products. There will be another action to change some new loading state, which we'll eventually tie to the withLoading HOC that we already have in our project.

Before we make a start on the Redux actions, let's create a fake API in ProductsData.ts for fetching products:

```
export const getProducts = async (): Promise<IProduct[]> => {
  await wait(1000);
  return products;
};
```

So, the function asynchronously waits a second before returning the products.

We need to start our action's implementation by creating some types. We'll do this next.

Creating state and action types

It's time to finally make a start on enhancing our React shop with Redux. We'll start by creating some types for the state and actions for our Redux store:

1. Let's create a new file called `ProductsTypes.ts` in the `src` folder with the following import statement at the top:

   ```
   import { IProduct } from "./ProductsData";
   ```

2. Let's create an enumeration for the two different action types that we are going to implement:

   ```
   export enum ProductsActionTypes {
     GETALL = "PRODUCTS/GETALL",
     LOADING = "PRODUCTS/LOADING"
   }
   ```

   Redux doesn't dictate the format of the action type strings. So, the format of the action type strings is our choice. We need to make sure the strings are unique though across the actions types in the store. So, we've included two bits of information in the string:

   - The area of the store the action is concerned with. In our case, this is `PRODUCTS`.
   - The specific operation within that area. In our case, we have `GETALL` for getting all the products and `LOADING` to indicate products are being fetched.

   We could have chosen `PRODUCTS-GETALL` or `Get All Products`. We just need to make sure the strings are unique. We have used an enumeration to give us nice IntelliSense when we consume these when implementing the action and reducer.

3. We can now create interfaces for the two actions:

   ```
   export interface IProductsGetAllAction {
     type: ProductsActionTypes.GETALL,
     products: IProduct[]
   }

   export interface IProductsLoadingAction {
     type: ProductsActionTypes.LOADING
   }
   ```

The IProductsGetAllAction interface is for an action that will be dispatched when the products need to be fetched. The IProductsLoadingAction interface is for an action that will cause the reducer to change the loading state.

4. Let's combine the action types together with a union type:

```
export type ProductsActions =
  | IProductsGetAllAction
  | IProductsLoadingAction
```

This will be the type for the action parameter passed into the reducer.

5. Lastly, let's create an interface for this area of the state in the store:

```
export interface IProductsState {
  readonly products: IProduct[];
  readonly productsLoading: boolean;
}
```

So, our state will contain an array of products, and whether products are being loaded.

Notice that the properties are prefixed with the readonly keyword. This will help us avoid changing the state directly.

Now that we have types in place for the actions and state, we can create some actions in the next section.

Creating actions

In this section, we are going to create two actions for getting the products and indicating that products are being loaded.

1. Let's start by creating a ProductsActions.ts file with the following import statement:

```
import { ActionCreator, AnyAction, Dispatch } from "redux";
```

These are a few types from Redux that we are going to use when implementing our actions.

2. One of our actions is going to be asynchronous. So, let's import a type from redux-thunk ready for when we implement this action:

```
import { ThunkAction } from "redux-thunk";
```

3. Let's add another import statement so that we can use our fake API:

```
import { getProducts as getProductsFromAPI } from "./ProductsData";
```

We've renamed the API function to `getProductsFromAPI` to avoid a name clash because we are going to create an action called `getProducts` a little later.

4. Let's also import the types we created in the last section:

```
import { IProductsGetAllAction, IProductsLoadingAction,
IProductsState, ProductsActionTypes } from "./ProductsTypes";
```

5. We are going to create what is called an action creator now. An action creator does what it says on the tin: it's a function that creates and returns an action! Let's create an action creator for creating the product loading action:

```
const loading: ActionCreator<IProductsLoadingAction> = () => {
  return {
    type: ProductsActionTypes.LOADING
  }
};
```

- We use the generic `ActionCreator` type containing the appropriate action interface for the function signature
- The function simply returns the required action object

We can write this function more succinctly using an implicit return statement as follows:

```
const loading: ActionCreator<IProductsLoadingAction> = () => ({
  type: ProductsActionTypes.LOADING
});
```

We'll use this shorter syntax from now on when implementing action creators.

6. Let's move on to implementing the action creator for getting products. This is more complex, so let's start with the function signature:

```
export const getProducts:
ActionCreator<ThunkAction<Promise<AnyAction>, IProductsState, null,
IProductsGetAllAction>> = () => {};
```

We again use the generic `ActionCreator` type, but this time it contains more than just the action interface that will eventually be returned. This is because this particular action is asynchronous.

We use `ThunkAction` inside `ActionCreator` for asynchronous actions, which is, in turn, a generic type with four parameters:

- The first parameter is the return type, which should ideally be `Promise<IProductsGetAllAction>`. However, the TypeScript compiler struggles to resolve this, so, we have opted for the slightly looser `Promise<AnyAction>` type.
- The second parameter is the state interface that the action is concerned with.
- The third parameter is the type of parameter passed into the action creator, which is `null` in our case because there is no parameter.
- The last parameter is the type of the action.

We export this action creator because this is going to be eventually called from the `ProductsPage` component.

7. Asynchronous actions need to return an asynchronous function that will eventually dispatch our action:

```
export const getProducts:
ActionCreator<ThunkAction<Promise<AnyAction>, IProductsState, null,
IProductsGetAllAction>> = () => {
  return async (dispatch: Dispatch) => {
  };
};
```

So, the first thing that function does is return another function, flagging that it is asynchronous, using the `async` keyword. The inner function takes the dispatcher from the store as a parameter.

8. Let's implement the inner function then:

```
return async (dispatch: Dispatch) => {
  dispatch(loading());
  const products = await getProductsFromAPI();
  return dispatch({
    products,
    type: ProductsActionTypes.GETALL
  });
};
```

- The first thing we do is dispatch our other action so that the loading state is eventually changed accordingly by the reducer
- The next step is to get the products asynchronously from the fake API
- The final step is to dispatch the required action

Now that we have created a couple of actions, we'll create a reducer in the next section.

Creating reducers

A reducer is a function that is responsible for creating new state for a given action. So, the function takes in an action with the current state and returns the new state. In this section, we'll create a reducer for the two actions we have created on products.

1. Let's start by creating a file called `ProductsReducer.ts` with the following import statements:

```
import { Reducer } from "redux";
import { IProductsState, ProductsActions, ProductsActionTypes }
from "./ProductsTypes";
```

We are importing the `Reducer` type from Redux along with types for the actions and state we created earlier.

2. Next, we need to define what the initial state is:

```
const initialProductState: IProductsState = {
  products: [],
  productsLoading: false
};
```

So, we are setting the products to an empty array and product loading state to `false`.

3. We can now start to create the reducer function:

```
export const productsReducer: Reducer<IProductsState,
ProductsActions> = (
  state = initialProductState,
  action
) => {
  switch (action.type) {
  // TODO - change the state
  }
  return state;
};
```

- We've typed the function with the `Reducer` generic type from Redux, passing in our state and action types. This gives us a nice level of type safety.

- The function takes in parameters for the state and action as required by Redux.
- The state defaults to the initial state object we just set in the previous step.
- At the end of the function, we return the default state if the action type is not recognized by the switch statement.

4. Let's carry on implementing our reducer:

```
switch (action.type) {
  case ProductsActionTypes.LOADING: {
    return {
      ...state,
      productsLoading: true
    };
  }
  case ProductsActionTypes.GETALL: {
    return {
      ...state,
      products: action.products,
      productsLoading: false
    };
  }
}
```

We have implemented a switch branch for each action. Both branches follow the same pattern by returning a new state object that has the old state spread into it and the appropriate properties merged over the top.

So, that's our first reducer complete. In the next section, we'll create our store.

Creating a store

In this section, we'll create a store that is going to hold our state and manage the actions and reducer:

1. Let's start off by creating a new file called `Store.tsx` with the following import statement to get the bits and pieces we need from Redux:

```
import { applyMiddleware, combineReducers, createStore, Store }
from "redux";
```

- `createStore` is a function we'll eventually use to create our store

- We need the `applyMiddleware` function because we need to use the Redux Thunk middleware to manage our asynchronous actions
- The `combineReducers` function is a function we can use to merge our reducers together
- `Store` is a TypeScript type we can use for the store

2. Let's import `redux-thunk`:

```
import thunk from "redux-thunk";
```

3. Finally, let's import our reducer and state type:

```
import { productsReducer } from "./ProductsReducer";
import { IProductsState } from "./ProductsTypes";
```

4. A key part of the store is the state. So, let's define an interface for this:

```
export interface IApplicationState {
  products: IProductsState;
}
```

At this point, the interface simply contains our products state.

5. Let's put our reducer in the Redux `combineReducer` function now:

```
const rootReducer = combineReducers<IApplicationState>({
  products: productsReducer
});
```

6. With the state and root reducer defined, we can create our store. We are actually going to create a function that creates the store:

```
export default function configureStore(): Store<IApplicationState>
{
  const store = createStore(rootReducer, undefined,
applyMiddleware(thunk));
  return store;
}
```

- The function that creates our store is called `configureStore` and returns the generic `Store` type with our specific store state passed in to it.
- The function uses the Redux `createStore` function to create and return the store. We pass in our reducer as well as the Redux Thunk middleware. We pass `undefined` as the initial state because our reducer takes care of the initial state.

We've made a great start on our store. In the next section, we'll start to connect our React shop to our store.

Connecting our React app to the store

In this section, we'll connect the `Products` page to our store. The first job is to add the React Redux `Provider` component which we'll do in the next section.

Adding the store Provider component

The `Provider` component can pass the store to components beneath it at any level. So, in this section we are going to add `Provider` right at the top of our component hierarchy so that all our components can access it:

1. Let's open our existing `index.tsx` and import the `Provider` component from React Redux:

   ```
   import { Provider} from "react-redux";
   ```

2. Let's also import the `Store` type from React Redux:

   ```
   import { Store } from "redux";
   ```

3. The final thing we need to import is the following from our store:

   ```
   import configureStore from "./Store";
   import { IApplicationState } from "./Store";
   ```

4. We are then going to create a little function component after the import statements:

   ```
   interface IProps {
     store: Store<IApplicationState>;
   }
   const Root: React.SFC<IProps> = props => {
     return ();
   };
   ```

   This `Root` component is going to be our new root element. It takes our store in as a prop.

5. So, we need to include the old root element, Routes, in our new root component:

```
const Root: React.SFC<IProps> = props => {
  return (
    <Routes />
  );
};
```

6. There's one more thing to add to this component, which is the Provider component from React Redux:

```
return (
  <Provider store={props.store}>
    <Routes />
  </Provider>
);
```

We've placed Provider at the top of the component tree with our store passed into it.

7. With our new root component complete, let's change our root render function:

```
const store = configureStore();
ReactDOM.render(<Root store={store} />, document.getElementById(
  "root"
) as HTMLElement);
```

We first create the store using our configureStore function and then pass this into our Root component.

So, this is the first step in connecting our components to the store. In the next section, we'll complete this connection for our ProductPage component.

Connecting components to the store

We are getting close to seeing our enhanced shop in action. In this section, we will connect our store to several components.

Connecting ProductsPage to the store

The first component we are going to connect to the store is going to be the ProductsPage component.

Let's open up `ProductsPage.tsx` and start to refactor it:

1. First, let's import the `connect` function from React Redux:

    ```
    import { connect } from "react-redux";
    ```

    We'll use the `connect` function at the end of this section to connect the `ProductsPage` component to the store.

2. Let's import the store state type and the `getProducts` action creator from our store:

    ```
    import { IApplicationState } from "./Store";
    import { getProducts } from "./ProductsActions";
    ```

3. The `ProductPage` component won't contain any state now because this will be held in the Redux store. So, let's start by removing the state interface, the static `getDerivedStateFromProps` method, as well as the constructor. The `ProductsPage` component should now have the following shape:

    ```
    class ProductsPage extends React.Component<RouteComponentProps> {
      public async componentDidMount() { ... }
      public render() { ... }
    }
    ```

4. The data is going to come from the store via props now. So, let's refactor our props interface:

    ```
    interface IProps extends RouteComponentProps {
      getProducts: typeof getProducts;
      loading: boolean;
      products: IProduct[];
    }

    class ProductsPage extends React.Component<IProps> { ... }
    ```

    So, we'll get the following data passed from the store to our component:

    - The `getProducts` action creator
    - A flag called `loading` that indicates whether products are being fetched
    - The array of products

5. So, let's adjust the `componentDidMount` life cycle method to invoke the `getProducts` action creator to start the process of products being fetched:

    ```
    public componentDidMount() {
    ```

```
      this.props.getProducts();
    }
```

6. We no longer reference the `products` array directly from `ProductsData.ts`. So, let's remove that from the input statement so that it looks as follows:

```
import { IProduct } from "./ProductsData";
```

7. There is still no sign of the `search` state we used to have. We are just going to pick this up at the start of the `render` method now and not store it in state at all:

```
public render() {
  const searchParams = new
URLSearchParams(this.props.location.search);
  const search = searchParams.get("search") || "";
  return ( ... );
}
```

8. Let's stay in the `render` method and replace the old `state` references:

```
<ul className="product-list">
  {this.props.products.map(product => {
    if (!search || (search &&
product.name.toLowerCase().indexOf(search.toLowerCase()) > -1)
    ) { ... }
  })}
</ul>
```

9. Under the class, but before the export statement, let's create a function that will map the state coming from the store to the component props:

```
const mapStateToProps = (store: IApplicationState) => {
  return {
    loading: store.products.productsLoading,
    products: store.products.products
  };
};
```

So, we are getting whether products are being loaded as well as the products from the store and passing these to our props.

10. There is one more prop we need to map to and that is the `getProducts` function prop. Let's create another function that will map this action from the store to this function prop in the component:

```
const mapDispatchToProps = (dispatch: any) => {
  return {
```

```
      getProducts: () => dispatch(getProducts())
    };
  };
```

11. There's one more job to do at the bottom of the file. This is to wrap the React Redux `connect` HOC around our `ProductsPage` component before it is exported:

```
export default connect(
  mapStateToProps,
  mapDispatchToProps
)(ProductsPage);
```

The `connect` HOC connects the component to our store, which is provided to us by the `Provider` component higher up in the component tree. The `connect` HOC also invokes the mapper functions that map the state and action creators from the store into the component props.

12. It's finally time to give our enhanced page a try. Let's start the dev server and the app via the terminal:

```
npm start
```

We should find the page behaves exactly the same as it did before. The only difference is now the state is being managed in our Redux store.

In the next section, we are going enhance our Products page by adding the loading spinner we already have in our project.

Connecting ProductsPage to the loading store state

In this section, we are going to add a loading spinner to the Products page. Before we can do this, we are going to extract the list of products out into its own component. We can then add the `withLoader` HOC to the extracted component:

1. Let's create a new file for the extracted component called `ProductsList.tsx` with the following imports:

```
import * as React from "react";
import { Link } from "react-router-dom";
import { IProduct } from "./ProductsData";
import withLoader from "./withLoader";
```

2. The component will take in props for the products array and the search string:

```
interface IProps {
  products?: IProduct[];
  search: string;
}
```

3. We'll call the component `ProductList` and it will be an SFC. Let's start to create the component:

```
const ProductsList: React.SFC<IProps> = props => {
  const search = props.search;
  return ();
};
```

4. We can now move the `ul` tag from the `ProductsPage` component JSX into our return statement in our new `ProductList` component:

```
return (
  <ul className="product-list">
    {props.products &&
      props.products.map(product => {
        if (
          !search ||
          (search &&
product.name.toLowerCase().indexOf(search.toLowerCase())
            > -1)
        ) {
          return (
            <li key={product.id} className="product-list-item">
              <Link to={`/products/${product.id}`}>{product.name}
              </Link>
            </li>
          );
        } else {
          return null;
        }
      })}
  </ul>
);
```

Note that we remove references to `this` after moving the JSX.

5. To finish off the `ProductList` component, let's export it wrapped with our `withLoader` HOC:

```
export default withLoader(ProductsList);
```

6. Let's change the return statement in `ProductPage.tsx` to reference the extracted component:

```
return (
  <div className="page-container">
    <p>
      Welcome to React Shop where you can get all your tools for
ReactJS!
    </p>
    <ProductsList
      search={search}
      products={this.props.products}
      loading={this.props.loading}
    />
  </div>
);
```

7. We mustn't forget to import the `ProductsList` component having referenced it:

```
import ProductsList from "./ProductsList";
```

8. Finally, we can remove the imported `Link` component in `ProductsPage.tsx` as this is no longer referenced.

   If we go to the running app and browse to the **Products** page, we should now see a loading spinner while the products load:

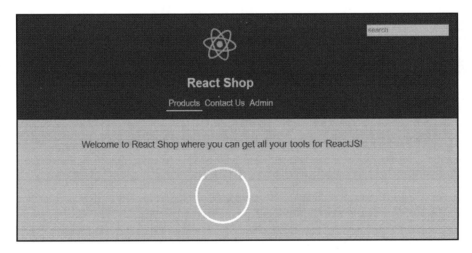

So, our **Products** page is nicely wired up to our Redux store now. In the next section, we'll wire up the **Product** page to the store.

Adding product state and actions to the store

Connecting the `ProductPage` component to our store is first going to require a little work in our store. We need additional state for the current product, as well as whether it has been added to the basket. We also need additional actions and reducer code to get a product and add it to the basket:

1. First, let's add additional state for the current product in `ProductsTypes.ts`:

```
export interface IProductsState {
  readonly currentProduct: IProduct | null;
  ...
}
```

2. While we are in `ProductTypes.ts`, let's add the action type for getting a product:

```
export enum ProductsActionTypes {
  GETALL = "PRODUCTS/GETALL",
  GETSINGLE = "PRODUCTS/GETSINGLE",
  LOADING = "PRODUCTS/LOADING"
}
```

3. Let's also add the action type for getting a product:

```
export interface IProductsGetSingleAction {
  type: ProductsActionTypes.GETSINGLE;
  product: IProduct;
}
```

4. We can then add this action type to our union actions type:

```
export type ProductsActions = IProductsGetAllAction |
IProductsGetSingleAction | IProductsLoadingAction;
```

5. Let's move on to creating the new action creator in `ProductsActions.ts`. First, let's import our fake API to get a product:

```
import { getProduct as getProductFromAPI, getProducts as
getProductsFromAPI} from "./ProductsData";
```

6. We can then import the type for the action creator we need to implement:

```
import { IProductsGetAllAction, IProductsGetSingleAction,
IProductsLoadingAction, IProductsState, ProductsActionTypes } from
"./productsTypes";
```

7. Let's implement the action creator for getting a product:

```
export const getProduct: ActionCreator<ThunkAction<Promise<any>,
IProductsState, null, IProductsGetSingleAction>> = (id: number) =>
{
  return async (dispatch: Dispatch) => {
    dispatch(loading());
    const product = await getProductFromAPI(id);
    dispatch({
      product,
      type: ProductsActionTypes.GETSINGLE
    });
  };
};
```

This is very similar to the `getProducts` action creator. The only difference in structure is that the action creator takes in a parameter for the product ID.

8. Move on to the reducer now in `ProductsReducer.ts`. Let's first set the current product to null in the initial state:

```
const initialProductState: IProductsState = {
  currentProduct: null,
  ...
};
```

9. In the `productReducer` function, let's add a branch in the switch statement for our new action type:

```
switch (action.type) {
  ...
  case ProductsActionTypes.GETSINGLE: {
    return {
      ...state,
      currentProduct: action.product,
      productsLoading: false
    };
  }
}
```

We spread the old state into a new object, overwrite the current project, and set the loading state to `false`.

So, that's some of the state management that the **Product** page needs in the Redux store. However, we aren't managing the basket yet in our store. We'll do this in the next section.

Adding basket state and actions to the store

We'll add state management for our basket in this section. We'll create a new section in our store for this.

1. First, let's create a new file for the types called `BasketTypes.ts` with the following content:

```
import { IProduct } from "./ProductsData";

export enum BasketActionTypes {
  ADD = "BASKET/ADD"
}

export interface IBasketState {
  readonly products: IProduct[];
}

export interface IBasketAdd {
  type: BasketActionTypes.ADD;
  product: IProduct;
}

export type BasketActions = IBasketAdd;
```

   - There is only one piece of state in our basket and that's an array of products in the basket.
   - There is only one action as well. This is to add a product to the basket.

2. Let's create a file called `BasketActions.ts` with the following content:

```
import { BasketActionTypes, IBasketAdd } from "./BasketTypes";
import { IProduct } from "./ProductsData";

export const addToBasket = (product: IProduct): IBasketAdd => ({
  product,
  type: BasketActionTypes.ADD
});
```

   This is the action creator for adding to the basket. The function takes in a product and returns it in the action with the appropriate action type.

3. On to the reducer now. Let's create a file called `BasketReducer.ts` with the following import statements:

```
import { Reducer } from "redux";
import { BasketActions, BasketActionTypes, IBasketState } from
"./BasketTypes";
```

4. Let's create an object for the initial basket state:

```
const initialBasketState: IBasketState = {
  products: []
};
```

5. Let's create the reducer now:

```
export const basketReducer: Reducer<IBasketState, BasketActions> =
(state = initialBasketState, action) => {
  switch (action.type) {
    case BasketActionTypes.ADD: {
      return {
        ...state,
        products: state.products.concat(action.product)
      };
    }
  }
  return state || initialBasketState;
};
```

This follows the same pattern as `productsReducer`.

One interesting point to note is how we elegantly add the `product` to the `products` array without mutating the original array. We use the JavaScript `concat` function, which creates a new array by merging the original with the parameter passed in. This is a great function to use in reducers where state changes involve adding items to arrays.

6. Let's open up `Store.ts` now and import the new reducer and state for the basket:

```
import { basketReducer } from "./BasketReducer";
import { IBasketState } from "./BasketTypes";
```

7. Let's add the basket state to the store:

```
export interface IApplicationState {
  basket: IBasketState;
```

```
        products: IProductsState;
    }
```

8. We have two reducers now. So, let's add the basket reducer to the
   `combineReducers` function call:

   ```
   export const rootReducer = combineReducers<IApplicationState>({
     basket: basketReducer,
     products: productsReducer
   });
   ```

Now that we've adjusted our store, we can connect our `ProductPage` component to it.

Connecting ProductPage to the store

In this section, we'll connect the `ProductPage` component to our store:

1. Let's first import the following into `ProductPage.tsx`:

   ```
   import { connect } from "react-redux";
   import { addToBasket } from "./BasketActions";
   import { getProduct } from "./ProductsActions";
   import { IApplicationState } from "./Store";
   ```

2. We are going to reference the store's `getProduct` now and not the one from
   `ProductsData.ts`. So, let's remove this from this import so that it looks like the
   following:

   ```
   import { IProduct } from "./ProductsData";
   ```

3. Next, let's move the state into props:

   ```
   interface IProps extends RouteComponentProps<{ id: string }> {
     addToBasket: typeof addToBasket;
     getProduct: typeof getProduct;
     loading: boolean;
     product?: IProduct;
     added: boolean;
   }

   class ProductPage extends React.Component<IProps> { ... }
   ```

   So, the `IState` interface and the `Props` type should be removed after this
   movement.

4. We can remove the constructor as we don't need to initialize any state now. This is all done in the store.

5. Let's change the `componentDidMount` life cycle method to call the action creator for getting the product:

```
public componentDidMount() {
  if (this.props.match.params.id) {
    const id: number = parseInt(this.props.match.params.id, 10);
    this.props.getProduct(id);
  }
}
```

Notice that we also remove the `async` keyword because the method is no longer asynchronous.

6. Moving on to the `render` function, let's replace the references to state with references to props:

```
public render() {
  const product = this.props.product;
  return (
    <div className="page-container">
      <Prompt when={!this.props.added}
message={this.navAwayMessage}
      />
      {product || this.props.loading ? (
        <Product
          loading={this.props.loading}
          product={product}
          inBasket={this.props.added}
          onAddToBasket={this.handleAddClick}
        />
      ) : (
        <p>Product not found!</p>
      )}
    </div>
  );
}
```

7. Let's look at the click handler now and refactor it to call the action creator for adding to the basket:

```
private handleAddClick = () => {
  if (this.props.product) {
    this.props.addToBasket(this.props.product);
  }
};
```

8. On to the final few steps now in the connection process. Let's implement the function that maps the action creators from the store into the component props:

```
const mapDispatchToProps = (dispatch: any) => {
  return {
    addToBasket: (product: IProduct) =>
dispatch(addToBasket(product)),
    getProduct: (id: number) => dispatch(getProduct(id))
  };
};
```

9. Mapping the state to the component props is a little more complex. Let's start with the simple mappings:

```
const mapStateToProps = (store: IApplicationState) => {
  return {
    basketProducts: store.basket.products,
    loading: store.products.productsLoading,
    product: store.products.currentProduct || undefined
  };
};
```

Note that we map a null `currentProduct` to `undefined`.

10. The remaining prop we need to map to is `added`. We need to check whether the current product in the store is in the basket state in order to set this `boolean` value. We can use the `some` function in the products array for this:

```
const mapStateToProps = (store: IApplicationState) => {
  return {
    added: store.basket.products.some(p =>
store.products.currentProduct ? p.id ===
store.products.currentProduct.id : false),
    ...
  };
};
```

11. The last step is to use the `connect` HOC from React Redux to wire the `ProductPage` component to the store:

```
export default connect(
  mapStateToProps,
  mapDispatchToProps
)(ProductPage);
```

We can now go to the running app, visit the product page, and add it to the basket. The **Add to basket** button should disappear after it is clicked. If we browse to a different product and then come back to a product we've already added to the basket, the **Add to basket** button shouldn't be present.

So, we now have both the **Products** and **Product** pages connected to our Redux store. In the next section, we'll create a basket summary component and connect that to the store.

Creating and connecting BasketSummary to the store

In this section, we'll create a new component called `BasketSummary`. This will show the number of items in the basket and will be located in the top right of our shop. The following screenshot shows what the basket summary will look like in the top right of the screen:

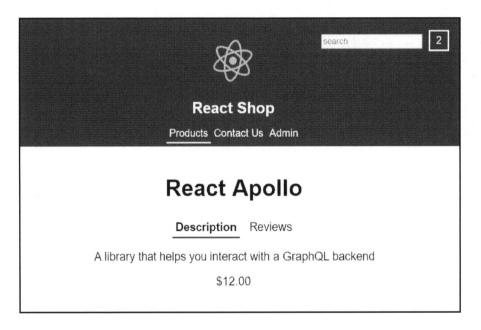

1. Let's create a file called `BasketSummary.tsx` with the following content:

```
import * as React from "react";

interface IProps {
  count: number;
}
```

```
const BasketSummary: React.SFC<IProps> = props => {
  return <div className="basket-summary">{props.count}</div>;
};

export default BasketSummary;
```

This is a simple component that takes in the number of products in the basket as a prop and displays this value in a `div` styled with a `basket-summary` CSS class.

2. Let's add the CSS class we have just referenced in `index.css`:

```
.basket-summary {
  display: inline-block;
  margin-left: 10px;
  padding: 5px 10px;
  border: white solid 2px;
}
```

3. We're going to add our basket summary to our header component. So, let's import it into `Header.tsx`:

```
import BasketSummary from "./BasketSummary";
```

4. Let's also import the `connect` function from React Redux:

```
import { connect } from "react-redux";
```

5. Let's import the state type for our store as well:

```
import { IApplicationState } from "./Store";
```

6. Add a prop for the number of products in the basket to the `Header` component:

```
interface IProps extends RouteComponentProps {
  basketCount: number;
}

class Header extends React.Component<IProps, IState> {
  public constructor(props: IProps) { ... }
  ...
}
```

We're going to keep the search state local in this component.

7. Let's add the `BasketSummary` component to the `Header` component JSX now:

```
<header className="header">
  <div className="search-container">
```

```
      <input ... />
      <BasketSummary count={this.props.basketCount} />
    </div>
    ...
  </header>
```

8. The next step is to map the number of products in the store basket to the `basketCount` prop:

```
const mapStateToProps = (store: IApplicationState) => {
  return {
    basketCount: store.basket.products.length
  };
};
```

9. Lastly, we can connect the `Header` component to the store:

```
export default connect(mapStateToProps)(withRouter(Header));
```

Now that the `Header` component is consuming the `BasketSummary` component and is also connected to the store, we should be able to add products to the basket in the running app and see the basket summary increase.

So, that completes this section on connecting components to the store. We have connected a few different components to the store, so hopefully this process is making good sense now.

In the next section, we'll explore a Redux-like approach for managing state within a component.

Managing state with useReducer

Redux is great for managing complex state across our app. It is a little heavy though if the state we are managing only exists within a single component. Obviously, we can manage these cases with `setState` (for class components) or `useState` (for function components). However, what if the state is complex? There may be lots of pieces of state and the state interactions may involve lots of steps with some of them being asynchronous. In this section, we'll explore an approach for managing these cases with the `useReducer` function in React. Our example will be contrived and simple but it will give us an understanding of this approach.

We are going to add a **Like** button to the **Product** page in our React shop. Users will be able to like a product several times. The `Product` component will keep track of the number of likes and the date and time of the last like in its state:

1. We'll start by opening `Product.tsx` and creating an interface, before the `Product` component, for our state, containing the number of likes and the date of the last like:

```
interface ILikeState {
  likes: number;
  lastLike: Date | null;
}
```

2. We'll create a variable to hold the initial state, also outside of `Product`:

```
const initialLikeState: ILikeState = {
  likes: 0,
  lastLike: null
};
```

3. Let's now create a type for the action:

```
enum LikeActionTypes {
  LIKE = "LIKE"
}

interface ILikeAction {
  type: LikeActionTypes.LIKE;
  now: Date;
}
```

4. We'll also create a union type containing all the action types. In our example, we only have one action type but let's do this to understand an approach that scales:

```
type LikeActions = ILikeAction;
```

5. Inside the `Product` component, let's call the `useReducer` function in React to get our state and `dispatch` function:

```
const [state, dispatch]: [
    ILikeState,
    (action: ILikeAction) => void
] = React.useReducer(reducer, initialLikeState);
```

Let's break this down:

- We pass into `useReducer` a function called `reducer` (which we haven't created yet).
- We also pass into `useReducer` our initial state.
- `useReducer` returns an array containing two elements. The first element is the current state and the second is a `dispatch` function to invoke an action.

6. Let's refactor this line and destructure the state so that we can reference the pieces of state directly:

```
const [{ likes, lastLike }, dispatch]: [
    ILikeState,
    (action: ILikeAction) => void
] = React.useReducer(reducer, initialLikeState);
```

7. At the bottom of the JSX in the `Product` component, let's add JSX to render how many likes we have and a button to add likes:

```
{!props.inBasket && (
    <button onClick={handleAddClick}>Add to basket</button>
)}
<div className="like-container">
    {likes > 0 && (
        <div>{`I like this x ${likes}, last at ${lastLike}`}</div>
    )}
    <button onClick={handleLikeClick}>
        {likes > 0 ? "Like again" : "Like"}
    </button>
</div>
```

8. Let's add the `like-container` CSS class we have just referenced into `index.css`:

```
.like-container {
  margin-top: 20px;
}

.like-container button {
  margin-top: 5px;
}
```

9. Let's also implement the click handler on the **Like** button:

```
const handleLikeClick = () => {
  dispatch({ type: LikeActionTypes.LIKE, now: new Date() });
};
```

10. Our last task is to implement the reducer function outside the `Product` component, just under the `LikeActions` type:

```
const reducer = (state: ILikeState = initialLikeState, action:
LikeActions) => {
  switch (action.type) {
  case LikeActionTypes.LIKE:
    return { ...state, likes: state.likes + 1, lastLike: action.now };
  }
  return state;
};
```

If we try this out, we'll initially see a **Like** button after we navigate to the **Product** page. If we click it, the button text turns to **Like again** and a piece of text appears above it indicating how many likes there are and the last time it was liked.

This implementation feels very similar to implementing actions and reducers in a Redux store but this is all within a component. This is overkill for the example we have just been through but could prove useful where we need to manage lots more pieces of state.

Summary

We started the chapter by introducing ourselves to Redux, learning the principles and key concepts. We learned that the state is stored in a single object and changed by pure functions called reducers when actions are dispatched.

We created our own store in our React shop to put the theory into practice. Here are some key points we learned in our implementation:

- Enumerations for action types give us nice IntelliSense when referencing them.
- Using interfaces to define the actions gives a nice level of type safety and allows us to create a union type that a reducer can use for the actions it has to deal with.
- Using read-only properties within the state interface helps us avoid mutating the state directly.
- Synchronous action creators simply return the required action object.
- Asynchronous action creators return a function that eventually returns the action object.
- The reducer contains a branch of logic for each action type it deals with, creating new state by spreading old state into a new object and then overwriting it with changed properties.
- A function called `createStore` from Redux creates the actual store. We pass all our reducers merged together along with Redux Thunk middleware to manage asynchronous actions.

We then connected some components to the store. Here are the key points in this process:

- A `Provider` component from React Redux needs to sit above all the components that want to consume the store. This takes in a prop that contains the store.
- A `connect` HOC from React Redux then wires up the individual components to the store. This takes in two parameters than can be used to map the state and action creators to the component props.

There are lots of bits and pieces to get our heads around when implementing Redux within our React apps. It does shine in scenarios where the state management is complex because Redux forces us to break the logic up into separate pieces that are easy to understand and maintain.

We learned that we can use a Redux-like approach within just a single component by leveraging React's useReducer function. This can be used when the state is complex and just exists in a single component.

One task that Redux actions often do is interact with a REST API. We are going to learn how we can interact with REST APIs in both class- and function-based components in the next chapter. We'll also learn about a native function we use to call to a REST API as well as a popular open source library.

Questions

Before we end this chapter, let's test our knowledge with some questions:

1. Is the type property in action objects required, and does this property need to be called type? Can we call it something else?
2. How many properties can the action object contain?
3. What is an action creator?
4. Why did we need Redux Thunk in our Redux store in our React shop app?
5. Could we have used something else other than Redux Thunk?
6. In our basketReducer we have just implemented, why didn't we just use the push function to add the item to the basket state? That is, what is wrong with the highlighted line?

```
export const basketReducer: Reducer<IBasketState, BasketActions> =
(
  state = initialBasketState,
  action
) => {
  switch (action.type) {
    case BasketActionTypes.ADD: {
      state.products.push(action.product);
    }
  }
  return state || initialBasketState;
};
```

Further reading

The following links are good resources of further information on React Redux:

- The Redux online docs are well worth reading at `https://redux.js.org`.
- In addition to these core Redux docs, the React Redux docs are worth looking at as well. These are at `https://react-redux.js.org/`.
- The Redux Thunk GitHub is at `https://github.com/reduxjs/redux-thunk`. The home page contains some useful information and samples.

Interacting with RESTful APIs

9

Interacting with RESTful APIs is a very common task we need to do when building an app, and it always results in us having to write asynchronous code. So, to begin with in this chapter, we'll have a detailed look at asynchronous code in general.

There are many libraries that we can use to help us interact with REST APIs. In this chapter, we'll look at both a native browser function and a popular open source library for interacting with REST APIs. We'll discover the additional features that the open source library has over the native function. We will also look at how we can interact with a REST API in both React class and function-based components.

In this chapter, we'll learn the following topics:

- Writing asynchronous code
- Using fetch
- Using axios with class components
- Using axios with function components

Technical requirements

We use the following technologies in this chapter:

- **TypeScript playground**: This is a website at `https://www.typescriptlang.org/play/` that allows us to play with asynchronous code without installing anything.
- **Node.js and** `npm`: TypeScript and React are dependent on these. We can install these from `https://nodejs.org/en/download/`. If we already have these installed, make sure `npm` is at least at version 5.2.
- **TypeScript**: This can be installed via `npm` with the following command in a terminal:

```
npm install -g typescript
```

- **Visual Studio Code**. We'll need an editor to write our React and TypeScript code, which can be installed from `https://code.visualstudio.com/`. We will also need the TSLint (by egamma) and Prettier (by Estben Petersen) extensions installed within Visual Studio Code.

- `jsonplaceholder.typicode.com`: We will use this online service to help us learn how to interact with a RESTful API.

 All the code snippets in this chapter can be found online at `https://github.com/carlrip/LearnReact17WithTypeScript/tree/master/09-RestfulAPIs`.

Writing asynchronous code

TypeScript code is executed synchronously by default, where each line of code is executed after each other. However, TypeScript code can also be asynchronous, which means things can happen independently of our code. Calling a REST API is an example of asynchronous code because the API request is handled outside of our TypeScript code. So, interacting with a REST API forces us to write asynchronous code.

In this section, we'll take the time to understand the approaches we can take when writing asynchronous code before using them to interact with RESTful APIs. We'll start in the next section by looking at callbacks.

Callbacks

A callback is a function we pass as a parameter to an asynchronous function to call when the asynchronous function is complete. In the next section, we'll go through an example of writing asynchronous code with a callback.

Callback execution

Let's go through an example of using callbacks in asynchronous code in the TypeScript playground. Let's enter the following code:

```
let firstName: string;
setTimeout(() => {
  firstName = "Fred";
  console.log("firstName in callback", firstName);
```

```
}, 1000);
console.log("firstName after setTimeout", firstName);
```

The code calls the JavaScript `setTimeout` function, which is asynchronous. It takes in a callback as the first parameter and the number of milliseconds the execution should wait until the callback is executed as the second parameter.

We use an arrow function as the callback function, where we set the `firstName` variable to "Fred" and output this to the console. We also log `firstName` in the console immediately after the call to `setTimeout`.

So, which `console.log` statement will get executed first? If we run the code and look at the console, we'll see that the last line is executed first:

```
firstName after setTimeout undefined                    VM53:6
firstName in callback Fred                              VM53:4
>
```

The key point is that after `setTimeout` is called, execution carries on to the next line of code. Execution doesn't wait for the callback to be called. This can make code that includes callbacks harder to read than synchronous code, particularly when we have callbacks nested within callbacks. This is referred to as **callback hell** by many developers!

So, how do we handle errors in asynchronous callback code? We'll find out in the next section.

Handling callback errors

In this section, we are going to explore how we can handle errors when using callback code:

1. Let's start by entering the following code in the TypeScript playground:

```
try {
  setTimeout(() => {
  throw new Error("Something went wrong");
  }, 1000);
} catch (ex) {
  console.log("An error has occurred", ex);
}
```

We are again using `setTimeout` to experiment with callbacks. This time, we throw an error inside the callback. We are hoping to catch the error outside the callback using a `try` / `catch` around the `setTimeout` function.

If we run the code, we see that we don't catch the error:

```
⊗ ▶Uncaught Error: Something went wrong                          VM1408:3
     at <anonymous>:3:15
>
```

2. We must handle errors within the callback. So, let's adjust our example to the following:

```
interface IResult {
  success: boolean;
  error?: any;
}
let result: IResult = { success: true };
setTimeout(() => {
  try {
    throw new Error("Something went wrong");
  } catch (ex) {
    result.success = false;
    result.error = ex;
  }
}, 1000);
console.log(result);
```

This time, the `try` / `catch` is within the callback. We use a variable, `result`, to determine whether the callback was executed successfully, along with any error. The `IResult` interface gives us a nice bit of type safety with the result `variable`.

If we run this code, we'll see that we successfully handle the error:

```
▼Object 🔘                                                        VM1784:11
  ▶error: Error: Something went wrong at <anonymous>:4:15
   success: false
  ▶ __proto__: Object
>
```

So, handling errors along with reading callback-based code is a challenge. Luckily, there are alternative approaches that deal with these challenges, which we'll go through in the next sections.

Promises

A promise is a JavaScript object that represents the eventual completion (or failure) of an asynchronous operation and its resulting value. We'll have a look at an example of consuming a promised-based function in the next section, followed by creating our own promised-based function after that.

Consuming a promised-based function

Let's have a quick look at some code that exposes a promise-based API:

```
fetch("https://jsonplaceholder.typicode.com/posts")
  .then(response => response.json())
  .then(data => console.log(data))
  .catch(json => console.log("error", json));
```

- This function is the native JavaScript `fetch` function for interacting with RESTful APIs
- The function takes in a URL for the request
- It has a `then` method to handle the response and reading of the response body
- It has a `catch` method to handle any errors

The code execution flows down as we would read it. We also don't have to do any additional work in the `then` methods to handle errors. So, this is much nicer than working with callback-based asynchronous code.

In the next section we'll create our own promised based function.

Creating a promised based function

In this section, we'll create a `wait` function to asynchronously wait a number of milliseconds that passed in as a parameter:

1. Let's enter the following into the TypeScript playground:

```
const wait = (ms: number) => {
  return new Promise((resolve, reject) => {
```

```
      if (ms > 1000) {
        reject("Too long");
      }
      setTimeout(() => {
        resolve("Sucessfully waited");
      }, ms);
    });
};
```

- The function starts by returning a `Promise` object, which takes in the function that needs to be executed asynchronously as its constructor parameter
- The `promise` function takes in a `resolve` parameter, which is a function that we call when the function has finished executing
- The promise function also takes in a `reject` parameter, which is a function that we call when the function errors
- Internally, we are using `setTimeout` with a callback to do the actual waiting

2. Let's consume our promised-based `wait` function:

```
wait(500)
  .then(result => console.log("then >", result))
  .catch(error => console.log("catch >", error));
```

The function simply outputs the result or error to the console after waiting 500 milliseconds.

So, let's give this a try and run it:

```
then >  Sucessfully waited                                    VM7199:12

>  |
```

As we can see, the output in the console indicates that the `then` method is executed.

3. If we call the `wait` function with a parameter greater than 1000, the `catch` method should be invoked. Let's give this a try:

```
wait(1500)
  .then(result => console.log("then >", result))
  .catch(error => console.log("catch >", error));
```

As expected, the `catch` method is executed:

```
catch >   Too long                                    VM7235:13
>
```

So, promises give us a nice way of writing asynchronous code. However, there's another approach that we have used a number of times earlier in this book. We'll go through this method in the next section.

async and await

`async` and `await` are two JavaScript keywords we can use to make asynchronous code read almost identically to synchronous code:

1. Let's look at an example of consuming our `wait` function we created in the last section by entering the following code into the TypeScript playground, after the `wait` function declaration:

```
const someWork = async () => {
  try {
    const result = await wait(500);
    console.log(result);
  } catch (ex) {
    console.log(ex);
  }
};

someWork();
```

- We have created an arrow function called `someWork` that is marked as asynchronous with the `async` keyword.
- We then call `wait` prefixed with the `await` keyword. This halts execution of the next line until `wait` has completed.
- The `try` / `catch` will catch any errors.

So, the code is very similar to how you would write it in a synchronous manner.

If we run this example, we get confirmation that the `console.log` statement in the `try` branch waited until the `wait` function had completely finished before executing:

```
then > Sucessfully waited                            VM7199:12
> |
```

2. Let's change the wait to `1500` milliseconds:

```
const result = await wait(1500);
```

If we run this, we see that an error is raised and caught:

```
Too long                                            VM9735:60
>
```

So, `async` and `await` make our code nice and easy to read. A bonus for using these in TypeScript is that the code can be transpiled to work in older browsers. So, for example, we can code with `async` and `await` and still support IE.

Now that we have a good understanding of writing asynchronous code, we'll put this into practice when we interact with RESTful APIs in the following sections.

Using fetch

The `fetch` function is a native JavaScript function that we can use to interact with RESTful APIs. In this section, we'll go through some common RESTful API interactions using `fetch`, starting with getting data. Throughout this section, we are going to interact with the fantastic `JSONPlaceholder` REST API.

Getting data with fetch

In this section, we'll use `fetch` to get some posts from the `JSONPlaceholder` REST API, starting with a basic `GET` request.

Basic GET request

Let's open up the TypeScript playground and enter the following:

```
fetch("https://jsonplaceholder.typicode.com/posts")
  .then(response => response.json())
  .then(data => console.log(data));
```

Here are some key points:

- The first parameter in the `fetch` function is the URL for the request
- `fetch` is a promised-based function
- The first `then` method handles the response
- The second `then` method handles when the body has been parsed as JSON

If we run the code, we should see an array of posts output to the console:

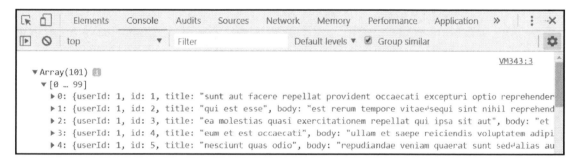

Getting response status

Very often, we need to check the status of the request. We can do this as follows:

```
fetch("https://jsonplaceholder.typicode.com/posts").then(response => {
  console.log(response.status, response.ok);
});
```

- The response `status` property gives the HTTP status code of the response
- The response `ok` property is a `boolean` and returns whether the HTTP status code is in the 200 range

If we run the previous code, we get **200** and **true** output to the console.

Let's try an example request where the post doesn't exist:

```
fetch("https://jsonplaceholder.typicode.com/posts/1001").then(response => {
  console.log(response.status, response.ok);
});
```

If we run the preceding code, we get **404** and **false** output to the console.

Handling errors

As we would expect with a promised-based function, we handle errors in the `catch` method:

```
fetch("https://jsonplaceholder.typicode.com/posts")
  .then(response => response.json())
  .then(data => console.log(data))
  .catch(json => console.log("error", json));
```

However, the `catch` method doesn't catch responses that aren't in the 200 range. An example of this was in the previous example, where we got 404 in the response status code. So, an HTTP error status code can be handled in the first `then` method and not the `catch` method.

So, what is the `catch` method for? The answer is to catch network errors.

So, that's how to get data using `fetch`. In the next section, we'll cover posting data.

Creating data with fetch

In this section, we'll use `fetch` to create some data with the JSONPlaceholder REST API.

Basic POST request

Creating data via a REST API usually involves using the HTTP POST method with the data we want to create in the request body.

Let's open up the TypeScript playground and enter the following:

```
fetch("https://jsonplaceholder.typicode.com/posts", {
  method: "POST",
  body: JSON.stringify({
```

```
      title: "Interesting post",
      body: "This is an interesting post about ...",
      userId: 1
    })
  })
    .then(response => {
      console.log(response.status);
      return response.json();
    })
    .then(data => console.log(data));
```

The `fetch` call is largely the same as for getting data. The key difference is the second parameter, which is an options object that can contain the method and body for the request. Notice also that the body needs to be a `string`.

If we run the preceding code, we get a **201** and an object containing the generated post ID in the console.

Request HTTP headers

Very often, we need to include HTTP headers in the request. We can specify these in the `options` object in a `headers` property:

```
fetch("https://jsonplaceholder.typicode.com/posts", {
  method: "POST",
  headers: {
    "Content-Type": "application/json",
    Authorization: "bearer some-bearer-token"
  },
  body: JSON.stringify({
    title: "Interesting post",
    body: "This is an interesting post about ...",
    userId: 1
  })
})
  .then(response => {
    console.log(response.status);
    return response.json();
  })
  .then(data => console.log(data));
```

Request headers can be used in this way for any HTTP method and not just an HTTP POST. For example, we can use this for a GET request as follows:

```
fetch("https://jsonplaceholder.typicode.com/posts/1", {
  headers: {
```

```
      "Content-Type": "application/json",
      Authorization: "bearer some-bearer-token"
    }
}).then(...);
```

So, that's how to use `fetch` to post data to a REST API. In the next section, we'll look at changing data.

Changing data with fetch

In this section, we'll use `fetch` to change some data via a REST API.

Basic PUT request

A common way to change data is via a `PUT` request. Let's open up the TypeScript playground and enter the following:

```
fetch("https://jsonplaceholder.typicode.com/posts/1", {
  method: "PUT",
  headers: {
    "Content-Type": "application/json"
  },
  body: JSON.stringify({
    title: "Corrected post",
    body: "This is corrected post about ...",
    userId: 1
  })
})
  .then(response => {
    console.log(response.status);
    return response.json();
  })
  .then(data => console.log(data));
```

So, the structure of a `fetch` call to do an HTTP `PUT` is very similar to a `POST` request. The only difference is that we specify the `method` property in the options object as `PUT`.

If we run the preceding code, we get **200** and the updated `POST` object output to the console.

Basic PATCH request

Some REST APIs offer PATCH requests, which allow us to submit changes to a portion of a resource. Let's open up the TypeScript playground and enter the following:

```
fetch("https://jsonplaceholder.typicode.com/posts/1", {
  method: "PATCH",
  headers: {
    "Content-type": "application/json"
  },
  body: JSON.stringify({
    title: "Corrected post"
  })
})
  .then(response => {
    console.log(response.status);
    return response.json();
  })
  .then(data => console.log(data));
```

So, we are submitting a change to the title of the post with the PATCH HTTP method. If we run the preceding code, we get **200** and the updated post object output to the console.

So, that's how to PUT and PATCH using fetch. In the next section, we'll delete some data.

Deleting data with fetch

Generally, we delete data via a DELETE HTTP method on a REST API. Let's enter the following in the TypeScript playground:

```
fetch("https://jsonplaceholder.typicode.com/posts/1", {
  method: "DELETE"
}).then(response => {
  console.log(response.status);
});
```

So, we are requesting to delete a post with the DELETE method.

If we run the preceding code, we get **200** output to the console.

So, we've learned how to interact with a RESTful API with the native fetch function. In the next section, we'll look at doing the same with a popular open source library and understanding its benefits over fetch.

Using axios with class components

axios is a popular open source JavaScript HTTP client. We're going to build a little React app that creates, reads, updates, and deletes posts from the JSONPlaceholder REST API. Along the way, we'll discover some of the benefits of axios over fetch. Our first job in the next section is to install axios.

Installing axios

Before we install axios, we are going to quickly create our little React app:

1. In a folder of our choice, let's open Visual Studio Code and its **Terminal** and enter the following command to create a new React and TypeScript project:

```
npx create-react-app crud-api --typescript
```

Note that the version of React we use needs to be at least version 16.7.0-alpha.0. We can check this in the package.json file. If the version of React in package.json is older than 16.7.0-alpha.0, then we can install this version using the following command:

```
npm install react@16.7.0-alpha.0
npm install react-dom@16.7.0-alpha.0
```

2. After the project is created, let's add TSLint as a development dependency to our project, along with some rules that work well with React and Prettier:

```
cd crud-api
npm install tslint tslint-react tslint-config-prettier --save-dev
```

3. Let's now add a tslint.json file containing some rules:

```
{
  "extends": ["tslint:recommended", "tslint-react", "tslint-config-prettier"],
  "rules": {
    "ordered-imports": false,
    "object-literal-sort-keys": false,
    "jsx-no-lambda": false,
    "no-debugger": false,
    "no-console": false,
  },
  "linterOptions": {
    "exclude": [
```

```
        "config/**/*.js",
        "node_modules/**/*.ts",
        "coverage/lcov-report/*.js"
    ]
  }
}
```

4. If we open `App.tsx`, there is a linting error. So, let's resolve this by adding `public` as the modifier on the `render` method:

```
class App extends Component {
  public render() {
    return ( ... );
  }
}
```

5. Now we can install `axios` using NPM:

    npm install axios

    Note that `axios` has TypeScript types within it, so, we don't need to install them.

6. Let's start our app running before we continue with development:

    npm start

The app will then start up and run in our browser. In the next section, we'll use axios to get posts from JSONPlaceholder.

Getting data with axios

In this section, we are going to render posts from `JSONPlaceholder` in the `App` component.

Basic GET request

We'll start off by getting the posts using a basic GET request with `axios`, and then rendering them in an unordered list:

1. Let's open `App.tsx` and add an import statement for `axios`:

    ```
    import axios from "axios";
    ```

2. Let's also create an interface for the posts that will come from JSONPlaceholder:

```
interface IPost {
  userId: number;
  id?: number;
  title: string;
  body: string;
}
```

3. We are going to store the posts in state, so let's add an interface for this:

```
interface IState {
  posts: IPost[];
}
class App extends React.Component<{}, IState> { ... }
```

4. Let's then initialize the post-state to an empty array in a constructor:

```
class App extends React.Component<{}, IState> {
  public constructor(props: {}) {
    super(props);
    this.state = {
      posts: []
    };
  }
}
```

5. When getting data from a REST API, we usually do this in the `componentDidMount` life cycle method. So, let's do this with `axios` to get our posts:

```
public componentDidMount() {
  axios
    .get<IPost[]>("https://jsonplaceholder.typicode.com/posts")
    .then(response => {
      this.setState({ posts: response.data });
    });
}
```

- We use the `get` function in `axios` to get data, which is a promised-based function like `fetch`
- This is a generic function that accepts the response body type as a parameter
- We pass the URL we are requesting as the parameter to the `get` function

- We can then handle the response in the `then` method
- We get access to the response body via the `data` property in the response object that is typed, as per the generic parameter

So, straight away this is nicer than `fetch` in two ways:

- We can easily type the response
- There is one step (rather than two) to get the response body

6. Now that we have the posts in the component state, let's render the posts in the `render` method. Let's also remove the `header` tag:

```
public render() {
  return (
    <div className="App">
      <ul className="posts">
        {this.state.posts.map(post => (
          <li key={post.id}>
            <h3>{post.title}</h3>
            <p>{post.body}</p>
          </li>
        ))}
      </ul>
    </div>
  );
}
```

We use the `posts` array's `map` function to display the posts in an unordered list.

7. We reference a `posts` CSS class, so let's add this to `index.css`:

```
.posts {
  list-style: none;
  margin: 0px auto;
  width: 800px;
  text-align: left;
}
```

If we look at the running app, it will now look like the following:

---

sunt aut facere repellat provident occaecati excepturi optio reprehenderit

quia et suscipit suscipit recusandae consequuntur expedita et cum reprehenderit molestiae ut ut quas totam nostrum rerum est autem sunt rem eveniet architecto

qui est esse

est rerum tempore vitae sequi sint nihil reprehenderit dolor beatae ea dolores neque fugiat blanditiis voluptate porro vel nihil molestiae ut reiciendis qui aperiam non debitis possimus qui neque nisi nulla

ea molestias quasi exercitationem repellat qui ipsa sit aut

et iusto sed quo iure voluptatem occaecati omnis eligendi aut ad voluptatem doloribus vel accusantium quis pariatur molestiae porro eius odio et labore et velit aut

---

So, a basic GET request with axios is nice and easy. We need to use the componentDidMount life cycle method in a class component to make a REST API call that will have data from the response rendered.

How do we handle errors though? We'll cover this in the next section.

Handling errors

1. Let's adjust the URL in our request:

   ```
   .get<IPost[]>("https://jsonplaceholder.typicode.com/postsX")
   ```

   If we look at the running app, the posts are no longer being rendered.

2. We want to handle this situation and give the user some feedback. We can do this using a catch method:

   ```
   axios
     .get<IPost[]>("https://jsonplaceholder.typicode.com/postsX")
     .then( ... )
     .catch(ex => {
       const error =
         ex.response.status === 404
           ? "Resource not found"
           : "An unexpected error has occurred";
       this.setState({ error });
     });
   ```

So, unlike `fetch`, HTTP status error codes can be handled in the `catch` method. The error object argument in `catch` contains a `response` property containing information about the response, including the HTTP status code.

3. We just referenced a piece of state called `error` in the `catch` method. We'll use this in the next step to render the error message. However, we first need to add this state to our interface and initialize it:

```
interface IState {
  posts: IPost[];
  error: string;
}
class App extends React.Component<{}, IState> {
  public constructor(props: {}) {
    super(props);
    this.state = {
      posts: [],
      error: ""
    };
  }
}
```

4. Let's then render the error if it contains a value:

```
<ul className="posts">
  ...
</ul>
{this.state.error && <p className="error">{this.state.error}</p>}
```

5. Let's add the `error` CSS class we just referenced to `index.css`:

```
.error {
  color: red;
}
```

If we look at the running app now, we'll see **Resource not found** in red.

6. Let's now change the URL to a valid URL so that we can move on to looking at how we can include HTTP headers in the next section:

```
.get<IPost[]>("https://jsonplaceholder.typicode.com/posts")
```

So, handling HTTP errors with `axios` is different than with `fetch`. We handle them in the first `then` method with `fetch`, whereas we handle them in the `catch` method with `axios`.

Request HTTP headers

In order to include HTTP headers in the request, we need to add a second parameter to the `get` function, which can contain various options, including HTTP headers.

Let's add an HTTP header for the content type in our request:

```
.get<IPost[]>("https://jsonplaceholder.typicode.com/posts", {
  headers: {
    "Content-Type": "application/json"
  }
})
```

So, we define the HTTP headers in an object in a property called `headers`.

If we look at the running app, it will be exactly the same. The JSONPlaceholder REST API doesn't require the content type, but other REST APIs that we interact with may do.

In the next section, we'll look at something that is not easily achieved in the `fetch` function, which is the ability to specify a timeout on the request.

Timeouts

Timing out requests after a certain amount of time can improve the user experience in our app:

1. Let's add a timeout to our request:

```
.get<IPost[]>("https://jsonplaceholder.typicode.com/posts", {
  headers: {
    "Content-Type": "application/json"
  },
  timeout: 1
})
```

So, adding a timeout to an `axios` request is super simple. We just add a `timeout` property to the options object with an appropriate number of milliseconds. We have specified just 1 millisecond, so that we can hopefully see the request timing out.

2. Let's handle a timeout now in the `catch` method:

```
.catch(ex => {
  const error =
    ex.code === "ECONNABORTED"
      ? "A timeout has occurred"
      : ex.response.status === 404
        ? "Resource not found"
        : "An unexpected error has occurred";
  this.setState({ error });
});
```

So, we check the `code` property in the caught error object in order to determine whether a timeout has occurred.

If we look at the running app, we should get confirmation that a timeout has occurred with **A timeout has occurred** displayed in red.

3. Let's now change the timeout to something more sensible so that we can move on to looking at how we can allow users to cancel requests in the next section:

```
.get<IPost[]>("https://jsonplaceholder.typicode.com/posts", {
  ...
  timeout: 5000
})
```

Canceling requests

Allowing the user to cancel a request can improve the user experience in our app. We'll do this with the help of `axios` in this section:

1. First, we are going to import the `CancelTokenSource` type from `axios`:

```
import axios, { CancelTokenSource } from "axios";
```

2. Let's add a cancel token and a loading flag to our state:

```
interface IState {
  posts: IPost[];
  error: string;
  cancelTokenSource?: CancelTokenSource;
  loading: boolean;
}
```

3. Let's initialize the loading state in the constructor:

```
this.state = {
  posts: [],
  error: "",
  loading: true
};
```

We've defined the cancel token as optional so we don't need to initialize it in the constructor.

4. Next, we'll generate the cancel token source and add it to the state, just before we make the GET request:

```
public componentDidMount() {
  const cancelToken = axios.CancelToken;
  const cancelTokenSource = cancelToken.source();
  this.setState({ cancelTokenSource });
  axios
    .get<IPost[]>(...)
    .then(...)
    .catch(...);
}
```

5. We can then use the token in the GET request as follows:

```
.get<IPost[]>("https://jsonplaceholder.typicode.com/posts", {
  cancelToken: cancelTokenSource.token,
  ...
})
```

6. We can handle cancellations in the `catch` method as follows. Let's also set the `loading` state to `false`:

```
.catch(ex => {
  const error = axios.isCancel(ex)
    ? "Request cancelled"
    : ex.code === "ECONNABORTED"
      ? "A timeout has occurred"
      : ex.response.status === 404
        ? "Resource not found"
        : "An unexpected error has occurred";
  this.setState({ error, loading: false });
});
```

So, we use the `isCancel` function in `axios` to check if the request has been canceled.

7. While we are in the `componentDidMount` method, let's set the `loading` state to `false` in the `then` method as well:

```
.then(response => {
  this.setState({ posts: response.data, loading: false });
})
```

8. In the `render` method, let's add a **Cancel** button, which will allow the user to cancel the request:

```
{this.state.loading && (
  <button onClick={this.handleCancelClick}>Cancel</button>
)}
<ul className="posts">...</ul>
```

9. Let's implement the **Cancel** button handler that we have just referenced:

```
private handleCancelClick = () => {
  if (this.state.cancelTokenSource) {
    this.state.cancelTokenSource.cancel("User cancelled
operation");
  }
};
```

In order to cancel the request, the cancel method is called on the cancel token source.

So, users can now cancel requests by clicking the **Cancel** button.

10. Now, this is going to be hard to test because the REST API we are using is really fast! So, in order to see a canceled request, let's cancel it in the `componentDidMount` method immediately after the request is sent:

```
axios
  .get<IPost[]>( ... )
  .then(response => { ... })
  .catch(ex => { ... });

cancelTokenSource.cancel("User cancelled operation");
```

If we look at the running app, we should see verification that the request was cancelled by **Request cancelled** being displayed in red.

So, `axios` makes it really easy to improve our app's user experience by adding the ability to cancel requests.

Before we move on to the next section, wherein we look at using `axios` to create data, let's remove the line we just added to cancel the request immediately after it was made.

Creating data with axios

Let's move on to creating data now. We are going to allow the user to enter a post title and body and save it:

1. Let's first create a new state for the title and body:

```
interface IState {
  ...
  editPost: IPost;
}
```

2. Let's initialize this new state as well:

```
public constructor(props: {}) {
  super(props);
  this.state = {
    ...,
    editPost: {
      body: "",
      title: "",
      userId: 1
    }
  };
}
```

3. We'll create an `input` and `textarea` to capture the post title and body from the user:

```
<div className="App">
  <div className="post-edit">
    <input
      type="text"
      placeholder="Enter title"
      value={this.state.editPost.title}
      onChange={this.handleTitleChange}
    />
    <textarea
      placeholder="Enter body"
      value={this.state.editPost.body}
```

```
      onChange={this.handleBodyChange}
    />
    <button onClick={this.handleSaveClick}>Save</button>
  </div>
  {this.state.loading && (
    <button onClick={this.handleCancelClick}>Cancel</button>
  )}
  ...
</div>
```

4. Let's implement the change handlers we have just referenced to update the state:

```
private handleTitleChange = (e:
React.ChangeEvent<HTMLInputElement>) => {
  this.setState({
    editPost: { ...this.state.editPost, title:
e.currentTarget.value }
  });
};

private handleBodyChange = (e:
React.ChangeEvent<HTMLTextAreaElement>) => {
  this.setState({
    editPost: { ...this.state.editPost, body: e.currentTarget.value
}
  });
};
```

5. We can add a bit of CSS in `index.css` to make this all look reasonable:

```
.post-edit {
  display: flex;
  flex-direction: column;
  width: 300px;
  margin: 0px auto;
}
.post-edit input {
  font-family: inherit;
  width: 100%;
  margin-bottom: 5px;
}

.post-edit textarea {
  font-family: inherit;
  width: 100%;
  margin-bottom: 5px;
}
```

```
.post-edit button {
  font-family: inherit;
  width: 100px;
}
```

6. We can also start work on the save click handler and POST the new post to the REST API using `axios`:

```
private handleSaveClick = () => {
  axios
    .post<IPost>(
      "https://jsonplaceholder.typicode.com/posts",
      {
        body: this.state.editPost.body,
        title: this.state.editPost.title,
        userId: this.state.editPost.userId
      },
      {
        headers: {
          "Content-Type": "application/json"
        }
      }
    )
};
```

7. We can handle response using the `then` method:

```
.then(response => {
  this.setState({
    posts: this.state.posts.concat(response.data)
  });
});
```

So, we concatenate the new post with the existing post to create a new posts array for the state.

The structure of the `post` function call is very similar to `get`. In fact, we could add error handling, a timeout, and the ability to cancel the request in the same way as we did for `get`.

If we add a new post in the running app and click the **Save** button, we see it added to the bottom of the posts list.

Next up, we will allow users to update posts.

Updating data with axios

Let's move on to updating data now. We are going to allow the user to click an **Update** button in an existing post to change and save it:

1. Let's first create an **Update** button in each list item in the posts:

```
<li key={post.id}>
  <h3>{post.title}</h3>
  <p>{post.body}</p>
  <button onClick={() => this.handleUpdateClick(post)}>
    Update
  </button>
</li>
```

2. We can now implement the **Update** button click handler, which sets the post being edited in the component state:

```
private handleUpdateClick = (post: IPost) => {
  this.setState({
    editPost: post
  });
};
```

3. In our existing save click handler, we need two branches of code now for the existing POST request and the PUT request we need to implement:

```
private handleSaveClick = () => {
  if (this.state.editPost.id) {
    // TODO - make a PUT request
  } else {
    axios
      .post<IPost>( ... )
      .then( ... );
  }
};
```

4. Let's implement the PUT request now:

```
if (this.state.editPost.id) {
  axios
    .put<IPost>(
      `https://jsonplaceholder.typicode.com/posts/${
        this.state.editPost.id
      }`,
      this.state.editPost,
      {
```

```
                    headers: {
                      "Content-Type": "application/json"
                    }
                  }
               )
               .then(() => {
                 this.setState({
                   editPost: {
                     body: "",
                     title: "",
                     userId: 1
                   },
                   posts: this.state.posts
                     .filter(post => post.id !== this.state.editPost.id)
                     .concat(this.state.editPost)
                 });
               });
          } else {
            ...
          }
```

So, we filter out and concatenate the updated post to create a new posts array for the state.

The structure of the put function call is very similar to get and post. Again, we could add error handling, a timeout, and the ability to cancel the request in the same way as we did for get.

In the running app, if we click an **Update** button in a post, change the title and body, and click the **Save** button, we see it removed from where it was and added to the bottom of the posts list with the new title and body.

If we want to PATCH a post, we can use the patch axios method. This has the same structure as put but instead of passing the whole object that is being changed, we can just pass the values that need updating.

In the next section, we will allow users to delete posts.

Deleting data with axios

Let's move on to deleting data now. We are going to allow the user to click a **Delete** button in an existing post to delete it:

1. Let's first create a **Delete** button in each list item in the posts:

```
<li key={post.id}>
  <h3>{post.title}</h3>
  <p>{post.body}</p>
  <button onClick={() => this.handleUpdateClick(post)}>
    Update
  </button>
  <button onClick={() => this.handleDeleteClick(post)}>
    Delete
  </button>
</li>
```

2. We can now create the **Delete** button click handler:

```
private handleDeleteClick = (post: IPost) => {
  axios
.delete(`https://jsonplaceholder.typicode.com/posts/${post.id}`)
    .then(() => {
      this.setState({
        posts: this.state.posts.filter(p => p.id !== post.id)
      });
    });
};
```

So, we use the `axios delete` method to make an HTTP `DELETE` request, which follows the same structure as the other methods.

If we go to the running app, we should see a delete button in each post. If we click one of the buttons, we'll see it removed from the list after a short delay.

So, that concludes this section on `axios` with class components. We've seen that the `axios` functions are a little cleaner than `fetch`, and features such as the ability to have typed responses, timeouts, and request cancellation make it a popular choice for many developers. In the next section, we'll refactor the `App` component we have just implemented to be a function component.

Using axios with function components

In this section, we'll implement REST API calls using `axios` in a function component. We'll refactor the `App` component we built in the last section:

1. First, we are going to declare a constant, called `defaultPosts` that is going to hold the default posts state we'll use a little later. We'll add this after the `IPost` interface and set this to an empty array:

```
const defaultPosts: IPost[] = [];
```

2. We'll remove the `IState` interface because the state will be structured as individual pieces of state now.

3. We'll also remove the previous `App` class component.

4. Next, let's start the `App` function component under the `defaultPosts` constant:

```
const App: React.SFC = () => {}
```

5. We can now create the state for the posts, error, cancel token, loading flag, and posts being edited:

```
const App: React.SFC = () => {
  const [posts, setPosts]: [IPost[], (posts: IPost[]) => void] =
React.useState(defaultPosts);

  const [error, setError]: [string, (error: string) => void] =
React.useState("");

  const cancelToken = axios.CancelToken;
  const [cancelTokenSource, setCancelTokenSource]:
[CancelTokenSource, (cancelSourceToken: CancelTokenSource) => void]
= React.useState(cancelToken.source());

  const [loading, setLoading]: [boolean, (loading: boolean) =>
void] = React.useState(false);

  const [editPost, setEditPost]: [IPost, (post: IPost) => void] =
React.useState({
    body: "",
    title: "",
    userId: 1
  });
}
```

So, we use the `useState` function to define and initialize all these pieces of state.

6. We want to make the REST API call to get the posts when the component has first been mounted. We can use the `useEffect` function, after the lines where the state is defined, to do this passing of an empty array as the second parameter:

```
React.useEffect(() => {
  // TODO - get posts
}, []);
```

7. Let's call the REST API to get the posts in the arrow function:

```
React.useEffect(() => {
  axios
    .get<IPost[]>("https://jsonplaceholder.typicode.com/posts", {
      cancelToken: cancelTokenSource.token,
      headers: {
        "Content-Type": "application/json"
      },
      timeout: 5000
    });
}, []);
```

8. Let's handle the response and set the post-state along with setting the loading state to `false`:

```
React.useEffect(() => {
  axios
    .get<IPost[]>(...)
    .then(response => {
      setPosts(response.data);
      setLoading(false);
    });
}, []);
```

9. Let's also handle any errors, setting the error state along with the loading state to `false`:

```
React.useEffect(() => {
  axios
    .get<IPost[]>(...)
    .then(...)
    .catch(ex => {
      const err = axios.isCancel(ex)
        ? "Request cancelled"
        : ex.code === "ECONNABORTED"
          ? "A timeout has occurred"
          : ex.response.status === 404
            ? "Resource not found"
```

```
        : "An unexpected error has occurred";
      setError(err);
      setLoading(false);
    });
  }, []);
```

10. We can move on to the event handlers now. These are very similar to the class component implementation, with `const` replacing the `private` access modifier, as well as `this.state` and `this.setState` being replaced by the specific state variables and state setter functions. We'll start with the **Cancel** button click handler:

```
const handleCancelClick = () => {
  if (cancelTokenSource) {
    cancelTokenSource.cancel("User cancelled operation");
  }
};
```

11. Next, we can add the change handlers for the title and body inputs:

```
const handleTitleChange = (e: React.ChangeEvent<HTMLInputElement>)
=> {
  setEditPost({ ...editPost, title: e.currentTarget.value });
};

const handleBodyChange = (e:
React.ChangeEvent<HTMLTextAreaElement>) => {
  setEditPost({ ...editPost, body: e.currentTarget.value });
};
```

12. The **Save** button click handler is next:

```
const handleSaveClick = () => {
  if (editPost.id) {
    axios
      .put<IPost>(
`https://jsonplaceholder.typicode.com/posts/${editPost.id}`,
        editPost,
        {
          headers: {
            "Content-Type": "application/json"
          }
        }
      )
      .then(() => {
        setEditPost({
          body: "",
          title: "",
```

```
                    userId: 1
                 });
                 setPosts(
                    posts.filter(post => post.id !==
       editPost.id).concat(editPost)
                 );
              });
          } else {
            axios
              .post<IPost>(
                "https://jsonplaceholder.typicode.com/posts",
                {
                   body: editPost.body,
                   title: editPost.title,
                   userId: editPost.userId
                },
                {
                   headers: {
                     "Content-Type": "application/json"
                   }
                }
              )
              .then(response => {
                 setPosts(posts.concat(response.data));
              });
          }
       };
```

13. Let's do the **Update** button next:

```
const handleUpdateClick = (post: IPost) => {
   setEditPost(post);
};
```

14. The last handler is for the **Delete** button:

```
const handleDeleteClick = (post: IPost) => {
   axios
.delete(`https://jsonplaceholder.typicode.com/posts/${post.id}`)
     .then(() => {
        setPosts(posts.filter(p => p.id !== post.id));
     });
};
```

15. Our final task is to implement the return statement. Again, this is very similar to the class component `render` method, with references to `this` removed:

```
return (
  <div className="App">
    <div className="post-edit">
      <input
        type="text"
        placeholder="Enter title"
        value={editPost.title}
        onChange={handleTitleChange}
      />
      <textarea
        placeholder="Enter body"
        value={editPost.body}
        onChange={handleBodyChange}
      />
      <button onClick={handleSaveClick}>Save</button>
    </div>
    {loading && <button
onClick={handleCancelClick}>Cancel</button>}
    <ul className="posts">
      {posts.map(post => (
        <li key={post.id}>
          <h3>{post.title}</h3>
          <p>{post.body}</p>
          <button onClick={() =>
handleUpdateClick(post)}>Update</button>
          <button onClick={() =>
handleDeleteClick(post)}>Delete</button>
        </li>
      ))}
    </ul>
    {error && <p className="error">{error}</p>}
  </div>
);
```

That's it! Our function component that interacts with a REST API is complete. If we try this, it should behave exactly as it did before.

The main difference in terms of REST API interaction is that we use the `useEffect` function to make a REST API call to get data that needs to be rendered. We still do this when the component has been mounted, like we do in class-based components. It's just a different way of tapping into that component life cycle event.

Summary

Callback-based asynchronous code can be difficult to read and maintain. Who's spent hours trying to track down the root cause of a bug in callback-based asynchronous code? Or just spent hours trying to understand what a piece of callback-based asynchronous code is trying to do? Thankfully, we now have alternative ways of writing asynchronous code.

Promise-based functions are a great improvement over callback-based asynchronous code because the code is a lot more readable and errors can be handled more easily. The `async` and `await` keywords arguably make reading asynchronous code even easier than promised-based function code because it is very close to what the synchronous equivalent would look like.

Modern browsers have a nice function called `fetch` for interacting with REST APIs. This is a promised-based function allowing us to easily make a request and nicely manage the response.

`axios` is a popular alternative to `fetch`. The API is arguably cleaner and allows us to better handle HTTP error codes. Timeouts and canceling requests are also made very simple using `axios`. `axios` is also TypeScript-friendly, having types baked into the library. Having played with both `axios` and `fetch`, which is your favorite?

We can interact with REST APIs in both class- and function-based components. When calling a REST API to get data to display in a first component render, we need to wait until just after the component has been mounted. In class components, we do this using the `componentDidMount` life cycle method. In function components, we do this using the `useEffect` function, passing an empty array as the second parameter. Having experienced interacting with REST APIs in both types of components, which component type are you going to use on your next React and TypeScript project?

REST APIs aren't the only type of API we are likely going to need to interact with. GraphQL is a popular alternative API server. We'll learn how we can interact with GraphQL servers in the next chapter.

Questions

Let's answer the following questions to help our knowledge of what we have just learned stick:

1. What will the output be in the console if we ran the following code in a browser?

```
try {
 setInterval(() => {
  throw new Error("Oops");
 }, 1000);
} catch (ex) {
  console.log("Sorry, there is a problem", ex);
}
```

2. Assuming that post 9999 doesn't exist, what would be the output in the console if we ran the following code in a browser?

```
fetch("https://jsonplaceholder.typicode.com/posts/9999")
  .then(response => {
    console.log("HTTP status code", response.status);
    return response.json();
  })
  .then(data => console.log("Response body", data))
  .catch (error => console.log("Error", error));
```

3. If we did a similar exercise with axios, what would be the output in the console when running the following code?

```
axios
  .get("https://jsonplaceholder.typicode.com/posts/9999")
  .then(response => {
    console.log("HTTP status code", response.status);
  })
  .catch(error => {
    console.log("Error", error.response.status);
  });
```

4. What is the benefit of using the native fetch over axios?
5. How can we add a bearer token to the following axios request?

```
axios.get("https://jsonplaceholder.typicode.com/posts/1")
```

6. We are using the following `axios` PUT request to update a post title?

```
axios.put("https://jsonplaceholder.typicode.com/posts/1", {
  title: "corrected title",
  body: "some stuff"
});
```

7. The body hasn't changed though—it's just the title we want to update. How can we change this to a PATCH request to make this REST call more efficient?

8. We have implemented a function component to display a post. It uses the following code to get the post from a REST API?

```
React.useEffect(() => {
  axios
    .get(`https://jsonplaceholder.typicode.com/posts/${id}`)
    .then(...)
    .catch(...);
});
```

What is wrong with the preceding code?

Further reading

The following links are good resources for further information on the topics we have covered in this chapter:

- More information about promises can be found at `https://developer.mozilla.org/en-US/docs/Web/JavaScript/Reference/Global_Objects/Promise`
- Additional information about `async` and `await` is at `https://developer.mozilla.org/en-US/docs/Web/JavaScript/Reference/Statements/async_function`
- More information about the `fetch` function can be found at `https://developer.mozilla.org/en-US/docs/Web/API/Fetch_API`
- The `axios` GitHub page is at `https://github.com/axios/axios`

Interacting with GraphQL APIs

10

GraphQL is an open source web API language for reading and writing data that is maintained by Facebook. It allows the client to specify exactly what data is returned and request multiple data areas in a single request. This efficiency and flexibility makes it a compelling alternative to a REST API. GraphQL also supports both reading and writing data.

In this chapter, we'll start by experimenting with some GraphQL queries against GitHub to get familiar with the syntax by using the *GitHub GraphQL API* explorer. We'll explore how we both read and write GraphQL data and how to specify exactly the way we want the data in the response returned to us.

We'll then consume the GitHub GraphQL server in a React and TypeScript application to build a little app that searches for a GitHub repository and returns some information about it. We'll use our knowledge from the last chapter on `axios` to interact with the GitHub GraphQL server to start off with. We'll then switch to using Apollo, which is a client library that makes interacting with GraphQL servers a breeze.

We'll cover the following topics in this chapter:

- GraphQL query and mutation syntax
- Using axios as a GraphQL client
- Using Apollo GraphQL client
- Working with cached data in Apollo

Technical requirements

We use the following technologies in this chapter:

- **Node.js and** npm: TypeScript and React are dependent on these. We can install them from https://nodejs.org/en/download/. If we already have these installed, make sure npm is at least at version 5.2.

- **Visual Studio Code**: We'll need an editor to write our React and TypeScript code, which can be installed from https://code.visualstudio.com/. We will also need the TSLint (by egamma) and Prettier (by Estben Petersen) extensions installed within Visual Studio Code.

- **GitHub**: We'll need a GitHub account. We can sign up at the following link if we haven't got an account: https://github.com/join.

- **GitHub GraphQL API Explorer**: We'll use this tool to play with the syntax of GraphQL queries and mutations. The tool is at https://developer.github.com/v4/explorer/.

All the code snippets in this chapter can be found online at https://github.com/carlrip/LearnReact17WithTypeScript/tree/master/10-GraphAPIs.

GraphQL query and mutation syntax

In this section, we'll use the GitHub GraphQL API explorer to start to get familiar with the syntax for interacting with a GraphQL server, starting with reading data in the next section.

Reading GraphQL data

In order to read GraphQL data, we make what is called a query. In this section, we'll start by covering the basic GraphQL syntax and move on to how to include nested objects in a query result, and then how we can create reusable queries by allowing parameters to be passed into them.

Basic query

In this section, we'll use the GitHub GraphQL API explorer to get information about our GitHub user account:

1. Let's open the following URL in a browser to open the tool:

    ```
    https://developer.github.com/v4/explorer/.
    ```

    We will need to be signed in to our GitHub account if we aren't already.

2. In the panel in the top-left corner, let's enter the following and click the **Execute Query** button:

    ```
    query {
      viewer {
        name
        }
    }
    ```

    This is our first GraphQL query. Here are some key points:

    -   We prefix a query with the `query` keyword. This is actually optional.
    -   `viewer` is the name of the object we want to get.
    -   `name` is a field within `viewer` that we want to return.

    The query result will appear on the right-hand side:

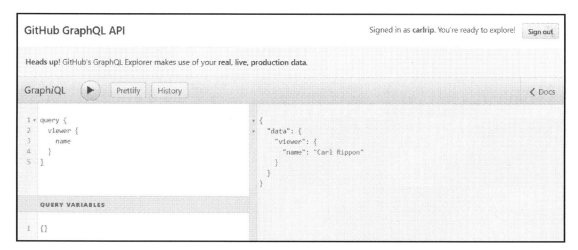

The data we requested is returned as a JSON object. The JSON contains a `data` object that contains a `viewer` object containing the `name` field. The `name` value should be our name, since this is the name stored in our GitHub account.

3. On the right-hand side of the results pane there is a **Docs** link. If we click this link, a **Documentation Explorer** appears:

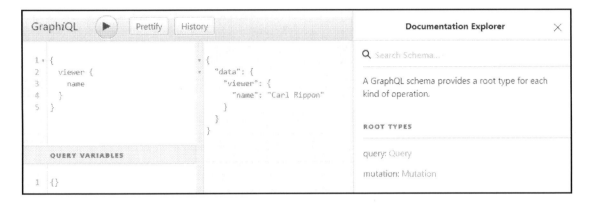

If we then click on the **Query** link, all the objects are shown that can be queried, including `viewer`, which is the one we just queried. If we click into this, we see all the fields that are available within `viewer`.

4. Let's add `avatarUrl` to our query, as this is an additional field available to us:

```
query {
  viewer {
    name
    avatarUrl
  }
}
```

So, we simply add the `avatarUrl` field inside the `viewer` object with a carriage return between the `name` and `avatarUrl` fields. If we execute the query, we see `avatarUrl` added to the JSON result. This should be a path to an image of us.

So, we are already seeing how flexible GraphQL is with being able to specify exactly which fields we want returned in the response. In the next section, we'll take this further by specifying the nested objects we want to return.

Returning nested data

Let's make a far more complex query in this section. We'll search for a GitHub repository, return information about it, including the number of stars it has and the last issues that have been raised as a nested array:

1. Let's start by entering the following query and executing it:

```
query {
  repository (owner:"facebook", name:"react") {
    name
    description
  }
}
```

This time, we are asking for the `repository` object, but passing two parameters for the `owner` and `name` of the repository. We are asking for the `name` and `description` of the repository to be returned.

We see that the repository and fields we asked for are returned:

```
1 ▾ query {
2     repository (owner:"facebook", name:"react") {
3       name
4       description
5     }
6   }

  ▾ {
      "data": {
        "repository": {
          "name": "react",
          "description": "A declarative, efficient, and flexible JavaScript library for
  building user interfaces."
        }
      }
    }
```

2. Let's now request the number of stars against the repository. To do this, we ask for the `totalCount` field within the `stargazers` nested object:

```
query {
  repository (owner:"facebook", name:"react") {
    name
    description
    stargazers {
      totalCount
    }
  }
}
```

If we execute the query, we see these results returned:

```
1 ▾ query {                                          ▾ {
2 ▾   repository (owner:"facebook", name:"react") {  ▾   "data": {
3       name                                         ▾     "repository": {
4       description                                        "name": "react",
5       stargazers {                                       "description": "A declarative, efficient, and flexible JavaScript library for
6         totalCount                             building user interfaces.",
7       }                                                  "stargazers": {
8     }                                                      "totalCount": 115001
9   }                                                      }
                                                         }
                                                       }
                                                     }
```

3. Let's now add an alias to `totalCount` within `stargazers`:

```
stargazers {
  stars:totalCount
}
```

If we execute the query, we see the stars count is returned against the alias we specified:

```
{
  "data": {
    "repository": {
      "name": "react",
      "description": "A declarative, efficient, and flexible
JavaScript library for building user interfaces.",
      "stargazers": {
        "stars": 114998
      }
    }
  }
}
```

4. Let's move on to requesting the last 5 issues within the repository:

```
{
  repository (owner:"facebook", name:"react") {
    name
    description
    stargazers {
      stars:totalCount
    }
    issues(last: 5) {
      edges {
        node {
          id
```

```
            title
            url
            publishedAt
          }
        }
      }
    }
  }
}
```

We request the `issues` object by passing 5 into the last parameter. We then request an `edges` object containing a `node` object that in turn contains the issue fields we are interested in.

So, what are the `edges` and `node` objects? Why can't we just request the fields we want directly? Well, this structure is in place to facilitate cursor-based pagination.

If we execute the query, we get the last 5 issues included in our result.

So, GraphQL allows us to make a single web request for different bits of data returning just the fields we require. Doing a similar thing with the GitHub REST API would probably require multiple requests and we'd get a lot more data than we need returned to us. It is these types of queries where GraphQL shines over REST.

Query parameters

The query we have just made is hardcoded to get data for a specific repository. In this section, we'll define variables in the query, which essentially allow parameters to be passed into it:

1. We can add query variables in parentheses after the `query` keyword, separated by commas. Each parameter is defined by declaring its name with its type after a semicolon. This is similar to defining parameters in a TypeScript function with type annotations. The variable names need to be prefixed with $. The ! after the type signifies that this is required. So, in our case, both variables are required in order for the query to be executed. The variables can then be referenced within the query, which, in our case, is where we request the repository object:

```
query ($org: String!, $repo: String!) {
  repository (owner:$org, name:$repo) {
    ...
  }
}
```

2. Before we execute the query, we need to specify the variable values. We do this in the **Query Variables** pane in the bottom-left corner in a JSON object:

```
{
  "org": "facebook",
  "repo": "react"
}
```

3. If we execute the query, we get the results for the repository we asked for:

We are now getting comfortable with reading data from a GraphQL server. But how can we create new data items or update data? We'll find out in the next section.

Writing GraphQL data

Let's turn our attention to writing to a GraphQL server now. We do this with what are called mutations. In this section, we'll create a `mutation` to add a GitHub star to a repository:

1. In order to star a repository, we need the repository `id`. So, let's add this to the query we have been working on to get this:

```
query ($org: String!, $repo: String!) {
  repository (owner:$org, name:$repo) {
    id
    ...
  }
}
```

2. Let's copy the `id` that is returned in the result. The `id` for the React repository is the shown in the following:

```
MDEwOlJlcG9zaXRvcnkxMDI3MDI1MA==
```

3. We can now write our first `mutation`:

```
mutation ($repoId: ID!) {
  addStar(input: { starrableId: $repoId }) {
    starrable {
      stargazers {
        totalCount
      }
    }
  }
}
```

Here are some key points on this `mutation`:

- We prefix a mutation with the `mutation` keyword.
- We put parameters to be passed into the `mutation` after the `mutation` keyword in parentheses. In our case, we have a single parameter for the repository `id` we want to star.
- `addStar` is the `mutation` function we are calling, which has a parameter called `input` that we need to pass to it.
- `input` is actually an object that has a field called `starrableId` we need to include. The value of this is the repository `id` we want to star, so we set it to our repository `id` variable `$repoId`.
- After the `mutation` parameters, we can specify what we want returned in the response. In our case, we want to return the number of stars on the repository.

4. We can specify the parameter value for the repository `id` in the **Query Variables** pane:

```
{
  "repoId": "MDEwOlJlcG9zaXRvcnkxMDI3MDI1MA=="
}
```

5. If we execute the `mutation`, the star will be added to the repository and the new total number of stars will be returned:

```
1 ▾ mutation ($repoId: ID!) {                    ▾ {
2 ▾   addStar(input: { starrableId: $repoId }) {   ▾   "data": {
3 ▾     starrable {                                ▾     "addStar": {
4       stargazers {                               ▾       "starrable": {
5         totalCount                                         "stargazers": {
6       }                                                      "totalCount": 115066
7     }                                                      }
8   }                                                      }
9 }                                                      }
10                                                      }
                                                      }

◄                                         ►

QUERY VARIABLES

1  {
2    "repoId": "MDEwOlJlcG9zaXRvcnkxMDI3MDI1MA=="
3  }
```

We have a good grasp on both GraphQL queries and mutations now. In the next section, we'll start to interact with a GraphQL server from a React and TypeScript app.

Using axios as a GraphQL client

Interacting with a GraphQL server is done via HTTP. We learned in Chapter 9, *Interacting with Restful APIs*, that `axios` is a great HTTP client. So, in this chapter, we'll cover how to interact with a GraphQL server using `axios`.

To help us learn, we'll create a React and TypeScript app to return information about our GitHub account. So, our first tasks are to get a token that will give us access to query the GitHub GraphQL server and scaffold a React and TypeScript app.

Getting a GitHub personal access token

The GitHub GraphQL server requires a bearer token for us to interact with it. So, let's go and generate a personal access token:

1. Let's sign in to our GitHub account and go to our **Settings** page by opening the menu under our avatar and choosing **Settings.**
2. In the left-hand menu, we then need to choose the **Developer settings** option. This will take us to the **Developer settings** page.
3. We can then choose the **Personal access tokens** option in the left-hand menu.
4. We will then see a **Generate new token** button that we can click to generate our bearer token. We will likely be prompted to input our password after clicking the button.
5. Before the token is generated, we are asked to specify the scopes. Let's enter a token description, tick **repo** and **user**, and then click the **Generate token** button.
6. The token is then generated and displayed in the page for us to copy and use in our React app.

Now that we have our bearer token, let's scaffold a React and TypeScript app in the next section.

Creating our app

We'll follow the usual steps for scaffolding a React and TypeScript app:

1. Let's open Visual Studio Code in a folder of our choice and open the terminal. Let's enter the following command to create a new React and TypeScript project:

```
npx create-react-app repo-search --typescript
```

Note that the version of React we use needs to be at least version `16.7.0-alpha.0`. We can check this in the `package.json` file. If the version of React in `package.json` is less than `16.7.0-alpha.0`, then we can install this version using the following command:

```
npm install react@16.7.0-alpha.0
npm install react-dom@16.7.0-alpha.0
```

2. After the project is created, let's add TSLint as a development dependency to our project, along with some rules that work well with React and Prettier:

```
cd repo-search
npm install tslint tslint-react tslint-config-prettier --save-
dev
```

3. Let's now add a `tslint.json` file containing some rules:

```
{
  "extends": ["tslint:recommended", "tslint-react", "tslint-
config-
    prettier"],
  "rules": {
    "ordered-imports": false,
    "object-literal-sort-keys": false,
    "jsx-no-lambda": false,
    "no-debugger": false,
    "no-console": false,
  },
  "linterOptions": {
    "exclude": [
      "config/**/*.js",
      "node_modules/**/*.ts",
      "coverage/lcov-report/*.js"
    ]
  }
}
```

4. If we open `App.tsx`, there is a linting error. So, let's resolve this by adding `public` as the modifier on the `render` method:

```
class App extends Component {
  public render() {
    return ( ... );
  }
}
```

5. Now we can install `axios` using `npm`:

```
npm install axios
```

6. Let's start our app running before we continue with the developments:

   ```
   npm start
   ```

7. Let's do a little more in our app before we make our first GraphQL query in `axios`. Let's create a new file called `Header.tsx` in the `src` directory containing the following `import`:

   ```
   import React from "react";
   import axios from "axios";
   ```

   This component will eventually contain our name and avatar from GitHub.

8. Let's return nothing from our `Header` component for the time being:

   ```
   export const Header: React.SFC = () => {
     return null;
   }
   ```

9. Now let's go back to `App.tsx` and import the `Header` component we have just created:

   ```
   import { Header } from "./Header";
   ```

10. We can now adjust the JSX in `App.tsx`, including our `Header` component:

    ```
    <div className="App">
      <header className="App-header">
        <Header />
      </header>
    </div>
    ```

11. As our final task in this section, let's change the `App-Header` CSS class in `App.css` so that the header isn't so tall:

    ```
    .App-header {
      background-color: #282c34;
      min-height: 200px;
      display: flex;
      flex-direction: column;
      align-items: center;
      justify-content: center;
      font-size: 16px;
      color: white;
    }
    ```

Querying the GraphQL server

Now that we have our React and TypeScript project in place, let's make a GraphQL query using `axios`:

1. In `Header.tsx`, we'll start by creating two interfaces for the GraphQL query response and the viewer data within it:

```
interface IViewer {
  name: string;
  avatarUrl: string;
}

interface IQueryResult {
  data: {
    viewer: IViewer;
  };
}
```

2. Let's create some state within our `Header` component for the `viewer`:

```
const [viewer, setViewer]: [
  IViewer,
  (viewer: IViewer) => void
] = React.useState({name: "", avatarUrl: ""});
```

3. It's nearly time to make the GraphQL query. We are going to do this when the component has just been mounted. We can use the `useEffect` function to do this:

```
React.useEffect(() => {
  // TODO - make a GraphQL query
}, []);
```

We pass an empty array as the second parameter so that the query only executes when the component is mounted and not on each render.

4. Let's use `axios` then to make the GraphQL query:

```
React.useEffect(() => {
  axios
    .post<IQueryResult>(
      "https://api.github.com/graphql",
      {
        query: `query {
          viewer {
            name
```

```
            avatarUrl
          }
        }`
      }
    )
  }, []);
```

Notice that we are doing an HTTP POST even though we are reading data. GraphQL requires us to use an HTTP POST because the details of the query are in the request body.

We are also using the interface we used earlier, IQueryResult, for the response data.

5. As mentioned earlier, we need to pass our bearer token in the HTTP Authorization header. So, let's do that:

```
axios
  .post<IQueryResult>(
    "https://api.github.com/graphql",
    {
      query: `query {
        viewer {
          name
          avatarUrl
        }
      }`
    },
    {
      headers: {
        Authorization: "bearer our-bearer-token"
      }
    }
  )
```

Obviously, we need to substitute in our real bearer token that we obtained earlier from GitHub.

6. We aren't handling the response yet, so let's do that and set the viewer state variable:

```
axios
  .post<IQueryResult>(
    ...
  )
  .then(response => {
```

```
        setViewer(response.data.data.viewer);
    });
```

7. Now that we have the data in state from the GraphQL query, let's render our avatar and name along with our app title:

```
return (
  <div>
    <img src={viewer.avatarUrl} className="avatar" />
    <div className="viewer">{viewer.name}</div>
    <h1>GitHub Search</h1>
  </div>
);
```

8. Let's add the avatar CSS class we just referenced into `App.css`:

```
.avatar {
  width: 60px;
  border-radius: 50%;
}
```

If we look at the running app, we should see our avatar and name in our app header:

So, we've just interacted with a GraphQL server using an HTTP library. All GraphQL requests are made using the HTTP POST method, even for reading data. All GraphQL requests are made to the same endpoint as well. The resource we want data from isn't in the URL, it's in the request body. So, whilst we can use an HTTP library, like `axios`, for querying GraphQL servers, it feels a little strange.

In the next section, we'll look at a GraphQL client that will help us query a GraphQL server in a more natural way.

Using Apollo GraphQL client

Apollo client is a client library for interacting with GraphQL servers. It has many benefits over using a generic HTTP library like `axios`, such as being able to read and write data declaratively with React components right in our JSX and having caching switched on right out of the box.

In this section, we'll refactor what we built in the last section with `axios` to use Apollo, and then extend our app a little more to include a GitHub repository search.

Installing Apollo client

Our first job is to install Apollo into our project.

1. To add Apollo client to our project, let's install the following packages via `npm`:

   ```
   npm install apollo-boost react-apollo graphql
   ```

   - `apollo-boost` contains everything we need to set up our Apollo client
   - `react-apollo` contains React components we are going to use to interact with the GraphQL server
   - `graphql` is a core package that we'll use to parse GraphQL queries

2. We'll also install some TypeScript types as well for `graphql`:

   ```
   npm install @types/graphql --save-dev
   ```

3. We need to make sure TypeScript includes the `es2015` and `esNext` libraries when it compiles our code. So, let's add the following `lib` field to `tsconfig.json`:

   ```
   {
     "compilerOptions": {
       "target": "es5",
       "lib": ["es2015", "dom", "esnext"],
       ...
     },
     ...
   }
   ```

We now have everything in place to start interacting with the GitHub GraphQL server with Apollo.

Migrating from axios to Apollo

Now that we have installed all the Apollo bits and pieces, let's migrate our `axios` code to Apollo.

Adding an Apollo provider

We are going to start in `App.tsx`, where we will define our Apollo client and *provide* it to all the components beneath the `App` in the component hierarchy:

1. In `App.tsx`, let's import `apollo-boost`, along with the `ApolloProvider` component from `react-apollo`:

   ```
   import ApolloClient from "apollo-boost";
   import { ApolloProvider } from "react-apollo";
   ```

2. Just above the `App` class component, let's create our `ApolloClient`:

   ```
   const client = new ApolloClient({
     uri: "https://api.github.com/graphql",
     headers: {
       authorization: `Bearer our-bearer-token`
     }
   });
   ```

   Obviously, we need to substitute in our real bearer token we obtained earlier from GitHub.

3. The last step is to use the `ApolloProvider` component to provide the `ApolloClient` we have created to all the other components in our app. We do this by putting `ApolloProvider` as the root component and passing it our `ApolloClient` object:

   ```
   public render() {
     return (
       <ApolloProvider client={client}>
         <div className="App">
           <header className="App-header">
             <Header />
           </header>
         </div>
       </ApolloProvider>
     );
   }
   ```

Now that the `ApolloClient` is set up, we can start interacting with the GraphQL server.

Using the query component to query GraphQL

We are now going to use the `Query` component to get our GitHub name and avatar, replacing the `axios` code:

1. Let's start by removing the `axios` import statement and instead of having the following imports:

    ```
    import gql from "graphql-tag";
    import { Query } from "react-apollo";
    ```

2. Our `IViewer` interface will remain the same, but we need to tweak our `IQueryResult` interface slightly:

    ```
    interface IQueryResult {
      viewer: IViewer;
    }
    ```

3. We are going to define our GraphQL query next:

    ```
    const GET_VIEWER = gql`
      {
        viewer {
          name
          avatarUrl
        }
      }
    `;
    ```

    So, we set the query to a `GET_VIEWER` variable and we have defined our query in a template literal. However, the `gql` function just before the template literal is a little odd. Shouldn't the template literal be in parentheses? This is actually called a tagged template literal, where the `gql` function from the core GraphQL library parses the template literal next to it. We end up with a query in `GET-VIEWER` that Apollo can use and execute.

4. We are now going to start to define our query. We can define our query directly in JSX using the `Query` component from `react-apollo`. However, in order to add some type safety, we are going to create a new component called `GetViewerQuery` that inherits from `Query` and defines the result type as a generic parameter:

```
class GetViewerQuery extends Query<IQueryResult> {}
```

5. We don't need any state anymore, so we can remove the `viewer` and `setViewer` variables.

6. We can also remove the `useEffect` function call that makes the `axios` query because we are going to do our query in JSX now.

7. So, let's use our `GetViewerQuery` component to invoke our query:

```
return (
  <GetViewerQuery query={GET_VIEWER}>
    {(({ data }) => {
      if (!data || !data.viewer) {
        return null;
      }
      return (
        <div>
          <img src={data.viewer.avatarUrl} className="avatar"
/>
          <div className="viewer">{data.viewer.name}</div>
          <h1>GitHub Search</h1>
        </div>
      );
    }}
  </GetViewerQuery>
);
```

- We pass the `GetViewerQuery` component our query we created earlier in a `query` prop.
- The query result is returned in the children function of `GetViewerQuery`.
- The children function argument contains an object containing the data in a `data` property. We destructure this data into a `data` variable.
- If there isn't any data, we escape early and return `null`.
- If we have data, we then return the JSX for our avatar and name referencing the `data` property.

> If we look at our running app, it should look exactly the same as the
> `axios` version. We may need to `npm start` the app again if it's showing
> an error.

8. There's other information that we can get from the children function argument.
   One piece of useful information is whether the data is being loaded. Let's use this
   to display a loading message:

```
return (
  <GetViewerQuery query={GET_VIEWER}>
    {(({ data, loading }) => {
      if (loading) {
        return <div className="viewer">Loading ...</div>;
      }
      ...
    }}
  </GetViewerQuery>
);
```

9. Another useful piece of information that we can get from the children function
   argument is information about an error that has occurred. Let's use this to
   display the error message, if there is one:

```
return (
  <GetViewerQuery query={GET_VIEWER}>
    {(({ data, loading, error }) => {
      if (error) {
        return <div
className="viewer">{error.toString()}</div>;
      }
      ...
    }}
  </GetViewerQuery>
);
```

This Apollo implementation is really elegant. It's clever how the `Query` component makes
the web request at the correct point in the component lifecycle and allows us to feed the rest
of the component tree the data.

In the next section, we'll continue to enhance our app with Apollo.

Adding a repository search component

In this section, we'll add a component to search for a GitHub repository and return some information about it:

1. Let's start by creating a new file called `RepoSearch.tsx` containing the following imports:

```
import * as React from "react";
import gql from "graphql-tag";
import { ApolloClient } from "apollo-boost";
```

2. We are going to take in `ApolloClient` as a prop. So, let's add an interface for that:

```
interface IProps {
  client: ApolloClient<any>;
}
```

3. Next, we'll scaffold our component:

```
const RepoSearch: React.SFC<IProps> = props => {
  return null;
}

export default RepoSearch;
```

4. Let's reference this in our `App` component, now in `App.tsx`, by first importing it:

```
import RepoSearch from "./RepoSearch";
```

5. We can now add this under the app header passing in `ApolloClient`:

```
<ApolloProvider client={client}>
  <div className="App">
    <header className="App-header">
      <Header />
    </header>
    <RepoSearch client={client} />
  </div>
</ApolloProvider>
```

Our repository `search` component is nicely set up now. In the next, section we can implement a search form.

Implementing the search form

Let's implement a search form that allows the user to supply an organization name and repository name:

1. Back in `RepoSearch.tsx`, let's start to define the state for the search fields, starting with the interface:

```
interface ISearch {
  orgName: string;
  repoName: string;
}
```

2. Now we can create a variable to hold our `search` state, along with a function to set it:

```
const RepoSearch: React.SFC<IProps> = props => {
  const [search, setSearch]: [
    ISearch,
    (search: ISearch) => void
  ] = React.useState({
    orgName: "",
    repoName: ""
  });

  return null;
}
```

3. Let's define the `search` form in our JSX:

```
return (
  <div className="repo-search">
    <form onSubmit={handleSearch}>
      <label>Organization</label>
      <input
        type="text"
        onChange={handleOrgNameChange}
        value={search.orgName}
      />
      <label>Repository</label>
      <input
        type="text"
        onChange={handleRepoNameChange}
```

```
        value={search.repoName}
      />
      <button type="submit">Search</button>
    </form>
  </div>
);
```

We've referenced a few bits that aren't implemented yet. So, we'll implement this one by one.

4. Let's add the `repo-search` class we referenced in `App.css`. We'll also style the labels and inputs along with the **Search** button as well:

```css
.repo-search {
  margin: 30px auto;
  width: 300px;
  font-family: Arial;
  font-size: 16px;
  text-align: left;
}

.repo-search label {
  display: block;
  margin-bottom: 3px;
  font-size: 14px;
}

.repo-search input {
  display: block;
  margin-bottom: 10px;
  font-size: 16px;
  color: #676666;
  width: 100%;
}

.repo-search button {
  display: block;
  margin-bottom: 20px;
  font-size: 16px;
}
```

5. Next, let's implement the input change handlers that simply update the `search` state:

```
const handleOrgNameChange = (e:
React.ChangeEvent<HTMLInputElement>) => {
  setSearch({ ...search, orgName: e.currentTarget.value });
};

const handleRepoNameChange = (e:
React.ChangeEvent<HTMLInputElement>) => {
  setSearch({ ...search, repoName: e.currentTarget.value });
};
```

6. The final bit we need to implement is the `search` handler:

```
const handleSearch = (e: React.FormEvent<HTMLFormElement>) => {
  e.preventDefault();

  // TODO - make GraphQL query
};
```

We call `preventDefault` on the event argument to stop a full postback occurring.

So, that's the search form started. We'll implement the GraphQL query in the next section.

Implementing the search query

We are now at the point where we need to make the GraphQL query to do the actual search:

1. Let's start by creating an interface for the repository data we expect to get back from the query:

```
interface IRepo {
  id: string;
  name: string;
  description: string;
  viewerHasStarred: boolean;
  stargazers: {
    totalCount: number;
  };
  issues: {
    edges: [
      {
        node: {
```

```
                    id: string;
                    title: string;
                    url: string;
                };
            }
        ];
    };
}
```

This is the structure we got back from the GitHub GraphQL Explorer in an earlier section.

2. We are going to need a default value for this state. So, let's define this:

```
const defaultRepo: IRepo = {
    id: "",
    name: "",
    description: "",
    viewerHasStarred: false,
    stargazers: {
      totalCount: 0
    },
    issues: {
      edges: [
        {
          node: {
            id: "",
            title: "",
            url: ""
          }
        }
      ]
    }
};
```

3. We can also define an interface for the query result as a whole:

```
interface IQueryResult {
    repository: IRepo;
}
```

4. Now we can create the query itself using a tagged template literal:

```
const GET_REPO = gql`
  query GetRepo($orgName: String!, $repoName: String!) {
    repository(owner: $orgName, name: $repoName) {
      id
      name
```

```
      description
      viewerHasStarred
      stargazers {
        totalCount
      }
      issues(last: 5) {
        edges {
          node {
            id
            title
            url
            publishedAt
          }
        }
      }
    }
  }
`;
```

This is the query we made in the GitHub GraphQL Explorer in an earlier section. Unlike our previous queries, this one has parameters that we'll need to include when we execute the query a little later.

5. We need to store the data we get from the query in state. So, let's create a state variable called `repo`, along with a function to set it:

```
const [repo, setRepo]: [
    IRepo,
    (repo: IRepo) => void
  ] = React.useState(defaultRepo);
```

6. We are also going to store any problems with the `search` in state as well:

```
const [searchError, setSearchError]: [
  string,
  (searchError: string) => void
] = React.useState("");
```

7. Let's update the `handleSearch` arrow function to clear any search error state before we do the `search`:

```
const handleSearch = (e: React.FormEvent<HTMLFormElement>) => {
  e.preventDefault();

  setSearchError("");
};
```

8. Let's go on and use `ApolloClient` passed in as a prop to make the query:

```
const handleSearch = (e: React.FormEvent<HTMLFormElement>) => {
  e.preventDefault();
  setSearchError("");

  props.client
    .query<IQueryResult>({
      query: GET_REPO
    });
};
```

9. There is more work to do here, though. First, we need to pass in the `query` parameters for the organization name and repository name from the values we have in our `search` state:

```
.query<IQueryResult>({
  query: GET_REPO,
  variables: { orgName: search.orgName, repoName:
  search.repoName }
})
```

10. Now it's time to handle the response in the `then` method and set the `repo` state to the data in the response:

```
props.client
  .query<IQueryResult>( ... )
  .then(response => {
    setRepo(response.data.repository);
  });
```

11. We will also handle any errors in the `catch` method and update the `searchError` state:

```
props.client
  .query<IQueryResult>(...)
  .then(...)
  .catch(error => {
    setSearchError(error.message);
  });
```

If we try a `search` in the running app, the query will be made okay, but we are not showing the results yet. Let's do that in the next section.

Rendering the search result

Let's render the data we have got from the repository query:

1. Let's render the repository name with its number of stars, along with its description, under the search form if we have a search result:

```
return (
  <div className="repo-search">
    <form ...>
      ...
    </form>
    {repo.id && (
      <div className="repo-item">
        <h4>
          {repo.name}
          {repo.stargazers ? ` ${repo.stargazers.totalCount}
          stars` : ""}
        </h4>
        <p>{repo.description}</p>
      </div>
    )}
  </div>
);
```

2. We'll also render the last 5 repository issues:

```
...
<p>{repo.description}</p>
<div>
  Last 5 issues:
  {repo.issues && repo.issues.edges ? (
    <ul>
      {repo.issues.edges.map(item => (
        <li key={item.node.id}>{item.node.title}</li>
      ))}
    </ul>
  ) : null}
</div>
```

3. If a problem has occurred, let's render the error message we have captured in state:

```
{repo.id && (
  ...
)}
{searchError && <div>{searchError}</div>}
```

4. Let's add a bit of CSS in `App.css` for the title of the repository in the search result:

```
.repo-search h4 {
  text-align: center;
}
```

If we search for a repository, we should now see information about the repository rendered:

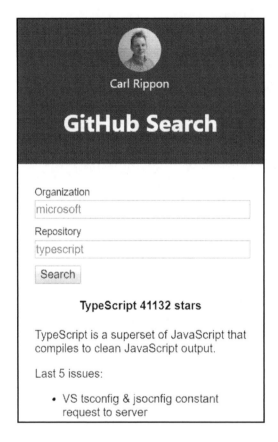

We are now getting comfortable querying a GraphQL server with Apollo. In the next section, we'll tackle mutations.

Implementing a mutation with Apollo

Let's allow users to star a GitHub repository in our app. This will involve sending a mutation via Apollo:

1. First, let's import the Mutation component from react-apollo:

```
import { Mutation } from "react-apollo";
```

2. Now let's create the mutation. The is the same query we executed in the GitHub GraphQL Explorer earlier:

```
const STAR_REPO = gql`
  mutation($repoId: ID!) {
    addStar(input: { starrableId: $repoId }) {
      starrable {
        stargazers {
          totalCount
        }
      }
    }
  }
`;
```

3. In the JSX, under where we render the description, let's place the Mutation component:

```
<p>{repo.description}</p>
<div>
  {!repo.viewerHasStarred && (
    <Mutation
      mutation={STAR_REPO}
      variables={{ repoId: repo.id }}
    >
      {() => (
        // render Star button that invokes the mutation when
          clicked
      )}
    </Mutation>
  )}
</div>
<div>
  Last 5 issues:
  ...
</div>
```

- We only render the `mutation` if the `viewer` hasn't already starred the repository
- The `Mutation` component takes in the mutation we just defined along with the variables, which is the repository `id` in our case

4. The `Mutation` component has a children function that gives us access to the `addStar` function. So, let's render a **Star!** button that calls `addStar` when clicked:

```
<Mutation
   ...
>
  {(addStar) => (
    <div>
      <button onClick={() => addStar()}>
        Star!
      </button>
    </div>
  )}
</Mutation>
)}
```

5. The `Mutation` component also tells us when the `mutation` is being executed via a `loading` property in a second argument in the children function. Let's use this to disable the button and inform the user that the star is being added:

```
<Mutation
   ...
>
  {(addStar, { loading }) => (
    <div>
      <button disabled={loading} onClick={() => addStar()}>
        {loading ? "Adding ..." : "Star!"}
      </button>
    </div>
  )}
</Mutation>
```

6. The `Mutation` component also tells us when there is an error. So, let's use this and render the error if one happens:

```
<Mutation
   ...
>
  {(addStar, { loading, error }) => (
    <div>
      <button ...>
```

```
      . . .
    </button>
    {error && <div>{error.toString()}</div>}
  </div>
  )}
</Mutation>
```

If we try to add a star to a repository, the star should be successfully added. We can go to the GitHub repository in github.com to verify this.

So, we are really getting to grips with Apollo now that we've implemented both queries and a mutation. There is one thing that was a little odd, though, that we may have spotted. The number of stars doesn't update in our app after we star a repository. Even if we search for the repository again, the number of stars is the number before we started it. However, if we refresh the browser and search for the repository again, we do get the correct number of stars. So, what's going on here? We'll find out in the next section.

Working with cached data in Apollo

We ended the last section with a bit of a mystery. Why aren't we getting the up-to-date number of stars in a repository search after we've started it? The answer is that Apollo caches the repository data after the initial search. When the same query is executed, it gets the results from its cache, rather than getting the data from the GraphQL server.

Let's double-check that this is the case:

1. Let's go to our app and open **Developer tools** on the **Network** tab and clear any previous requests:

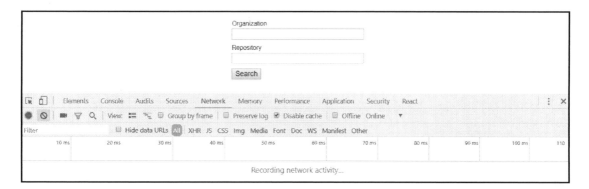

2. Let's do a search. We'll see a couple of requests to the GitHub GraphQL server:

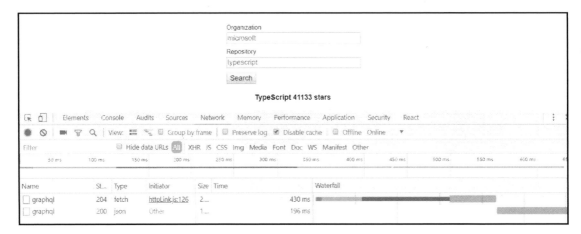

3. Under the **Developer tools**, **Network** tab, let's clear the requests, and then in our app let's click the **Search** button again. We'll see that no network requests will be made, but the data is rendered. So, the data must be coming from a local cache.

So, our `ApolloClient` that we configured using `apollo-boost` automatically caches queries in an in-memory cache. In the next section, we'll learn how to clear the cache so that our app shows the correct number of stars after a repository has been starred.

Clearing the caching using refetchQueries

We need a way of clearing the cached query result after a `mutation` has happened. One way of doing this is to use the `refetchQueries` prop on the `Mutation` component:

1. Let's give this a go. The `refetchQueries` prop takes in an array of objects that contain the queries with the corresponding variable values that should be removed from the cache:

```
<Mutation
  mutation={STAR_REPO}
  variables={{ repoId: repo.id }}
  refetchQueries={[
    {
      query: GET_REPO,
      variables: {
        orgName: search.orgName,
        repoName: search.repoName
```

```
            }
          }
        ]}
      >
        ...
      </Mutation>
```

2. If we star a repository now, the number of stars doesn't update straight away. However, if the **Search** button is pressed, the stars are updated.

So, the cache was cleared but the experience still isn't ideal. Ideally, we want the number of stars to be updated immediately after the **Star!** button is clicked.

If we think through what we have just done, we are trying to bypass the cache. However, the cache is in place to help our app perform well.

So, this approach doesn't feel great. The user experience still isn't ideal, and we have just made our app less performant. There must be a better way! We'll explore a different approach in the next section.

Updating the cache after a Mutation

Let's think through the problem one more time:

- We have some information about a repository in a cache that includes the number of stars it has.
- When we star the repository, we want to see that the number of stars has been incremented by one.
- What if we could just increment the number of stars in the cache by one? This should hopefully resolve the problem.

So, let's give this a go and update the cache after the `mutation` has finished:

1. First, let's remove the `refetchQueries` prop we implemented in the last section.
2. There is an `update` prop on the `Mutation` component that we can leverage to update the cache. So, let's start to implement this:

```
<Mutation
  mutation={STAR_REPO}
  update={cache => {
    // Get the cached data
    // update the cached data
    // update our state
  }}
```

```
        >
          ...
        </Mutation>
```

3. So, we need to implement an arrow function that updates the cache that is
   available as an argument:

```
<Mutation
  ...
  update={cache => {
    const data: { repository: IRepo } | null =
cache.readQuery({
      query: GET_REPO,
      variables: {
        orgName: search.orgName,
        repoName: search.repoName
      }
    });
    if (data === null) {
      return;
    }
  }}
>
  ...
</Mutation>
```

So, the cache has a `readQuery` function that we can use to get the cached data. If
no data is found in the cache then we can exit the function without doing
anything else.

4. So, now that we have the data from the cache, we can increment the number of
   stars. To do this, we create a new object and spread the props from the cached
   repository into it and overwrite it with the incremented number of stars and the
   fact that the viewer has starred the repository:

```
update={cache => {
  ...
  if (data === null) {
    return;
  }
  const newData = {
    ...data.repository,
    viewerHasStarred: true,
    stargazers: {
      ...data.repository.stargazers,
      totalCount: data.repository.stargazers.totalCount + 1
    }
```

```
      };
    }}
```

5. We can then update the cache with its `writeQuery` function. We pass in the query with the variable values and the new data to store in the cache:

```
update={cache => {
  . . .
  const newData = {
    . . .
  };
  cache.writeQuery({
    query: GET_REPO,
    variables: {
      orgName: search.orgName,
      repoName: search.repoName
    },
    data: { repository: newData }
  });
}}
```

6. There's one more job to do, which is to update the `repo` state so that the number of stars updates immediately onscreen:

```
update={cache => {
  . . .
  cache.writeQuery(...);
  setRepo(newData);
}}
```

That should be it. If we try to star a repository in our app again, we should see that the number of stars is immediately incremented.

Caching is one of the great features that Apollo gives us out-of-the-box. The `update` prop on the `Mutation` component gives us a precise way to update our cache.
The `refetchQueries` prop on the `Mutation` component is a more heavy-handed and less efficient way of forcing a cache to be updated.

Summary

GraphQL shines over REST because it allows us to efficiently get the data we need in the shape we need with far less effort. The GitHub GraphQL Explorer is a great tool for getting comfortable with the syntax. There are two main types of requests we can make to a GraphQL server:

- We can execute a `query` to read data
- We can execute a `mutation` to write data

Queries allow us to specify the objects and fields we want in the response. We can rename them by using aliases. We can parameterize a query by defining variables. We can give variables types and specify whether each one is required or not with `!` at the end. There are query features that we didn't cover in this chapter, such as conditionally including fields and the powerful paging capability. In summary, it's an extremely powerful query language!

Mutations share some of the same features as queries, such as being able to pass parameters into them. It's great how we get to control what data is included in the response as well.

GraphQL operates over HTTP with HTTP `POST` requests to a single URL. The HTTP body contains the query or `mutation` information. We can use an HTTP client to interact with a GraphQL server, but we'll probably be more productive with a library like Apollo that is built specifically to interact with GraphQL servers.

React Apollo is a set of React bits and pieces that work with the core Apollo library. It gives us nice `Query` and `Mutation` React components for including queries and mutations right in our JSX, making our code arguably easier to read. Before we can use these components, we need to set up our `ApolloClient` object with the URL to the GraphQL server and any credentials. We also need to include an `ApolloProvider` component high in our component tree, above all the components that need GraphQL data.

Caching is switched on out-of-the-box when we scaffold our project with `apollo-boost`. The `Mutation` component gives us `update` and `refetchQueries` props to manage cache updates.

All in all, GraphQL is a very productive way to interact with backends, and it works really nicely with React and TypeScript apps.

So, we've learned many different aspects of React and TypeScript in this book so far. One big topic that we haven't covered yet is how we can robustly test the apps we build. We'll cover this in the next chapter.

Questions

Let's have a go at some questions to test our knowledge on what we have just learned:

1. In the GitHub GraphQL Explorer, create a query to return the last five open issues in the React project. Return the issue title and the URL in the response.

2. Enhance the last query and make the number of issues that are returned a parameter and make this default to five.

3. Create a `mutation` in the **GitHub GraphQL Explorer** to unstar a starred repository. The `mutation` should take a required repository `id` in as a parameter.

4. What part of the HTTP request does the GraphQL query go in?

5. What part of the HTTP request does the GraphQL `mutation` go in?

6. How can we make the response from the `react-apollo` `Query` component type safe?

7. Is caching on or off by default when you scaffold a project with `react-boost`?

8. What prop can we use on the `Mutation` component to update the local cache?

Further reading

The following links are good resources of further information on GraphQL in general, along with React and Apollo:

- The GraphQL docs are at `https://graphql.org/learn/`
- The Apollo docs are at `https://www.apollographql.com/docs/`
- The React section of the Apollo docs is at `https://www.apollographql.com/docs/react/`

11
Unit Testing with Jest

Building a robust suite of unit tests that catches real bugs and doesn't flag false positives as we refactor our code is one of the hardest tasks we do as software developers. Jest is a great testing tool that helps us meet this challenge, as we'll find out in this chapter.

Perhaps the easiest bits of an app to unit test are pure functions, because there are no side effects to deal with. We'll revisit the validator functions we built in `Chapter 7`, *Working with Form*, and implement some unit tests against them in order to learn how to unit test pure functions.

Unit testing components is the most common type of unit test we'll be carrying out while building our apps. We'll learn about it in detail, and leverage a library to help us implement tests that don't unnecessarily break when we refactor our code.

We'll learn what snapshot testing is, and how we can leverage it to implement our tests quicker. Snapshots can be used for testing pure functions as well as components, so they are a very useful tool to have at our disposal.

Mocking is a challenging topic because if we mock too much, we aren't really testing our app. However, there are certain dependencies that make sense to mock, such as a REST API. We'll revisit the app we built in `Chapter 9`, *Interacting with Restful APIs*, in order to implement some unit tests against it and learn about mocking.

When implementing a suite of unit tests for our app, it is useful to know which bits we've tested and which bits we haven't. We'll learn how to use a code coverage tool to help us quickly identify areas of our app that need more unit tests.

The following topics will be covered in this chapter:

- Testing pure functions
- Testing components
- Using Jest snapshot tests
- Mocking dependencies
- Getting code coverage

Technical requirements

We use the following technologies in this chapter:

- **Node.js and** npm: TypeScript and React are dependent on these. Install them from the following link: https://nodejs.org/en/download/. If you already have these installed, make sure npm is at least version 5.2.

- **Visual Studio Code**: We'll need an editor to write our React and TypeScript code, which can be installed from https://code.visualstudio.com/. We'll also need the TSLint extension (by egamma) and the Prettier extension (by Estben Petersen).

- **React shop**: We'll be implementing unit tests on the React shop we created. This is available on GitHub at the following link: https://github.com/carlrip/LearnReact17WithTypeScript/tree/master/08-ReactRedux%EF%BB%BF.

- **Chapter 9 code**: We'll be implementing unit tests on the app we created in Chapter 9, *Interacting with RESTful APIs*. This is available on GitHub at the following link: https://github.com/carlrip/LearnReact17WithTypeScript/tree/master/09-RestfulAPIs/03-AxiosWithClass.

> In order to restore code from a previous chapter, the LearnReact17WithTypeScript repository at https://github.com/carlrip/LearnReact17WithTypeScript can be downloaded. The relevant folder can then be opened in Visual Studio Code and npm install entered in the terminal to do the restore. All the code snippets in this chapter can be found online at the following link: https://github.com/carlrip/LearnReact17WithTypeScript/tree/master/11-UnitTesting.

Testing pure functions

We'll start our unit testing journey in this section by implementing a unit test on a pure function.

> A pure function has a consistent output value for a given set of parameter values. Pure functions only depend on the function arguments, and on nothing outside the function. These functions also don't change any of the argument values passed into them.

The fact that these functions only depend on their parameter values makes them straightforward to unit test.

We are going to implement a unit test on the `required` validator function we created in our `Form` component in the React shop we built. If you haven't already, open this project in Visual Studio Code.

We are going to use Jest, which is very popular for unit testing React apps, as our unit testing framework. Luckily the `create-react-app` tool installs and configures this for us when creating a project. So, Jest is ready to be used in our React shop project.

Creating a basic pure function test

Let's create our first unit test in our project to test the `required` function in `Form.tsx`:

1. Start by creating a file called `Form.test.tsx` in the `src` folder. We'll use this file for our test code, to test the code in `Form.tsx`.

> The `test.tsx` extension is important because Jest automatically looks for files with this extension when finding tests to execute. Note that if our tests don't contain any JSX, we could use a `test.ts` extension.

2. Let's import the function we want to test, along with a TypeScript type we need for a parameter value:

```
import { required, IValues } from "./Form";
```

3. Let's start to create our test using the Jest `test` function:

```
test("When required is called with empty title, 'This must be populated' should be returned", () => {
  // TODO: implement the test
});
```

The `test` function takes in two parameters:

- The first parameter is a message telling us whether the test passed or not, which will be shown in the test output
- The second parameter is an arrow function that will contain our test

4. We'll move on to calling the `required` function with a `values` parameter that contains an empty `title` property:

```
test("When required called with title being an empty string, an
error should be 'This must be populated'", () => {
  const values: IValues = {
    title: ""
  };
  const result = required("title", values);
  // TODO: check the result is correct
});
```

5. Our next task in this test is to check that the result from the `required` function is what we expect. We can use the Jest `expect` function to do this:

```
test("When required called with title being an empty string, an
error should be 'This must be populated'", () => {
  const values: IValues = {
    title: ""
  };
  const result = required("title", values);
  expect(result).toBe("This must be populated");
});
```

We pass the variable we are checking into the `expect` function. We then chain a `toBe` matcher function onto this, which checks that the result from the `expect` function is the same as the parameter supplied to the `toBe` function.

 `toBe` is one of many Jest matcher functions we can use to check a variable value. The full list of functions can be found at `https://jestjs.io/docs/en/expect`.

6. Now that our test is complete, we can run the test by typing the following in the terminal:

```
npm test
```

This starts the Jest test runner in watch mode, which means that it will continuously run, executing tests when we change the source files.

Jest will eventually find our test file, execute our test, and output the result to the terminal, as follows:

```
> react-scripts test
 PASS  src/Form.test.tsx
  √ When required called with title being an empty string,
an error should be 'This must be populated' (3ms)

Test Suites: 1 passed, 1 total
Tests:       1 passed, 1 total
Snapshots:   0 total
Time:        2.613s
Ran all test suites.

Watch Usage
 › Press f to run only failed tests.
 › Press o to only run tests related to changed files.
 › Press p to filter by a filename regex pattern.
 › Press t to filter by a test name regex pattern.
 › Press q to quit watch mode.
 › Press Enter to trigger a test run.
```

7. Let's change the expected result in the test to make the test fail:

```
expect(result).toBe("This must be populatedX");
```

When we save the test file, Jest automatically executes the test and outputs the failure to the terminal, as follows:

```
 FAIL  src/Form.test.tsx
  x When required called with title being an empty string, an error should be 'This must be pop
ulated' (19ms)

  ● When required called with title being an empty string, an error should be 'This must be pop
ulated'

    expect(received).toBe(expected) // Object.is equality

    Expected: "This must be populatedX"
    Received: "This must be populated"

       6 |   };
       7 |   const result = required("title", values);
    >  8 |   expect(result).toBe("This must be populatedX");
         |                  ^
       9 | });
      10 |

      at Object.toBe (src/Form.test.tsx:8:18)

Test Suites: 1 failed, 1 total
Tests:       1 failed, 1 total
Snapshots:   0 total
Time:        3.412s
Ran all test suites.
```

Jest gives us valuable information about the failure. It tells us this:

- Which test failed
- What the expected result was, in comparison to the actual result
- The line in our test code where the failure occurred

This information helps us quickly resolve test failures.

8. Before we move on, let's correct our test code:

```
expect(result).toBe("This must be populated");
```

When we save the change, the test should now pass.

Understanding Jest watch options

After Jest executes our tests, it provides us with the following options:

```
> Press f to run only failed tests.
> Press o to only run tests related to changed files.
> Press p to filter by a filename regex pattern.
> Press t to filter by a test name regex pattern.
> Press q to quit watch mode.
> Press Enter to trigger a test run.
```

These options let us specify what tests should be executed, which is really useful as the number of tests grows. Let's explore some of these options:

1. If we press *F*, Jest will execute only the tests that have failed. In our code, we get confirmation that we have no failing tests:

```
No failed test found.
Press `f` to quit "only failed tests" mode.

Watch Usage: Press w to show more.
```

2. Let's press *F* to exit this option and take us back to all the options that are available.

3. Now, let's press *P*. This allows us to test a specific file or a collection of files with names matching a regular expression pattern. Let's enter `form` when prompted for the filename pattern:

```
Pattern Mode Usage
 › Press Esc to exit pattern mode.
 › Press Enter to filter by a filenames regex pattern.

pattern › form█
```

Our test in `Form.test.tsx` will then be executed.

4. We are going to leave the filename filter on and press *T*. This will allow us to add an additional filter by test name. Let's enter `required`:

```
Active Filters: filename /form/

Pattern Mode Usage
 › Press Esc to exit pattern mode.
 › Press Enter to filter by a tests regex pattern.

pattern › required█
```

Our test on the `required` function will then be executed.

5. To clear the filters, we can press *C*.

 If we receive an error—**watch is not supported without git/hg, please use --watchAll,** this will be because our project isn't in a Git repository. We can resolve the issue by entering the `git init` command in the Terminal.

We have a good handle on the options available to execute our tests now.

Adding structure to unit test results

As we implement more unit tests, it is useful to add some structure to the unit test results so that we can read them more easily. There is a Jest function called `describe` that we can use to group the results of certain tests together. It may make reading test results easier if all the tests for a function are grouped together.

Let's do this and refactor the unit test we created earlier, using the `describe` function in Jest:

```
describe("required", () => {
  test("When required called with title being an empty string, an error
should be 'This must be populated'", () => {
    const values: IValues = {
      title: ""
    };
    const result = required("title", values);
    expect(result).toBe("This must be populated");
  });
});
```

The describe function takes in two parameters:

- The first parameter is the title for the group of tests. We have used the function name we are testing for this.
- The second parameter is an arrow function that contains the tests to execute. We have placed our original test here.

When we save our test file, the tests will automatically run, and our improved output is shown in the terminal with our test result under a `required` heading:

```
PASS  src/Form.test.tsx
  required
    √ When required called with title being an empty string, an error should be 'This must be populated' (1ms
)

Test Suites: 1 passed, 1 total
Tests:       1 passed, 1 total
Snapshots:   0 total
Time:        1.388s
Ran all test suites related to changed files.

Watch Usage: Press w to show more.[]
```

We're starting to get familiar with Jest, having implemented and executed a unit test. In the next section, we will move on to the more complex topic of unit testing components.

Testing components

Unit testing a component is challenging because a component has dependencies such as the browser's DOM and the React library. How exactly can we render a component in our test code before we do the necessary checks? How can we trigger DOM events when coding a user interaction, such as clicking a button?

We'll answer these questions in this section, by implementing some tests on the `ContactUs` component we created in our React shop.

Creating a basic component test

We are going to start by creating a unit test to verify that submitting the **Contact Us** form without filling in the fields results in errors being displayed on the page:

1. We are going to implement a unit test on the `ContactUs` component. We'll start by creating a file called `ContactUs.test.tsx` in the `src` folder.

2. We are going to use `ReactDOM` to render a test instance of the `ContactUs` component. Let's import `React` and `ReactDOM`:

   ```
   import React from "react";
   import ReactDOM from "react-dom";
   ```

3. We are going to simulate the form submit event, so let's import the `Simulate` function from the React testing utilities:

   ```
   import { Simulate } from "react-dom/test-utils";
   ```

4. Let's now import the component we need to test:

   ```
   import ContactUs from "./ContactUs";
   ```

5. We also need to import the submission result interface from `Form.tsx` as well:

   ```
   import { ISubmitResult } from "./Form";
   ```

6. Let's start to create our test using the Jest `test` function, with the results outputting to a `ContactUs` group:

```
describe("ContactUs", () => {
  test("When submit without filling in fields should display
errors", () => {
    // TODO - implement the test
  });
});
```

7. The first task in our test implementation is to create our React component in the DOM:

```
test("When submit without filling in fields should display errors",
() => {
  const handleSubmit = async (): Promise<ISubmitResult> => {
    return {
      success: true
    };
  };

  const container = document.createElement("div");
  ReactDOM.render(<ContactUs onSubmit={handleSubmit} />,
container);

  // TODO - submit the form and check errors are shown

  ReactDOM.unmountComponentAtNode(container);
});
```

First, we create a container `div` tag and then render our `ContactUs` component into this. We have also created a handler for the `onSubmit` prop, which returns success. The last line in the test cleans up by removing the DOM elements that were created in the test.

8. Next, we need to get a reference to the form, and then submit it:

```
ReactDOM.render(<ContactUs onSubmit={handleSubmit} />, container);

const form = container.querySelector("form");
expect(form).not.toBeNull();
Simulate.submit(form!);

// TODO - check errors are shown

ReactDOM.unmountComponentAtNode(container);
```

Here is the step-by-step description:

- We use the `querySelector` function, passing in the `form` tag to get a reference to the `form` tag.
- We then check that the form is not `null` by using the Jest `expect` function with the `not` and `toBeNull` functions chained together.
- The `submit` event is simulated using the `Simulate` function from the React testing utilities. We use an `!` after the `form` variable to inform the TypeScript compiler that it is not `null`.

9. Our final task is to check that the validation errors are displayed:

```
Simulate.submit(form!);

const errorSpans = container.querySelectorAll(".form-error");
expect(errorSpans.length).toBe(2);

ReactDOM.unmountComponentAtNode(container);
```

Let's see this step-by-step:

- We use the `querySelectorAll` function on the container DOM node, passing in a CSS selector to find the `span` tags that should contain the errors
- We then use the Jest `expect` function to verify that two errors are displayed

10. When the test runs, it should pass successfully, giving us two passing tests:

```
PASS  src/Form.test.tsx
PASS  src/ContactUs.test.tsx

Test Suites: 2 passed, 2 total
Tests:       2 passed, 2 total
Snapshots:   0 total
Time:        4.359s
Ran all test suites related to changed files.

Watch Usage: Press w to show more.
```

In this test, Jest is rendering the component in a fake DOM. The form `submit` event is also simulated, using the `simulate` function from standard React testing utilities. So, there's a lot of mocking going on in order to facilitate an interactive component test.

Also note that we are referencing internal implementation details in our test code. We reference a `form` tag, along with a `form-error` CSS class. What if we later change this CSS class name to `contactus-form-error`? Our test would break, without there necessarily being a problem with our app.

This is called a **false positive**, and can make code bases with these kinds of tests very time-consuming to change.

Improving our tests with react-testing-library

react-testing-library is a set of utilities that helps us write maintainable tests for React components. It focuses heavily on helping us remove implementation details from our test code.

We'll use this library to remove the CSS class references in our test code, and also the tight coupling to React's event system.

Installing react-testing-library

Let's install `react-testing-library` first as a development dependency via the terminal:

```
npm install --save-dev react-testing-library
```

After a few seconds, this will be added to our project.

Removing CSS class references from our tests

We'll make our first improvement to our test by removing the dependencies on the `form-error` CSS class. Instead, we will get a reference to the errors via the error text, which is what the user sees onscreen and not an implementation detail:

1. We'll import a `render` function from `react-testing-library`, which we will now use to render our component. We'll also import a `cleanup` function, which we'll use at the end of our tests to remove the test component from the DOM:

   ```
   import { render, cleanup} from "react-testing-library";
   ```

2. We can render our component using the `render` function we have just imported, rather than using `ReactDOM.render`, as follows:

```
test("When submit without filling in fields should display
errors", () => {
  const handleSubmit = async (): Promise<ISubmitResult> => {
    return {
      success: true
    };
  };
  const { container, getAllByText } = render(
    <ContactUs onSubmit={handleSubmit} />
  );

  const form = container.querySelector("form");
  ...
});
```

We get the container DOM node back in a `container` variable, along with a `getallByText` function, which we'll use to get a reference to the displayed errors.

3. Let's now use the `getAllByText` function to get the errors displayed on the page:

```
Simulate.submit(form!);

const errorSpans = getAllByText("This must be populated");
expect(errorSpans.length).toBe(2);
```

4. The last change we are going to make is to clean up our DOM at the end of the test using the `cleanup` function we just imported, rather than `ReactDOM.unmountComponentAtNode`. We are also going to do this outside our test, in Jest's `afterEach` function. Our completed test should now look like the following:

```
afterEach(cleanup);

describe("ContactUs", () => {
  test("When submit without filling in fields should display
errors", () => {
    const handleSubmit = async (): Promise<ISubmitResult> => {
      return {
        success: true
      };
    };
```

```
        const { container, getAllByText } = render(
          <ContactUs onSubmit={handleSubmit} />
        );

        const form = container.querySelector("form");
        expect(form).not.toBeNull();
        Simulate.submit(form!);

        const errorSpans = getAllByText("This must be populated");
        expect(errorSpans.length).toBe(2);
      });
    });
```

When the test runs, it should still execute okay and the tests should pass.

Using fireEvent for user interaction

We are now going to switch to depending on the native event system, rather than React's event system which sits on top of it. This gets us closer to testing what happens when users are using our app, and increases our confidence in our test:

1. Let's start by adding the `fireEvent` function to the import statement from `react-testing-library`:

   ```
   import { render, cleanup, fireEvent } from "react-testing-library";
   ```

2. We are going to add the `getByText` function to the destructured variables from the call to the `render` function:

   ```
        const { getAllByText, getByText } = render(
          <ContactUs onSubmit={handleSubmit} />
        );
   ```

   We can also remove the destructured `container` variable, as that won't be needed anymore.

3. We can then use this function to get a reference to the **Submit** button. After that, we can use the `fireEvent` function we imported to click the button:

   ```
        const { getAllByText, getByText } = render(
          <ContactUs onSubmit={handleSubmit} />
        );

        const submitButton = getByText("Submit");
        fireEvent.click(submitButton);
   ```

```
const errorSpans = getAllByText("This must be populated");
expect(errorSpans.length).toBe(2);
```

The previous code that referenced the form tag has now been removed.

When the test runs, it still passes.

So, our test references items that the user sees, rather than implementation details, and is far less likely to unexpectedly break.

Creating a second test for a valid form submission

Now that we have got the gist of how to write robust tests, let's add a second test to check that no validation errors are shown when the form is filled incorrectly:

1. We'll start by creating a new test in our ContactUs group:

```
describe("ContactUs", () => {
  test("When submit without filling in fields should display
errors", () => {
    ...
  });

  test("When submit after filling in fields should submit
okay", () => {
    // TODO – render component, fill in fields, submit the form
and check there are no errors
  });
});
```

2. We'll render the component in the same way as the first test, but destructuring slightly different variables:

```
test("When submit after filling in fields should submit okay",
() => {
  const handleSubmit = async (): Promise<ISubmitResult> => {
    return {
      success: true
    };
  };
  const { container, getByText, getByLabelText } = render(
    <ContactUs onSubmit={handleSubmit} />
  );
});
```

Now:

- We'll need the `container` object to check whether there are any errors displayed
- We'll use the `getByText` function to locate the **Submit** button
- We'll use the `getByLabelText` function to get references to our inputs

3. We can now get a reference to the name input using the `getByLabelText` function. After that, we do a little check to verify that the name input does exist:

```
const { container, getByText, getByLabelText } = render(
  <ContactUs onSubmit={handleSubmit} />
);

const nameField: HTMLInputElement = getByLabelText(
  "Your name"
) as HTMLInputElement;
expect(nameField).not.toBeNull();
```

4. We then need to simulate the user filling in this input. We do this by calling the native `change` event, passing in the required event argument, which includes our input value:

```
const nameField: HTMLInputElement = getByLabelText(
  "Your name"
) as HTMLInputElement;
expect(nameField).not.toBeNull();
fireEvent.change(nameField, {
  target: { value: "Carl" }
});
```

We have simulated the user setting the name field as `Carl`.

 We use a type assertion after the call to `getByLabelText` to inform the TypeScript compiler that the returned element is of type `HTMLInputElement`, so that we don't get a compilation error.

5. We then can follow the same pattern for filling in the email field:

```
const nameField: HTMLInputElement = getByLabelText(
  "Your name"
) as HTMLInputElement;
expect(nameField).not.toBeNull();
fireEvent.change(nameField, {
  target: { value: "Carl" }
```

```
});

const emailField = getByLabelText("Your email address") as
HTMLInputElement;
expect(emailField).not.toBeNull();
fireEvent.change(emailField, {
  target: { value: "carl.rippon@testmail.com" }
});
```

Here, we have simulated the user setting the email field as
carl.rippon@testmail.com.

6. We can then submit the form by clicking the **Submit** button, in the same way as
in our first test:

```
fireEvent.change(emailField, {
  target: { value: "carl.rippon@testmail.com" }
});

const submitButton = getByText("Submit");
fireEvent.click(submitButton);
```

7. Our final task is to verify there are no errors displayed on the screen.
Unfortunately, we can't use the getAllByText function we used in the last test,
as this expects to find at least one element, and in our case we expect there to be
no elements. So, before we carry out this check, we are going to add a wrapping
div tag around errors. Let's go to Form.tsx and do this:

```
{context.errors[name] && context.errors[name].length > 0 && (
  <div data-testid="formErrors">
    {context.errors[name].map(error => (
      <span key={error} className="form-error">
        {error}
      </span>
    ))}
  </div>
)}
```

We've given the div tag a data-testid attribute, which we'll use in our test.

8. Let's go back to our test. We can now locate the div tag around the errors using the data-testid attribute. We can then verify that this div tag is null, because no errors are displayed:

```
fireEvent.click(submitButton);

const errorsDiv = container.querySelector("[data-
testid='formErrors']");
expect(errorsDiv).toBeNull();
```

When the test runs in our suite of tests, we'll find we now have three passing tests.

Isn't referencing the data-testid attribute an implementation detail, though? The user doesn't see or care about the data-testid attribute—this seems to contradict what we said earlier.

It is kind of an implementation detail, but it is specifically for our test. So, an implementation refactor is unlikely to unexpectedly break our test.

In the next section, we are going to add another test, this time using Jest snapshot tests.

Using Jest snapshot tests

A snapshot test is one where Jest compares all the elements and attributes in a rendered component to a previous snapshot of the rendered component. If there are no differences, then the test passes.

We are going to add a test to verify the ContactUs component renders OK, by checking the DOM nodes using a Jest snapshot test:

1. We'll create a test with the title Renders okay in the ContactUs group of tests, rendering the component in the same way as previously:

```
describe("ContactUs", () => {
  ...
  test("Renders okay", () => {
    const handleSubmit = async (): Promise<ISubmitResult> => {
      return {
        success: true
      };
    };
    const { container } = render(<ContactUs
onSubmit={handleSubmit} />);
    // TODO - do the snapshot test
```

```
    });
  });
```

2. We can now add the line to carry out the snapshot test:

```
test("Renders okay", () => {
  const handleSubmit = async (): Promise<ISubmitResult> => {
    return {
      success: true
    };
  };
  const { container } = render(<ContactUs
onSubmit={handleSubmit} />);

  expect(container).toMatchSnapshot();
});
```

Doing a snapshot test is pretty simple. We pass the DOM node we want to compare into Jest's `expect` function, and then chain the `toMatchSnapshot` function after it.

When the test runs, we'll get confirmation that the snapshot has been written in the terminal, as follows:

```
> 1 snapshot written.

Snapshot Summary
> 1 snapshot written from 1 test suite.

Test Suites: 2 passed, 2 total
Tests:       4 passed, 4 total
Snapshots:   1 written, 1 total
Time:        4.241s
Ran all test suites related to changed files.

Watch Usage: Press w to show more.
```

3. If we look at our `src` folder, we'll see it now contains a `__snapshots__` folder. If we look in this folder, we'll see a file called `ContactUs.test.tsx.snap`. Opening the file, we'll see the following content:

```
// Jest Snapshot v1, https://goo.gl/fbAQLP

exports[`ContactUs Renders okay 1`] = `
<div>
  <form
    class="form"
```

```
          novalidate=""
      >
        <div
          class="form-group"
        >
          <label
            for="name"
          >
            Your name
          </label>
          <input
            id="name"
            type="text"
            value=""
          />
        </div>
        . . .
      </form>
    </div>
    `;
```

Some of the content is stripped out in this snippet, but we get the gist: we have a copy of every DOM node including their attributes from the `container` element we passed into the `toMatchSnapshot` function.

This test is heavily coupled to our implementation, though. So, any change to our DOM structure or attributes will break our test.

4. As an example, let's add a `div` tag inside our `Form` component in `Form.tsx`:

```
<form ...>
  <div>{this.props.children}</div>
  . . .
</form>
```

When the test runs, we'll see confirmation that our test has broken. Jest does a great job of showing us the difference in the terminal:

```
Received value does not match stored snapshot "ContactUs Renders okay 1".

- Snapshot
+ Received

@@ -1,89 +1,91 @@
  <div>
    <form
      class="form"
      novalidate=""
    >
-     <div
-       class="form-group"
-     >
-       <label
-         for="name"
+     <div>
+       <div
+         class="form-group"
        >
          Your name
-       </label>
-       <input
-         id="name"
-         type="text"
-         value=""
-       />
-     </div>
```

5. We are happy that this is a valid change, so we can press *U* to let Jest update the snapshot:

```
Snapshot Summary
  > 1 snapshot updated from 1 test suite.

Test Suites: 2 passed, 2 total
Tests:       4 passed, 4 total
Snapshots:   1 updated, 1 total
Time:        2.901s, estimated 3s
Ran all test suites related to changed files.

Watch Usage: Press w to show more.█
```

So, are snapshot tests a good thing or a bad thing? They are volatile because they are tightly coupled to the implementation of a component. However they are super-easy to create, and when they do break, Jest does a great job of highlighting the problem area and allowing us to efficiently correct the test snapshot. They are well worth a try to see if your team gains value from them.

We have learned a lot already in this chapter about unit testing React and TypeScript apps. Next up, we'll learn how we can mock dependencies.

Mocking dependencies

Mocking a component's dependencies can make the component easier to test. However, if we mock too many things, is the test really verifying that the component will work in our real app?

Establishing what to mock is one of the hardest tasks when writing unit tests. There are some things that make a lot of sense to mock, though, such as REST APIs. A REST API is a pretty fixed contract between the frontend and backend. Mocking a REST API also allows our tests to run nice and fast.

In this section, we'll eventually learn how to mock REST API calls made with `axios`. First, though, we'll learn about Jest's function mocking feature.

Using a mock function in Jest

We are going to make another improvement to the test that verified that submitting the **Contact Us** form without filling in the fields results in errors being displayed on the page. We are going to add an additional check, to make sure the submit handler is not executed:

1. Let's go back to the first component test we wrote: `ContactUs.test.tsx`. We manually created a `handleSubmit` function that we referenced in our instance of the `ContactUs` component. Let's change this to a Jest mock function:

   ```
   const handleSubmit = jest.fn();
   ```

   Our test will run correctly, as it did before, but this time Jest is mocking the function for us.

2. Now that Jest is mocking the submit handler, we can check whether it was called as an additional check at the end of our test. We do this using the `not` and `toBeCalled` Jest matcher functions:

```
const errorSpans = container.querySelectorAll(".form-error");
expect(errorSpans.length).toBe(2);

expect(handleSubmit).not.toBeCalled();
```

This is really nice, because we've not only simplified our submit handler function, but we've also really easily added a check to verify that it hasn't been called.

Let's move on to the second test we implemented, which verified that a valid **Contact Us** form was submitted okay:

1. We'll again change the `handleSubmit` variable to reference a Jest mock function:

```
const handleSubmit = jest.fn();
```

2. Let's verify that the submit handler is called. We do this using the `toBeCalledTimes` Jest function to pass in the number of times we expect the function to be called, which is 1 in our case:

```
const errorsDiv = container.querySelector("[data-
testid='formErrors']");
expect(errorsDiv).toBeNull();

expect(handleSubmit).toBeCalledTimes(1);
```

When the test executes, it should still pass.

3. There is one other useful check we can do. We know that the submit handler is being called, but does it have the correct arguments? We can use the `toBeCalledWith` Jest function to check this:

```
expect(handleSubmit).toBeCalledTimes(1);
expect(handleSubmit).toBeCalledWith({
  name: "Carl",
  email: "carl.rippon@testmail.com",
  reason: "Support",
  notes: ""
});
```

Again, when the test executes, it should still pass.

So, by letting Jest mock our submit handler, we've quickly added a few valuable additional checks to our tests.

Mocking Axios with axios-mock-adapter

We are going to move to the project we created in Chapter 9, *Interacting with Restful APIs.* We are going to add a test that verifies the posts are rendered on the page correctly. We'll mock the JSONPlaceholder REST API so we are in control of the data that is returned, and so that our test will execute nicely and quickly:

1. First, we need to install the `axios-mock-adapter` package as a development dependency:

   npm install axios-mock-adapter --save-dev

2. We are also going to install `react-testing-library`:

   npm install react-testing-library --save-dev

3. The project already has a test file, `App.test.tsx`, which includes a basic test on the `App` component. We'll remove the test, but leave the imports, as we'll need these.

4. In addition, we are going to import some functions from react-testing-library, `axios` and a `MockAdapter` class that we'll use to mock the REST API calls:

   ```
   import { render, cleanup, waitForElement } from "react-testing-library";
   import axios from "axios";
   import MockAdapter from "axios-mock-adapter";
   ```

5. Let's add the usual cleanup line that will execute after each test:

   ```
   afterEach(cleanup);
   ```

6. We'll create our test with an appropriate description, and place it under an `App` group:

   ```
   describe("App", () => {
     test("When page loads, posts are rendered", async () => {

       // TODO - render the app component with a mock API and
       check that the posts in the rendered list are as expected
   ```

```
        });
    });
```

Note that the `arrow` function is marked with the `async` keyword. This is because we'll eventually make an asynchronous call in our test.

7. Our first job in our test is to mock the REST API call using the `MockAdapter` class:

```
test("When page loads, posts are rendered", async () => {
    const mock = new MockAdapter(axios);
mock.onGet("https://jsonplaceholder.typicode.com/posts").reply(
200, [
    {
      userId: 1,
      id: 1,
      title: "title test 1",
      body: "body test 1"
    },
    {
      userId: 1,
      id: 2,
      title: "title test 2",
      body: "body test 2"
    }
  ]);
});
```

We use the `onGet` method to define the response HTTP status code and body we want when the URL to get the posts is called. So, the call to the REST API should return two posts containing our test data.

8. We need to check that the posts are rendered correctly. In order to do this, we are going to add a `data-testid` attribute to the unordered posts list in `App.tsx`. We are also only going to render this when we have data:

```
{this.state.posts.length > 0 && (
  <ul className="posts" data-testid="posts">
    ...
  </ul>
)}
```

9. Moving back to our test, we can now render the component and destructure the `getByTestId` function:

```
mock.onGet("https://jsonplaceholder.typicode.com/posts").reply(...)
;
const { getByTestId } = render(<App />);
```

10. We need to check that the rendered posts are correct, but this is tricky, because these are rendered asynchronously. We need to wait for the posts list to be added to the DOM before doing our checks. We can do this using the `waitForElement` function from react-testing-library:

```
const { getByTestId } = render(<App />);
const postsList: any = await waitForElement(() =>
getByTestId("posts"));
```

The `waitForElement` function takes in an arrow function as a parameter, which in turn returns the element we are waiting for. We use the `getByTestId` function to get the posts list, which finds it using its `data-testid` attribute.

11. We can then use a snapshot test to check that the content in the posts list is correct:

```
const postsList: any = await waitForElement(() =>
getByTestId("posts"));
expect(postsList).toMatchSnapshot();
```

12. Before our test can execute successfully, we need to make a change in `tsconfig.json` so that the TypeScript compiler knows that we are using `async` and `await`:

```
{
  "compilerOptions": {
    "target": "es5",
    "lib": ["dom", "es2015"],
    ...
  },
  "include": ["src"]
}
```

When the test executes, the snapshot is created. If we inspect the snapshot, it will contain the two list items containing data that we told the REST API to return.

We've learned about some great features in Jest and react-testing-library that help us write maintainable tests on pure functions and React components.

How can we tell what bits of our app are covered by unit tests, though—and, more importantly, what bits are uncovered? We'll find out in the next section.

Getting code coverage

Code coverage is how we refer to how much of our app code is covered by unit tests. As we write our unit tests, we'll have a fair idea of what code is covered and what code is not covered, but as the app grows and time passes, we'll lose track of this.

Jest comes with a great code coverage tool, so we don't have to keep what is covered in our heads. In this section, we'll use this to discover the code coverage in the project we worked on in the previous section, where we mocked `axios`:

1. Our first task is to add an `npm` script that will run the tests with the coverage tracking tool switched on. Let's add a new script called `test-coverage` that includes the `--coverage` option when `react-scripts` is executed:

```
"scripts": {
  "start": "react-scripts start",
  "build": "react-scripts build",
  "test": "react-scripts test",
  "test-coverage": "react-scripts test --coverage",
  "eject": "react-scripts eject"
},
```

2. We can then run this command in the terminal:

```
npm run test-coverage
```

After a few seconds, Jest will render some nice high-level coverage statistics on each file in the terminal:

```
 App
   √ When page loads, posts are rendered (43ms)


-----------------------------|---------|----------|---------|----------|--------------------|
File                         | % Stmts | % Branch | % Funcs | % Lines | Uncovered Line #s  |
-----------------------------|---------|----------|---------|----------|--------------------|
All files                    |    8.74 |     4.35 |    10.2 |    8.74 |                    |
 App.tsx                     |   33.33 |    21.43 |   26.32 |   33.33 |... 71,177,180,181  |
 index.tsx                   |       0 |      100 |     100 |       0 |     1,2,3,4,5,12    |
 registerServiceWorker.ts    |       0 |        0 |       0 |       0 |... 11,118,119,120  |
 serviceWorker.ts            |       0 |        0 |       0 |       0 |... 31,138,139,140  |
-----------------------------|---------|----------|---------|----------|--------------------|
Test Suites: 1 passed, 1 total
Tests:       1 passed, 1 total
Snapshots:   1 passed, 1 total
Time:        3.97s
Ran all test suites.
```

3. If we look in our project file structure, we'll see that a coverage folder has been added with a lcov-report folder within it. There is an index.html file within the lcov-report folder that contains more detailed information on the coverage within each file. Let's open this and have a look:

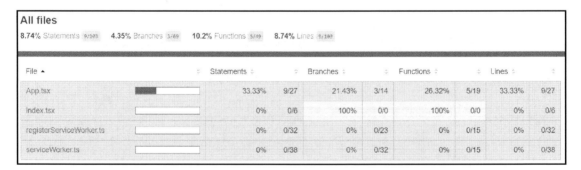

We see the same information as presented in the terminal.

What do these four columns of statistics mean?

- The Statements column shows how many statements in the code have been executed
- The Branches column shows how many branches in the conditional statements in the code have been executed

- The `Function` column shows how many functions in the code have been called
- The `Line` column shows how many lines in the code have been executed. Generally, this will be the same as the `Statements` figure. However, it can be different if multiple statements have been placed on a single line. For example, the following is counted as a single line, but two statements:

```
let name = "Carl"; console.log(name);
```

4. We can drill into each file to find which specific bits of code aren't covered. Let's click on the `App.tsx` link:

```
35        public componentDidMount() {
36   1x     const cancelToken = axios.CancelToken;
37   1x     const cancelTokenSource = cancelToken.source();
38   1x     this.setState({ cancelTokenSource });
39   1x     axios
40           .get<IPost[]>("https://jsonplaceholder.typicode.com/posts", {
41             cancelToken: cancelTokenSource.token,
42             headers: {
43               "Content-Type": "application/json"
44             },
45             timeout: 5000
46           })
47           .then(response => {
48   1x         this.setState({ posts: response.data, loading: false });
49           })
50           .catch(ex => {
51             const error = axios.isCancel(ex)
52               ? "Request cancelled"
53               : ex.code === "ECONNABORTED"
54               ? "A timeout has occurred"
55               : ex.response.status === 404
56               ? "Resource not found"
57               : "An unexpected error has occurred";
58             this.setState({ error, loading: false });
59           });
60
61           // cancelTokenSource.cancel("User cancelled operation");
62         }
```

The `1x` with a green background to the left of the lines of code indicates that those lines have been executed by our tests once. The code highlighted in red is code that isn't covered by our tests.

So, getting coverage statistics and identifying additional tests that we may want to implement is pretty easy. It's something well worth using to give us confidence that our app is well-tested.

Summary

In this chapter, we learned how to test pure functions written in TypeScript using Jest. We simply execute the function with the parameters we want to test, and use Jest's `expect` function chained with one of Jest's matcher functions, such as `toBe`, to validate the result.

We looked at how to interact with Jest's test runner, and how to apply filters so that only the tests we are focusing on are executed. We learned that testing React and TypeScript components is more involved than testing pure functions, but Jest and react-testing-library give us a great deal of help.

We also learned how to render a component using the `render` function, and how to interact with and inspect elements using various functions such as `getByText` and `getLabelByText` from react-testing-library.

We learned that we can easily test asynchronous interactions using the `waitForElement` function in react-testing-library as well. We now understand the benefit of not referencing implementation details in our tests, which will help us build more robust tests.

We also discussed Jest's clever snapshot testing tool. We looked at how these tests can regularly break, but also why they are incredibly easy to create and change.

The ability to mock and spy into functions is another great Jest feature we now know about. Checking that functions for component event handlers have been called with the right parameters can really add value to our tests.

We discussed the `axios-mock-adapter` library which we can use for mocking `axios` REST API requests. This allows us to easily test container components that interact with RESTful APIs.

We now know how to quickly identify the additional tests that we need to implement to give us confidence that our app is well-tested. We created an `npm` script command to enable us to do this, using `react-scripts` and the `--coverage` option.

Overall, we now have the knowledge and the tools to robustly create unit tests for our apps with Jest.

Jasmine and Mocha are two popular alternative testing frameworks to Jest. The big advantage of Jest is that it is configured by `create-react-app` to work out the box. We would have to configure Jasmine and Mocha manually if we wanted to use them. Jasmine and Mocha are worth considering, though, if your team is already experienced with either of these tools, rather than learning another testing framework.

Enzyme is another popular library used with Jest to test React apps. It supports shallow rendering, which is a way of rendering only the top-level elements in a component and not child components. It is well worth exploring, but remember that the more we mock, the further from the truth we get, and the less confidence we have that our app is well-tested.

Questions

1. Let's say we are implementing a Jest test and we have a variable called `result`, which we want to check isn't `null`. How can we do this with Jest matcher functions?

2. Let's say we have a variable called `person` that is of type `IPerson`:

   ```
   interface IPerson {
     id: number;
     name: string;
   }
   ```

   We want to check that the `person` variable is `{ id: 1, name: "bob" }`. How can we do this with Jest matcher functions?

3. Is it possible to carry out our check in the last question with a Jest snapshot test? If so, how?

4. We have implemented a component called `CheckList` which renders text from an array in a list. Each list item has a checkbox so that the user can select list items. The component has a function prop called `onItemSelect` that is called when a user selects an item by checking the checkbox. We are implementing a test to verify that the `onItemSelect` prop works. The following line of code renders the component in the test:

   ```
   const { container } = render(<SimpleList data={["Apple",
   "Banana", "Strawberry"]} onItemSelect={handleListItemSelect}
   />);
   ```

   How can we use a Jest mock function for `handleListItemSelect` and check that it is called?

5. In the implementation of `SimpleList` in the last question, the `onItemSelect` function takes in a parameter called `item`, which is the `string` value that the user has selected. In our test, let's pretend we have already simulated the user selecting `Banana`. How can we check the `onItemSelect` function was called, with the item parameter being `Banana`?

6. In the implementation of `SimpleList` in the last two questions, the text is displayed using a label that is tied to the checkbox using the `for` attribute. How can we use functions in react-testing-library to firstly locate the `Banana` checkbox and then check it?

7. In this chapter, we found that the coverage was low in our code that rendered posts from the JSONPlaceholder REST API. One of the areas that wasn't covered was handling HTTP error codes in the `componentDidMount` function when we get the posts from the REST API. Create a test to cover this area of code.

Further reading

The following resources are useful for finding more information on unit testing React and TypeScript apps:

- Official Jest documentation can be found at the following link: `https://jestjs.io/`
- The React Testing Library GitHub repository is at the following link: `https://github.com/kentcdodds/react-testing-library`
- Read the documentation for Enzyme at the following link: `https://airbnb.io/enzyme/docs/api/`
- The Jasmine GitHub page is as follows: `https://jasmine.github.io/index.html`
- The Mocha homepage can be found at `https://mochajs.org/`

Answers

Chapter 1: TypeScript Basics

1. What are the five primitive types?

   - `string`: Represents a sequence of Unicode characters
   - `number`: Represents both integers and floating-point numbers
   - `boolean`: Represents a logical true or false
   - `undefined`: Represents a value that hasn't been initialized yet
   - `null`: Represents no value

2. What will the inferred type be for the `flag` variable be in the following code?

   ```
   const flag = false;
   ```

   `flag` will be inferred as the `boolean` type.

3. What's the difference between an interface and a type alias?

   The main difference is that type aliases can't be extended or implemented from, like you can with interfaces.

4. What is wrong with the following code?

   ```
   class Product {
     constructor(public name: string, public unitPrice: number) {}
   }

   let table = new Product();
   table.name = "Table";
   table.unitPrice = 700;
   ```

   The constructor requires `name` and `unitPrice` to be passed. Here are two ways to resolve the problem.

Pass the values in the constructor:

```
let table = new Product("Table", 700);
```

Make the parameters optional:

```
class Product {
  constructor(public name?: string, public unitPrice?: number) {}
}
```

5. If we want our TypeScript program to support IE11, what should the `--target` compiler option be?

This should be `es5` because IE11 only supports up to ES5 features.

6. Is it possible to get the TypeScript compiler to transpile ES6 JavaScript files? If so, how?

Yes! We can use the `--allowJS` setting to get the compiler to transpile JavaScript files.

7. How can we prevent `console.log()` statements from getting into our code?

We can use tslint and the `"no-console"` rule to enforce this. This would be the rule in `tslint.json`:

```
{
 "rules": {
 "no-console": true
 }
}
```

Chapter 2: What is New in TypeScript 3

1. We have the following function that draws a point:

```
function drawPoint(x: number, y: number, z: number) {
  ...
}
```

We also have the following `point` variable:

```
const point: [number, number, number] = [100, 200, 300];
```

How can we call the `drawPoint` function in a terse manner?

```
drawPoint(...point);
```

2. We need to create another version of the `drawPoint` function that can call by passing the x, y, and z point values as parameters:

```
drawPoint(1, 2, 3);
```

Internally in the implementation of `drawPoint` we draw the point from a tuple data type, `[number, number, number]`. How can we define the method parameter(s) with the required tuple?

```
function drawPoint(...point: [number, number, number]) {
  ...
}
```

3. In your implementation of `drawPoint`, how can you make the z point optional?

```
function drawPoint(...point: [number, number, number?]) {
  ...
}
```

4. We have a function called `getData` that calls a web API to get some data. The number of different API resources is still growing, so we've chosen to use `any` as the return type:

```
function getData(resource: string): any {
  const data = ... // call the web API
  if (resource === "person") {
    data.fullName = `${data.firstName} ${data.surname}`;
  }
  return data;
}
```

How can we make `getData` more type-safe by leveraging the `unknown` type?

```
class Person {
  firstName: string;
  surname: string;
  fullName: string;
}

function getData(resource: string): unknown {
  const data = {};
  if (data instanceof Person) {
    data.fullName = `${data.firstName} ${data.surname}`;
```

```
    }
    return data;
  }
```

5. What `build` flag can we use to determine which projects are out of date and need to be rebuilt without doing a rebuild?

```
tsc --build ... --dry --verbose
```

Chapter 3: Getting Started with React and TypeScript

1. During development, what are the `TSLint` settings for allowing debugger statements and logging to the console?

```
"rules": {
  "no-debugger": false,
  "no-console": false,
},
```

2. In JSX, how can we display a button with a label from a prop called `buttonLabel` in a class component?

```
<button>{this.props.buttonLabel}</button>
```

3. How can we make the `buttonLabel` prop optional and default to **Do It**?

Use a ? before the type annotation in the interface for the props:

```
interface IProps {
  buttonLabel?: string
}
```

Implement a static `defaultProps` object at the top of the class component:

```
public static defaultProps = {
  buttonLabel: "Do it"
};
```

4. In JSX, how can we display the preceding button only if the state called `doItVisible` is true? Assume we already have a state type declared containing `doItVisible` and it has already been initialized in the constructor

```
{this.state.doItVisible &&
<button>{this.props.buttonLabel}</button>}
```

5. How would we create a click handler for this button?

```
<button
onClick={this.handleDoItClick}>{this.props.buttonLabel}</button>

private handleDoItClick = () => {
  // TODO: some stuff!
};
```

6. We have a state type declared containing `doItDisabled`. It has also been initialized in the constructor. How would we set this state to disable the **Do it** button after we click it?

```
private handleDoItClick = () => {
   this.setState({doItDisabled: true})
};

<button
disabled={this.state.doItDisabled}>{this.props.buttonLabel}</button
>
```

7. If the button is clicked when it is disabled, is the click handler still be invoked?

No

8. Which life cycle method would be used in a class component to add event handlers to a none React web component that lives in our React component?

`componentDidMount`

9. Which life cycle method would we then use to remove this event handler?

`componentWillUnmount`

10. We have a function component called `Counter`. It needs to contain a piece of state called `count` and a function to update it called `setCount`. How can we define this state and default the initial count to 10?

```
const count, setCount = React.useState(10);
```

11. In the preceding `Counter` component, we have a `decrement` function that needs to reduce `count` by 1:

```
const decrement = () => {
  // TODO - reduce count by 1
};
```

How can this be implemented?

```
const decrement = () => {
  setCount(count - 1);
};
```

Chapter 4: Routing with React Router

1. We have the following `Route` that shows a list of customers:

```
<Route path="/customers" component={CustomersPage} />
```

Will the `CustomersPage` component render when the page is `"/customers"`?
Yes

2. Will the `CustomersPage` component render when the page is `"/customers/24322"`?
Yes

3. We only want the `CustomersPage` component to render when the path is `"/customers"`. How can we change the attributes on `Route` to achieve this?

We can use the `exact` attribute:

```
<Route exact={true} path="/customers" component={CustomersPage} />
```

4. What would be the `Route` that could handle the path `"/customers/24322"`? It should put `"24322"` in a route parameter called `customerId`:

```
<Route exact={true} path="/customers/:customerId"
component={CustomerPage} />
```

5. We can then use `RouteComponentProps` as the `CustomerPage` props type and get access to `customerId` via `props.match.params.customerId`.

   How can we catch paths that don't exist so that we can inform the user?

   Make sure all the `Route` components are wrapped in a `Switch` component. We can then add a `Route` to a component that renders a **not found** message to the user as the last `Route` in `Switch`:

   ```
   <Switch>
     <Route path="/customers/:customerId" component={CustomerPage} />
     <Route exact={true} path="/customers" component={CustomersPage}
   />
     <Route component={NotFoundPage} />
   </Switch>
   ```

6. How would we implement a `search` query parameter in `CustomersPage`? So, `"/customers/?search=Cool Company"` would show customers the name **Cool Company**.

   First we need the props type to be `RouteComponentProps` in our class:

   ```
   import { RouteComponentProps } from "react-router-dom";

   class CustomersPage extends React.Component<RouteComponentProps,
   IState> { ... }
   ```

   We can the use `URLSearchParams` to get the `search` query parameter and do the search in the `componentDidMount` life cycle method:

   ```
   public componentDidMount() {
     const searchParams = new URLSearchParams(props.location.search);
     const search = searchParams.get("search") || "";

     const products = await ... // make web service call to do search
     this.setState({ products });
   }
   ```

7. After a while we decide to change the "customer" paths to "clients". How can we implement this so that users can still use the existing "customer" paths but have the paths automatically redirect to the new "client" paths.

We can use the Redirect component to redirect the old paths to the new paths:

```
<Switch>
 <Route path="/clients/:customerId" component={CustomerPage} />
 <Route exact={true} path="/clients" component={CustomersPage} />

 <Redirect from="/customers/:customerId" to="/clients/:customerId"
 />
 <Redirect exact={true} from="/customers" to="/clients" />

 <Route component={NotFoundPage} />
</Switch>
```

Chapter 5: Advanced Types

1. We have an interface that represents a course result as follows:

```
interface ICourseMark {
  courseName: string;
  grade: string;
}
```

We can use this interface as follows:

```
const geography: ICourseMark = {
  courseName: "Geography",
  grade: "B"
}
```

The grades can only be A, B, C, or D. How can we create a stronger typed version of the grade property in this interface?

We can use a union type:

```
interface ICourseMark {
  courseName: string;
  grade: "A" | "B" | "C" | "D";
}
```

2. We have the following functions, which validate that numbers and strings are populated with a value:

```
function isNumberPopulated(field: number): boolean {
  return field !== null && field !== undefined;
}

function isStringPopulated(field: string): boolean {
  return field !== null && field !== undefined && field !== "";
}
```

How can we combine these into a single function called `isPopulated` with signature overloads?

We can use overload signatures and then a union type for `field` in the main function. We can then use the `typeof` type guard in the function to deal with the different branches of logic:

```
function isPopulated(field: number): boolean
function isPopulated(field: string): boolean
function isPopulated(field: number | string): boolean {
  if (typeof field === "number") {
  return field !== null && field !== undefined;
  } else {
  return field !== null && field !== undefined && field !== "";
  }
}
```

3. How can we implement a more flexible version of the `isPopulated` function with generics?

We can use a generic function with a `typeof` type guard for the special branch of code for strings:

```
function isPopulated<T>(field: T): boolean {
  if (typeof field === "string") {
    return field !== null && field !== undefined && field !== "";
  } else {
    return field !== null && field !== undefined;
  }
}
```

4. We have the follow type alias of stages:

```
type Stages = {
  pending: 'Pending',
  started: 'Started',
```

```
    completed: 'Completed',
  };
```

How can we programmatically turn this into the union type `'Pending'` | `'Started'` | `'Completed'`?

We can use the `keyof` keyword:

```
type StageUnion = keyof Stages
```

5. We have the following union type:

```
type Grade = 'gold' | 'silver' | 'bronze';
```

How can we programmatically create the following type?

```
type GradeMap = {
  gold: string;
  silver: string;
  bronze: string
};
```

We can map the type as follows:

```
type GradeMap = { [P in Grade]: string }
```

Chapter 6: Component Patterns

1. What special property does React give us to access a components children?

   A property called `children`

2. How many components can share state with React context?

   As many components as we like that are under the provider component in the component hierarchy

3. When consuming the React context, what pattern does it use to allow us to render our content with the context?

   The render props pattern

4. How many render props can we have in a component?

As many as we like

5. How many children props do we have in a component?

1

6. We only used `withLoader` on the product page. We have the following function in `ProductData.ts` to get all the products:

```
export const getProducts = async (): Promise<IProduct[]> => {
  await wait(1000);
  return products;
};
```

Can you use this to implement a loader spinner on the products page by consuming the `withLoader` HOC.

First we split `ProductPage` into a container and presentational component. The presentational component will render the product list exporting it wrapped in the `withLoader` HOC:

```
import * as React from "react";
import { Link } from "react-router-dom";
import { IProduct } from "./ProductsData";
import withLoader from "./withLoader";

interface IProps {
  products: IProduct[];
  search: string;
}
const ProductList: React.SFC<IProps> = props => {
  const { products, search } = props;
  return (
    <ul className="product-list">
      {products.map(product => {
        if (
          !search ||
          (search &&
product.name.toLowerCase().indexOf(search.toLowerCase()) > -1)
        ) {
          return (
            <li key={product.id} className="product-list-item">
              <Link
to={`/products/${product.id}`}>{product.name}</Link>
            </li>
```

```
            );
          } else {
            return null;
          }
        })}
      </ul>
    );
};

export default withLoader(ProductList);
```

We then can consume this in `ProductPage` as follows in its `render` method:

```
public render() {
  return (
  <div className="page-container">
  <p>
  Welcome to React Shop where you can get all your tools for
  ReactJS!
  </p>
  <ProductList
  loading={this.state.loading}
  products={this.state.products}
  search={this.state.search}
  />
  </div>
  );
}
```

7. Is it possible to create a loader spinner using the children props pattern? So, the consuming JSX would be something like this:

```
<Loader loading={this.state.loading}>
  <div>
    The content for my component ...
  </div>
</Loader>
```

If so, have a go at implementing it?

Yes

```
import * as React from "react";

interface IProps {
  loading: boolean;
}
```

```
const Loader: React.SFC<IProps> = props =>
  props.loading ? (
    <div className="loader-overlay">
      <div className="loader-circle-wrap">
        <div className="loader-circle" />
      </div>
    </div>
  ) : props.children ? (
    <React.Fragment>{props.children}</React.Fragment>
  ) : null;

export default Loader;
```

Chapter 7: Working with Forms

1. Extend our generic `Field` component to include a number editor using the native number input.

   - Firstly, add `"Number"` to the `type` prop:

     ```
     interface IFieldProps {
       ...
       type?: "Text" | "Email" | "Select" | "TextArea" | "Number";
     }
     ```

   - Include the `"Number"` type when rendering the `input`:

     ```
     {(type === "Text" || type === "Email" || type === "Number") &&
     (
       <input
         type={type.toLowerCase()}
         id={name}
         value={context.values[name]}
         onChange={e => handleChange(e, context)}
         onBlur={e => handleBlur(e, context)}
       />
     )}
     ```

2. Implement an urgency field on the **Contact Us** form to indicate how urgent a response is. The field should be numeric.

   Add the following field immediately after the notes field:

   ```
   <Form.Field name="urgency" label="How urgent is a response?"
   type="Number" />
   ```

3. Implement a new validator function in the generic `Form` component, that validates a number is between two other numbers.

    Add the following function in `Form.tsx`:

    ```
    export const between: Validator = (
      fieldName: string,
      values: IValues,
      bounds: { lower: number; upper: number }
    ): string =>
      values[fieldName] &&
      (values[fieldName] < bounds.lower || values[fieldName] >
    bounds.upper)
        ? `This must be between ${bounds.lower} and ${bounds.upper}`
        : "";
    ```

4. Implement a validation rule on the urgency field to ensure it is between 1 and 10.

    - Firstly import the `between` validator into `ContactUs.tsx`:

        ```
        import { between, Form, ISubmitResult, IValues, minLength,
        required } from "./Form";
        ```

    - Add the rule on urgency in the `validationRules` prop in `ContactUs.tsx`:

        ```
        validationRules={{
          email: { validator: required },
          name: [{ validator: required }, { validator: minLength, arg:
        3 }],
          urgency: [{ validator: between, arg: { lower: 1, upper: 10 }
        }]
        }}
        ```

5. Our validation triggers when a users clicks in and out of a field without typing anything. How can we just trigger validation, still when a field loses focus but only when it has been changed? Have a go at an implementation for this.

    - We need to track whether a field has been touched in the form state:

        ```
        interface ITouched {
          [key: string]: boolean;
        }

        interface IState {
        ```

```
        touched: ITouched;
        ...
    }
```

- We initialize the `touched` values for each field to `false` in the constructor:

```
constructor(props: IFormProps) {
  super(props);
  const errors = {};
  const touched = {};
  Object.keys(props.defaultValues).forEach(fieldName => {
    errors[fieldName] = [];
    touched[fieldName] = false;
  });
  this.state = {
    errors,
    submitted: false,
    submitting: false,
    touched,
    values: props.defaultValues
  };
}
```

- In the `setValue` method, we update the `touched` value to `true` for the field being updated:

```
private setValue = (fieldName: string, value: any) => {
  const newValues = { ...this.state.values, [fieldName]:
   value };
  const newTouched = { ...this.state.touched, [fieldName]:
   true };
  this.setState({ values: newValues, touched: newTouched
});
};
```

- At the top of the validate method, we check whether the field has been touched and if not, we return an empty array to indicate the field is valid:

```
private validate = (fieldName: string, value: any): string[] =>
{
  if (!this.state.touched[fieldName]) {
    return [];
  }
  ...
};
```

Chapter 8: React Redux

1. Is the `type` property in action objects required? And does this property need to be called `type`? Can we call it something else?

   The `type` property is required in the action objects and must be called `type`.

2. How many properties can the action object contain?

   As many as we like! It needs to include at least one for the `type` property. It can then include as many other properties as we need in order for the reducer to change the state but this is generally lumped in one additional property. So, generally an action will have one or two properties.

3. What is an action creator?

   An action creator is a function that returns an action object. Components invoke these functions in order to make a change to the state in the store.

4. Why did we need Redux Thunk in our Redux store in our React shop app?

   By default, a Redux store can't manage asynchronous action creators. Middleware needs to be added to the Redux store in order to facilitate asynchronous action creators. Redux Thunk is the middleware we added to do this.

5. Could we have used something else other than Redux Thunk?

   Yes! We could have created our own middleware. There are other well-established libraries that we could have used as well, such as Redux Saga.

6. In our `basketReducer` we have just implemented, why didn't we just use the `push` function to add the item to the basket state? What is wrong with the highlighted line?

```
export const basketReducer: Reducer<IBasketState, BasketActions> =
(
  state = initialBasketState,
  action
) => {
  switch (action.type) {
    case BasketActionTypes.ADD: {
      state.products.push(action.product);
    }
  }
```

```
      return state || initialBasketState;
    };
```

This mutates the product's state directly and makes the function impure. This is because we have changed the state argument, which lives outside the scope of our function. Breaking this rule, in this case, results in the basket summary not incrementing on the rendered page when the **Add to basket** button is clicked.

Chapter 9: Interacting with RESTful APIs

1. What will the output be in the console if we run the following code in a browser?

```
try {
 setInterval(() => {
  throw new Error("Oops");
 }, 1000);
} catch (ex) {
  console.log("Sorry, there is a problem", ex);
}
```

We'd get a message saying that an uncaught error (Oops) has occurred. The console.log statement wouldn't be reached.

2. Assuming that post 9999 doesn't exist, what would be the output in the console if we ran the following code in a browser:

```
fetch("https://jsonplaceholder.typicode.com/posts/9999")
  .then(response => {
    console.log("HTTP status code", response.status);
    return response.json();
  })
  .then(data => console.log("Response body", data))
  .catch (error => console.log("Error", error));
```

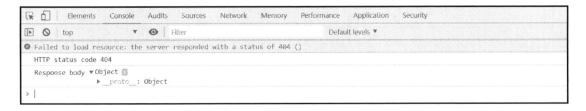

The key thing is that an HTTP error doesn't get handled in the catch method with the fetch function.

3. If we did a similar exercise with `axios`, what would be the output in the console when running the following code?

```
axios
  .get("https://jsonplaceholder.typicode.com/posts/9999")
  .then(response => {
    console.log("HTTP status code", response.status);
  })
  .catch(error => {
    console.log("Error", error.response.status);
  });
```

The key thing is that an HTTP error does get handled in the `catch` method with `axios`.

4. What is a benefit of using the native `fetch` over `axios`?

If we are targeting modern browsers (and not IE) and only require simple REST API interaction then `fetch` is arguably more favorable than `axios` because our code isn't dependent on third-party code. It will also probably run a little faster because there is less non-native code being executed.

5. How can we add a bearer token to the following `axios` request?

```
axios.get("https://jsonplaceholder.typicode.com/posts/1")
```

6. The second parameter is an object literal that has a `header` property that can contain HTTP headers for the request:

```
axios
  .get("https://jsonplaceholder.typicode.com/posts/1", {
    headers: {
      "Authorization": `Bearer ${token}`
    }
  });
```

7. We are using the following `axios` PUT request to update a post title:

```
axios.put("https://jsonplaceholder.typicode.com/posts/1", {
  title: "corrected title",
  body: "some stuff"
});
```

The body hasn't changed though – it's just the title we want to update. How can we change this to a PATCH request to make this REST call more efficient?

```
axios.patch("https://jsonplaceholder.typicode.com/posts/1", {
  title: "corrected title"
});
```

8. We have implemented a function component to display a post. It uses the following code to get the post from a REST API:

```
React.useEffect(() => {
  axios
    .get(`https://jsonplaceholder.typicode.com/posts/${id}`)
    .then(...)
    .catch(...);
});
```

What is wrong with the preceding code?

The second parameter in the `useEffect` function is missing, which means the REST API will be called every time the component is rendered. An empty array should be supplied as the second parameter so that the REST API is only called on the first render:

```
React.useEffect(() => {
  axios
    .get(`https://jsonplaceholder.typicode.com/posts/${id}`)
    .then(...)
    .catch(...);
}, []);
```

Chapter 10: Interacting with GraphQL APIs

1. In the **GitHub GraphQL Explorer**, create a query to return the last five open issues in the React project. Return the issue title and the URL in the response:

```
query {
  repository (owner:"facebook", name:"react") {
    issues(last: 5, states:[OPEN]) {
      edges {
        node {
          title
          url
        }
      }
    }
  }
}
```

2. Enhance the last query, make the number of issues that is returned a parameter, and make this default to 5:

```
query ($lastCount: Int = 5) {
  repository (owner:"facebook", name:"react") {
    issues(last: $lastCount, states: [OPEN]) {
      edges {
        node {
          title
          url
        }
      }
    }
  }
}
```

3. Create a mutation in the **GitHub GraphQL Explorer** to unstar a starred repository. The mutation should take a repository ID as a parameter:

```
mutation ($repoId: ID!) {
  removeStar(input: { starrableId: $repoId }) {
    starrable {
      stargazers {
        totalCount
      }
    }
  }
}
```

4. What part of the HTTP request does the GraphQL query go in?

   The HTTP body

5. What part of the HTTP request does the GraphQL mutation go in?

   The HTTP body

6. How can we make the response from the `react-apollo` `Query` component type safe?

   Create another component that extends `Query` passing in a type for the result as a generic parameter:

   ```
   class MyQuery extends Query<IResult> {}
   ```

   We can then use the `MyQuery` component in our JSX.

7. Is caching on or off by default when you scaffold a project with `react-boost`?

   On

8. What prop can we use on the `Mutation` component to update the local cache?

   The `update` prop.

Chapter 11: Unit Testing with Jest

1. Let's say we are implementing a Jest test and we have a variable called `result`, which we want to check isn't `null`. How can we do this with Jest matcher functions?

   ```
   expect(result).not.toBeNull()
   ```

2. Let's say we have variable called `person` that is of type `IPerson`:

   ```
   interface IPerson {
     id: number;
     name: string;
   }
   ```

We want to check that the `person` variable is `{ id: 1, name: "bob" }`. How can we do this with Jest matcher functions?

```
expect(person).not.toBeEqual({ id: 1, name: "bob" });
```

3. Is it possible to carry out our check in the last question with a Jest snapshot test? If so how?

Yes:

```
expect(person).toMatchSnapshot();
```

4. We have implemented a component called `CheckList`, which renders text from an array in a list. Each list item has a checkbox so that the user can select list items. The component has a function prop called `onItemSelect` that is called when a user selects an item by checking the checkbox. We are implementing a test to verify that the `onItemSelect` prop works. The following line of code renders the component in the test:

```
const { container } = render(<SimpleList data={["Apple", "Banana",
"Strawberry"]} onItemSelect={handleListItemSelect} />);
```

How can we use a Jest mock function for `handleListItemSelect` and check that it is called?

```
const handleListItemSelect = jest.fn();
const { container } = render(<SimpleList data={["Apple", "Banana",
"Strawberry"]} onItemSelect={handleListItemSelect} />);

// TODO - select the list item

expect(handleListItemSelect).toBeCalledTimes(1);
```

5. In the implementation of `SimpleList` in the last question, the `onItemSelect` function takes in a parameter called `item` which is the `string` value that the user has selected. In our test, let's pretend we have already simulated the user selecting `"Banana"`. How can we check the `onItemSelect` function was called with the item parameter being `"Banana"`?

```
expect(handleListItemSelect).toBeCalledWith("Banana");
```

6. In the implementation of `SimpleList` in the last two questions, the text is displayed using a label that is tied to the checkbox is using the `for` attribute. How can we use functions in React Testing Library to firstly locate the `"Banana"` checkbox and then check it?

```
const checkbox = getByLabelText("Banana") as HTMLInputElement;
fireEvent.change(checkbox, {
  target: { checked: true }
});
```

7. In this chapter, we found out the coverage was low in our code that rendered posts from the JSONPlaceholder REST API. One of the areas that wasn't covered was handling HTTP error codes in the `componentDidMount` function when we get the posts from the REST API. Create a test to cover this area of code:

```
test("When the post GET request errors when the page is loaded, an
error is shown", async () => {
  const mock = new MockAdapter(axios);
  mock.onGet("https://jsonplaceholder.typicode.com/posts").reply(404)
  ;

  const { getByTestId } = render(<App />);

  const error: any = await waitForElement(() =>
getByTestId("error"));

  expect(error).toMatchSnapshot();
});
```

A test ID needs to be added to the `App` component code:

```
{this.state.error && <p className="error" data-
testid="error">{this.state.error}</p>}
```

Other Books You May Enjoy

If you enjoyed this book, you may be interested in these other books by Packt:

React Cookbook
Carlos Santana Roldan

ISBN: 9781783980727

- Gain the ability to wield complex topics such as Webpack and server-side rendering
- Implement an API using Node.js, Firebase, and GraphQL
- Learn to maximize the performance of React applications
- Create a mobile application using React Native
- Deploy a React application on Digital Ocean
- Get to know the best practices when organizing and testing a large React application

Full-Stack React Projects
Shama Hoque

ISBN: 9781788835534

- Set up your development environment and develop a MERN application
- Implement user authentication and authorization using JSON Web Tokens
- Build a social media application by extending the basic MERN application
- Create an online marketplace application with shopping cart and Stripe payments
- Develop a media streaming application using MongoDB GridFS
- Implement server-side rendering with data to improve SEO
- Set up and use React 360 to develop user interfaces with VR capabilities
- Learn industry best practices to make MERN stack applications reliable and scalable

Leave a review - let other readers know what you think

Please share your thoughts on this book with others by leaving a review on the site that you bought it from. If you purchased the book from Amazon, please leave us an honest review on this book's Amazon page. This is vital so that other potential readers can see and use your unbiased opinion to make purchasing decisions, we can understand what our customers think about our products, and our authors can see your feedback on the title that they have worked with Packt to create. It will only take a few minutes of your time, but is valuable to other potential customers, our authors, and Packt. Thank you!

Index

including, in request 362

Made in the USA
Lexington, KY
27 February 2019